The San Francisco Nexus in World War II

The San Francisco Nexus in World War II

Freedoms Found, Liberties Lost, and the Atomic Bomb

Philip E. Meza

LEXINGTON BOOKS
Lanham • Boulder • New York • London

Published by Lexington Books
An imprint of The Rowman & Littlefield Publishing Group, Inc.
4501 Forbes Boulevard, Suite 200, Lanham, Maryland 20706
www.rowman.com

86-90 Paul Street, London EC2A 4NE

Copyright © 2023 by Philip E. Meza

All rights reserved. No part of this book may be reproduced in any form or by any electronic or mechanical means, including information storage and retrieval systems, without written permission from the publisher, except by a reviewer who may quote passages in a review.

British Library Cataloguing in Publication Information Available

Library of Congress Cataloging-in-Publication Data

Names: Meza, Philip E., author.
Title: The San Francisco nexus in World War II : freedoms found, liberties lost, and the atomic bomb / Philip E. Meza.
Other titles: San Francisco nexus in WWII
Description: Lanham : Lexington Books, 2023. | Includes bibliographical references and index.
Identifiers: LCCN 2023026476 (print) | LCCN 2023026477 (ebook) | ISBN 9781666941579 (cloth) | ISBN 9781666941593 (paperback) | ISBN 9781666941586 (ebook)
Subjects: LCSH: World War, 1939-1945—California—San Francisco Bay Area. | San Francisco Bay Area (Calif.)—Civilization—20th century. | San Francisco Bay Area (Calif.)—Ethnic relations—History—20th century. | Lawrence Radiation Laboratory—History—20th century. | Atomic bomb—Design and construction—History.
Classification: LCC D769.85.C21 S246 2023 (print) | LCC D769.85.C21 (ebook) | DDC 940.53/79461—dc23/eng/20230608
LC record available at https://lccn.loc.gov/2023026476
LC ebook record available at https://lccn.loc.gov/2023026477

To my parents Edward and Grace Meza, who lived in these eventful times as children, separated by a continent, an ocean, and a language.

Contents

Acknowledgments		ix
1	The Crucible by the Bay	1
2	Bridging the New World	7
3	Gold Comes to Berkeley	13
4	Making the Desert Bloom	21
5	A Hit on Treasure Island	35
6	Fission from the Old World	41
7	Panic in California	49
8	Drumbeat to Internment	61
9	Developing the Means	73
10	Sketching the Atomic Bomb	83
11	A National Disgrace	93
12	Nearer to Free: Black Migration to San Francisco	115
13	The Baritone Who Broke the Jim Crow Union	131
14	Out of LeConte and into Los Alamos	145
15	The World Comes to San Francisco	157

16	Jack Kennedy Present at the Creation	167
17	Trinity and After	185
18	Gold in Peace, Iron in War	193
Bibliography		201
Index		213
About the Author		221

Acknowledgments

I received a lot of help from people writing this book. It is a pleasure to acknowledge them here.

Connie Perez-Wong with the InterContinental Mark Hopkins Hotel, home of the storied Top of the Mark, kindly shared with me log books of the revived tradition of squadron bottles at that bar. In these books veterans who fought in World War II and America's wars in Korea, Vietnam, Afghanistan, and Iraq share stories of the precious hours they spent at the Top of the Mark while on leave. Included in one of these log books is an entry from former Navy Lieutenant Lupei Chou, a veteran of America's war in Afghanistan. I am grateful to her for allowing me to share her Top of the Mark story.

Abigail Malangone, archivist from the John F. Kennedy Presidential Library and Museum helped me navigate the intricacies of that wonderful collection where researchers can look up from papers and take in a view of the entrance to Boston Harbor framed by IM Pei's expansive glass-and-steel pavilion. Thanks also to James Hill and Maryrose Grossman at the Kennedy Library and Jennifer Quan with the John F. Kennedy Library Foundation for their help with photos and permissions.

The San Francisco Public Library is an invaluable resource to me. In particular the Main branch, which serves a wide variety of patrons with patience and skill, and the Marina branch, whose librarians are all terrific and exhibit a small-town neighborliness that befits the attractive parkside mid-century modern building in which they work. One especially compelling asset of the SFPL is its extensive photography archive with two million photos of San Francisco and California from 1850 to the present. Special thanks to Christina Moretta and Lisa Palella who helped me steer through this treasure trove.

On the subject of photos, Erin Hurley at Cal's beautiful Doe Library and Lorna Kirwan at the incomparable Bancroft Library both were wonderful representatives of those important institutions. Thanks also to Thor Swift and Alice Muller at Lawrence Berkeley Labs for their help with photos and clearances. Similarly, I owe special thanks to Sarah Bseirani at the National Archives and Records Administration for going above and beyond.

I also benefited from the help of small museums and historical societies. These places are often staffed by people who work there because they love the subjects of their collections. That is true of the Sausalito Historical Society and the Treasure Island Museum. Barbara Rycerski, Sharon Seymour, and Dana Whitson with the SHS helped me better understand the life and work of Joseph James. Look for Tami Bell's compelling interpretative portrayal of Joseph James on YouTube. Melanie Garduno with the TIM dug deep into their archives to provide me with information about the Golden Gate International Exhibition. So too, I want to thank Sandra Fye and Meghan Beaudet at the National Museum of Nuclear Science and History for their help clearing texts. My thanks also to musicologist Leta E. Miller whose research informs much of what we know about Joseph James's career as a performer and the environment in which he worked.

I want to thank my friends Ingo Schmoldt for his advice and guidance concerning the photographs I selected and Amitabh Sharma who read the text and made helpful comments.

One inspiration for this book has been the wonderful writing of the late Kevin Starr, the unofficial dean of California history. The books in his "California Dream" series are recommended reading to anyone interested in learning about the cultural history of this fascinating place. As a native of San Francisco who lived in that city but taught as a university professor at USC in Los Angeles, his ambit spanned the Golden State.

Another inspiration was my friendship with a wonderful photographer, the late Fred Lyon. I first learned about bassist Vernon Alley from Fred. They met in 1944 when Lyon was a navy aviation cadet at St Mary's and Alley was stationed there as a navy musician playing with the "Jive Bombers." After the war, they shared fun times in the Fillmore and at the Monterey Jazz Festival. They remained lifelong friends. The two men personify the artistry that has long flourished in San Francisco.

At Lexington Books, my thanks to Eric Kuntzman, who acquired this book; Sydney Wedbush who edited it; Nicolette Amstutz, Rachel Kirkland, Emilia Rivera, and Samuel Withers who helped guide the book through the production process; and Kathi Ha who designed its cover and Nancy Bryan who proofread the text. Thanks also to Harry Bego whose Textract software helped me produce the index. This book also benefited from the insightful comments of an anonymous peer reviewer, which I appreciated.

Closer to home, I want to acknowledge my siblings and siblings-in-law Robert, Sara, Robbie, and Juliana. I wrote this book with the next generation in mind. These include Caitlin and Alex, Kristen, Scarlett, Tara, and Reid.

My greatest thanks goes to my wife Marjorie, who encourages my "writing habit"; and my parents, Grace and the late Edward, to whom this book is dedicated.

1

The Crucible by the Bay

It is a small region, but it has a big impact in the world. Known today for its leadership in technology, venture capital, and creative industries as well as for its diverse and influential culture, San Francisco and the twin poles of the nearby world class universities at Berkeley and Stanford attract people from all over the world. They come for the opportunity to create something new and thrive in the distinct vibes generated by that city and those universities. It can be astonishing to consider that so many qualities that define this region—public and private partnerships to fund research, technological leadership, ethnic and racial diversity, and global outlook to name only a few—were created or reinforced in the crowded years around World War II when San Francisco and the Bay Area were a crucible in which the elements and practices that define the region also shaped the future of the country and the world.[1]

The city of San Francisco is the nexus of this region. Its grid of streets was laid out in 1847 before the gold rush, before the Civil War, and before the transcontinental railroad. By contrast, its rival city to the south, Los Angeles, came of age well after all of these things. It is less than forty-nine square miles in size, located at the tip of a peninsula surrounded by ocean and bay, tiny compared to the vastness of LA. But San Francisco's bustling port that greets Pacific trade meant it was more international than most places in America and more open to new ideas and ways of thinking. The residual wealth and spirit of the gold rush meant there was entrepreneurialism and deep pockets of money in San Francisco sometimes willing to finance wild dreams. This fed optimism about life and the opportunities in the region that attracted visionaries from all over the country and the world.

What did Californians new and old find in San Francisco and the Bay Area before World War II? In terms of industry and commerce, San Francisco contained multitudes. It could build entire locomotives as early as 1860, by 1875 it repaired ships using parts manufactured in the city, and by the turn of the twentieth century whole battleships were built in its shipyards. Not content just to build ships, San Francisco firms and entrepreneurs got involved with trading and insuring the goods carried on ships, creating markets that supported banks and insurance companies.[2] At its peak, before San Francisco had its two bridges, the Beaux-Art style Ferry Building that still graces the Embarcadero hosted fifty thousand transits each workday, making it one of the busiest terminals in the world, second to London's Charing Cross.[3]

San Francisco was a cosmopolitan yet provincial town. For decades, its politics were slightly center right.[4] Its residents were mostly White, but diverse in their Whiteness, with Irish, Italians, Russians, Slavs, and others living in between and upon its seven hills. The native Ohlone and other indigenous people mostly had been displaced in the nineteenth century. Jews from Germany and Eastern Europe fared well in the city. Asian people from China and Japan and some Black people from elsewhere in America were willing to endure bigotry and prejudice written into state and local laws to come to San Francisco to make better lives for themselves and their children. Latinos had been a small but constant presence in the city. In the 1870s, Chinese immigrants made up nearly ten percent of the state's population, but their relative numbers dwindled into the twentieth century due to "death, a shortage of women and children, immigration exclusion, and return migration to China."[5] Chinese and Japanese immigrants were prohibited by law from becoming citizens.

Today, the population of Southern California far exceeds that of Northern California, but it wasn't always thus. In the first years of the twentieth century, sixty percent of the people in California lived in the San Francisco Bay Area.[6] It wasn't until 1920 that Los Angeles exceeded San Francisco in population, an event significant enough to be reported on the front page of the *New York Times*.[7] In both the northern and the southern halves of the state, the people of California: farmers, ranchers, miners, small merchants, manufacturing workers and others were willing to invest in infrastructure like roads and bridges, and in public schools, colleges and universities, to support their dreams for the future. In 1911, at a time when there were fewer than seven cars for every thousand people in the country, California passed its first highway construction act. The initial miles were constructed in Burlingame, twenty-five miles south of the city.[8]

Financing for infrastructure projects often came from daring, innovative and successful homegrown banks, especially San Francisco-based Bank of Italy, later known as Bank of America, founded in the Italian neighborhood of North Beach in 1904 by A. P. Giannini, the son of Italian immigrants. This bank, which grew to become the second largest in the country by 1939, and others in California helped free the state from relying on capital from elsewhere and accelerated economic growth in San Francisco and across the West.[9]

In the first half of the twentieth century, Californians and their legislature enthusiastically supported public higher education, making post-high school education and training widely available to all its citizens at low cost. Colleges to train teachers had been established at larger cities across the state. In 1919, the state teacher college in Los Angeles moved to its new home in Westwood and was transformed into the University of California, Los Angeles (UCLA), joining the state's flagship university at Berkeley that had been founded in 1868, and ever after known as Cal. Over time, other universities were created to join Cal and UCLA in the University of California (UC) system. An additional network of state colleges and community colleges grew throughout California complementing the UC system. At its inception and until 1970, tuition at Cal, UCLA and the other campuses in the growing UC system was free for state residents. As early as 1897 the state provided some financial aid for needy students to help them pay for books and materials. Thus, Cal and later UCLA educated many students who could not afford to attend private colleges like Stanford University, founded in 1885, located forty-five miles south of San Francisco, which began charging tuition in 1920; the University of Southern California, located in Los Angeles, founded in 1880 and which had always charged tuition; and the California Institute of Technology, better known as Caltech, in Pasadena close to Los Angeles. Caltech's forerunner was founded in 1891 as a modest private school focused on vocational training before it made itself into a world class private sciences and engineering university beginning in the 1920s.

The California legislature funded its public universities well in the fat times of the roaring 1920s and more sparingly in the lean times of the Great Depression. Cal's Bay Area rival Stanford was a private institution that did not receive public funding. Former US President Herbert Hoover, alumnus of the first graduating class at Stanford and a university trustee after losing the White House to Franklin Delano Roosevelt in 1932, held enormous sway at his alma mater. His contempt for FDR's Depression-era spending influenced Stanford's leaders to not seek research money or other funding from the state or federal government.[10] Research funding at Stanford thus was circumscribed, and it remained only a highly distinguished regional university until a change of leadership during the middle of World War II brought more government funding that boosted research performed there and raised its profile. By contrast, the leaders at

Berkeley had always looked for money from governments and wherever else they could find it, especially during the Great Depression.

Before World War II, much of the costly work going on at the frontiers of physics at Berkeley under the young, gifted, and dynamic experimental physicist Ernest Lawrence had been financed through philanthropies and industry-university partnerships. It was Lawrence who ushered in the era of "Big Science" with its big costs. At about this time, Stanford's science and especially engineering faculty began to work closely with established as well as new technology companies in the Bay Area. This did not lead to big money financing big projects like at Berkeley during the 1930s and 1940s, but it did create a symbiosis that made Stanford a veritable nursery for start-ups, some of which became very successful during the Cold War and later, reinforcing the area's commercial dynamism and swelling the university's endowment. By the end of the 1940s Berkeley and Stanford grew into world class universities that helped shape the intellectual and entrepreneurial environments in the Bay Area for many years to come. Here is one measure: in 1960, almost forty percent of the world's Nobel Prize winners lived in California and most of them worked at Berkeley or Sanford.[11]

After decades of presidential leadership that promoted a laissez-faire executive branch of federal government, no place better showed the impact of President Franklin Roosevelt's strong exercise of executive powers—for good and for bad—than San Francisco. One of the most consequential leaders to hold the White House, in the third of the four terms FDR would win, he issued two executive orders that deeply affected San Francisco and the Bay Area. One order desegregated labor unions and workplaces involved in defense work. Because war production was about to touch most of the economy, this executive order was a tool that one Black San Franciscan, a singer and actor turned ship worker named Joseph James and his lawyer from the NAACP, Thurgood Marshall, a man destined to the Supreme Court, would use to bring Black Americans into the middle class and add to the patchwork of races in San Francisco. While this was happening, a different executive order had the effect of forcibly removing American citizens from their homes solely because of their Japanese ancestry and interning them in camps for the duration of the war. It was a disgraceful action born of the fears and outright racism of many California leaders, done in haste by the president who was distracted by America's precipitous entry into the global war, and upheld by the US Supreme Court in perhaps its worst decision since the Dred Scott case that determined Black Americans could not be American citizens. Japanese Americans, most of whom lived in San Francisco and Los Angeles, were removed from their homes and sent at rifle point to internment camps, showing the fragility of liberty in America, a lesson that remains relevant today.

An estimated 1.6 million soldiers and sailors shipped out under the Golden Gate Bridge heading to the war.[12] For most, it was their first time in California and many spent their last leaves in the city. Many of those vowed to come back to the Bay Area to live if they survived the war. Black workers left the Jim Crow South and found good paying industrial work in the shipyards of the Bay Area, and a less oppressive environment in which to live. California's Black population doubled during the war.[13] Black emigrants from the South moved into Fillmore district homes of Japanese Americans forced out by internment, joining—sometimes uneasily—Black San Franciscans who had lived in that neighborhood for generations. They contributed to the lifeblood of the city. In the late 1940s, Black culture in the Fillmore pulsed. Starting then and until redevelopment tore out its heart by the 1970s, the Fillmore was described as the "Harlem of the West." For a brief time, Black and White jazz fans, rich, poor, and in-between, mingled together in the dozen or so jazz clubs that dotted the Fillmore. This vibrant scene was witnessed by a young single mother, Marguerite Johnson, who lived there. She later became famous as the writer, poet, and activist Maya Angelou. In her memoir, *I Know Why the Caged Bird Sings*, she writes about her teenage years in San Francisco, "The city became for me the ideal of what I wanted to be as a grownup. Friendly but never gushing, cool but not frigid or distant, distinguished without the awful stiffness."[14]

Distinguished and unstuffy are components of a good environment for invention and innovation to thrive. This is the story of some of the ways it happened around San Francisco in the years when the world was aflame with war.

NOTES

1. Sometimes elements literally were created in the region. Berkeley researchers have been responsible for discovering sixteen elements to date, more than any other university in the world. These include Berkelium and Californium.

2. Kevin Starr, *The Dream Endures* (Oxford: Oxford University Press, 1997), 118.

3. Starr, *The Dream Endures*, 123.

4. Most San Franciscans voted Republican and posted voter turnout percentages that exceed those of today. Until the early 1960s, every mayor and most of the members of the board of supervisors were Republican. Of course, it was a very different Republican party then.

5. Kevin Starr, "The Gold Rush and the California Dream," *California History* 77, no 1 (Spring 1998): 66.

6. Kevin Starr, On the Same Page Lecture given at the San Francisco Public Library, June 19, 2012. See 14:05.

7. "Los Angeles with 575,480 of Population Passes San Francisco and Leads the West," *New York Times*, June 9, 1920.

8. Kevin Starr, On the Same Page Lecture given at the San Francisco Public Library, June 19, 2012. See 20:15.

9. Gerald D. Nash, "Stages of California's Economic Growth, 1870–1970: An Interpretation," *California Historical Quarterly* 51, no. 4 (Winter 1972): 324.

10. Stephen B. Adams, "Regionalism in Stanford's Contribution to the Rise of Silicon Valley," *Enterprise and Society* 4 no. 3 (September 2003): 532.

11. Gerald D. Nash, *The American West in the Twentieth Century* (Englewood Cliffs, NJ: Prentice-Hall, 1973), 267.

12. Kevin Starr, On the Same Page Lecture given at the San Francisco Public Library, June 19, 2012. See 45:38.

13. Nash, *The American West in the Twentieth Century*, 198.

14. Maya Angelou, *I Know Why the Caged Bird Sings* (New York: Ballentine Books, 2015), 211.

2

✢

Bridging the New World

It called for more than a party, it called for a world's fair. The Golden Gate International Exhibition was intended to celebrate the completion of two ambitious construction projects—bridges to span the San Francisco Bay and the Golden Gate strait. The San Francisco-Oakland Bay Bridge is a mash up of three parts: a cantilevered trusswork bridge from Oakland that fed onto a span leading to Yerba Buena Island which in turn joined an ordinary looking suspension bridge leading to San Francisco. All of it double decked to accommodate automobiles on its upper spans and commuter train traffic on the lower decks. Painted battleship grey, it was a product of necessity and looked like one. Feeding into San Francisco's Embarcadero lined with busy ports, this bridge was built for work. By contrast, the Golden Gate Bridge was an art deco beauty with a single deck suspended between two elegant towers. Most bridges were painted gray or silver to better fade into their surroundings. Not this one. San Francisco artist Maynard Dixon called for an "eye-filling" shade of red to work in harmony and stand with its surroundings.[1] Irving Miller, the architect in charge of designing the color and lighting for the bridge did not disappoint. He selected a vibrant color called International Orange to enhance the grandeur of the structure and complement the sometimes green, sometimes golden and sometimes brown hillsides at either of its ends, and the regularly present fog in its varying shades of grey. Anchored upon stunning and storied terrain, the Golden Gate Bridge was designed for beauty and meant for adventure. Together, these two bridges captured the spirit of the city that was part broad-shouldered port town and part glittering city on seven hills.[2]

Work on both bridges started in 1933 within months of each other in the worst of the Great Depression. San Francisco was a more rough-and-tumble town then: only one-third of its population was female, and fully a quarter of the population were blue collar men, "truckers, stevedores, merchant sailors, the majority of them single."[3] There was ethnic diversity in the city. The most numerous groups were Italians, Irish, and Germans, but there were also large numbers of Scandinavians, Chinese, Russians, and other groups too. San Francisco also had a small but well-established Black community that built California's earliest Black institutions like schools, newspapers, and churches.[4]

This population, however, remained small throughout the 1930s and there was not a growing industrial Black working class in the city as there were elsewhere in the country, especially in cities like Chicago and Detroit. Black workers remained outside of and often explicitly excluded from the growing organized labor movement in the country.[5] At the time of the fair, there were fewer than five thousand Black people living in the city. This was slightly smaller than the population of Japanese Americans in the city. Many Black San Franciscans lived in the Western Addition, also called the Fillmore, the site of the city's Japantown, where most of the ethnically Japanese San Franciscans lived. In a time of little residential integration anywhere in the nation, Black Americans and Japanese Americans intermingled together fairly well in the Fillmore. But if San Francisco at this time did not have as much ethnic or racial unrest as some other American cities, it had its share of labor strife.

At a time when the region that became Silicon Valley was still covered with orchards, agriculture was an important part of the Bay Area economy, and remains so today in many parts of California. In 1933, strikes among farm workers had the prominent Alameda District Attorney Earl Warren, who would go on to higher office and the leadership of the US Supreme Court, roll up his sleeves to combat what he saw as communist provocateurs stirring up unrest during the hard times of the Great Depression and ecological catastrophe that was the Dust Bowl. If San Francisco did not suffer from the Depression as much as some areas, there was still much hunger and despair, a moment of which was captured in photographer Dorothea Lange's poignant image of a destitute and forlorn man standing amid a San Francisco bread line.

Jobs were scarce, but San Francisco's ports remained active. Conditions there, however, were difficult and often humiliating for workers. For example, longshoremen had to belong to a bogus employer-sponsored association that refused to tie with real labor unions. To get work, longshoremen had to assemble pre-dawn at the Ferry Building on the Embarcadero to participate in a "shape-up" where they presented themselves to a "straw boss," a private contractor hired by wharfside employers to maintain an arm's length separation from the transaction. Straw bosses made the decisions about which men were hired and which ships those longshoremen worked. Abuses like favoritism and kickbacks to straw bosses were common. The hours longshoremen worked varied depending upon what a given ship carried, some longshoremen might find work for only a few hours in a day while others had to work for "twenty-four to thirty-six hours at a stretch, depending upon the cargo." Foremen drove the longshoremen relentlessly and some workers dropped dead from heart attacks or collapsed from exhaustion on the job.[6]

Several earlier attempts to unionize the ports had been beaten back, sometimes literally, by management. But by 1933 workers and the burgeoning labor movement found a friend in President Franklin D. Roosevelt, then in the first year of his first term. Militancy among and between labor and employers increased as the Depression wore on. Some of the worst violence came during a general strike lasting four days on San Francisco's waterfront in 1934. It was the first time a major US port city was completely shut down by a strike. Riots between San Francisco police, strikers, and "punchers" hired by labor and management respectively to add muscle to their chosen sides, all of whom numbered in the thousands, led to bloodshed and a few deaths. In the end, labor won most of their demands for better pay and improved working conditions. The following year, federal laws were enacted that protected the rights of workers to organize into unions. Overlooked by many in labor's celebrations was the fact that non-White workers were excluded from most of these unions, as they had been from most skilled and semiskilled jobs.

As the hard times of the 1930s began to ebb with the end of the decade, San Francisco and California were in a mood to celebrate. Much had changed in the country and in the world while those bridges were being built. Opening in early 1939, the Golden Gate International Exhibition, with its theme "Pageant of the Pacific," was meant to showcase a new San Francisco in a new California which instead of looking eastward from the far end of the continent was now gazing west from the beginning of the Pacific Rim. The exhibition took over Treasure Island, an island made of landfill built by the Army Corps of Engineers on the shoals of Yerba Buena Island from mud dredged out of San Francisco Bay. The US government paid for this work and the site was slated to become an airport, but first it would host an exhibition that celebrated the rise of California and San Francisco as economic and cultural forces in the Pacific region. Visitors to the exhibition found an eclectic mix of attractions intended to characterize San Francisco and California. There were rides, pageants, agricultural exhibits, and impressive displays of the latest in science and commerce. Of course, there was some kitsch too, such as monkeys driving racing cars along a track and other excitements like burlesque dancer

Sally Rand's Nude Ranch, featuring "women wearing cowboy hats, gun belts and boots, and little else."[7] Business was brisk at the ranch.

Fine arts and performing arts were also featured, including a superb performance of "Swing Mikado," a recent reinterpretation of the Gilbert and Sullivan comic opera performed by an all-Black touring cast of one hundred performers financed by the Federal Theater Project, a part of President Roosevelt's Works Progress Administration, intended to employ theater people across the country put out of work by the Depression. FTP shows entertained audiences in the millions who had stopped going to live theater or had never seen a live professional show.[8] The play featured musical numbers that had been rescored from the original Mikado to better suit swing syncopation and added popular dance routines and dialog in supposed Black dialect. The show had successful runs in Chicago and on Broadway before coming to the exhibition, where it was a popular attraction seen by thousands including First Lady Eleanor Roosevelt who greeted cast members backstage. In the production was a talented baritone named Joseph James who had been acting in an FTP touring company in southern California and working as a day player actor for movies in Hollywood before joining the cast at Treasure Island.

The japonaiserie flavor of "Swing Mikado" fit the vibe of much of the exhibition. Although more than twenty countries mostly from Latin American and Pacific nations exhibited their cultures, food, and trade at the fair, the centerpiece of the national displays was the Japanese pavilion. One of the largest and most popular foreign exhibits at the fair, Japan's pavilion exceeded three acres of exquisitely landscaped gardens with running streams and rocky outcrops along with tea houses and impressive replicas of important shrines. The main structure, "one of the finest and most interesting sights at the exhibition" according to the official guidebook, was "an original combination of the architecture of a feudal castle and a Samurai house of the 17th Century."[9] Here visitors observed traditional tea services, watched artisans create raw silk fabric from cocoon to loom, and enjoyed traditional Japanese opera and dance. *Time* called it the "best foreign exhibit—obviously designed to win U. S. friends."[10] Japan's reputation among nations at the time needed repair. It had invaded the Chinese province of Manchuria in 1931 in search of raw materials to fuel its growing industries. By the time of the exhibition, Japan controlled large sections of China, and war crimes against the Chinese were commonplace. After touring the pavilion, a representative from the Museum of Greater Shanghai in China said with tremendous understatement that Japan had spent so much money on its World's Fair propaganda because, "they are very much in need of good will at the present time."[11]

A short walk from the Japanese pavilion along the promenade named for Japan's Tokaido Road led visitors toward the exhibition's Hall of Science. There they could learn about the serious research being done in California at universities that were then just beginning to gain prominence, including Caltech, Stanford, UCLA, and above all Berkeley. Attractions included exhibitions on atomic structure, radiation, and a full-scale model of the cyclotron, "one of the most powerful tools in physics," producing high energy particles that it smashed into the nuclei of atoms to create new elements that had never been seen in nature.[12] Alchemists had dreamed of doing this for centuries. Developed by a twenty-nine-year-old professor of physics at Berkeley in 1930, the cyclotron was the rare device that had the potential to change the world. Physics is a science that yields its secrets to the young.[13] Lawrence, an experimental physicist, and his close friend and colleague, theoretical physicist J. Robert Oppenheimer were in their early thirties when they led a group of graduate students and junior faculty at Cal that were developing the latest tools and theories to understand atomic structure and harness its power. Together, these two men were pulling the center of gravity of atomic research from Europe to Berkeley.

NOTES

1. See Maynard Dixon's letter in support of the color choice in Irving F. Morrow, "Golden Gate Bridge Report on Color and Lighting," April 6, 1935, 20.

2. Because it carries one-third of the traffic of all California's state-owned bridges, the San Francisco-Oakland Bay Bridge is often described as a workhorse. In 2013 the east span of the bridge was replaced by a dramatic suspension bridge and the old span was dismantled. That same year, the west span was enhanced by a dazzling and ever-changing lighting installation designed by artist Leo Villareal. Maynard Dixon wanted all Bay Area bridges to evoke a sense of "wonder." After that, the workhorse Bay Bridge looked more like a wonderful show horse, especially at night. Alas, the Bay Bridge light show stopped in 2023 as organizers sought more funding.

3. Kevin Starr, *Endangered Dreams: The Great Depression in California* (New York: Oxford University Press, 1996), 84.

4. Albert S. Broussard, *Black San Francisco: The Struggle for Racial Equality in the West, 1900–1954* (Lawrence: University Press of Kansas, 1993), 2.

5. Albert S. Broussard, *Black San Francisco: The Struggle for Racial Equality in the West, 1900–1954*, 3.

6. Starr, *Endangered Dreams*, 87.

7. "Sally Rand (1904–1979)." The Museum of the City of San Francisco. Sfmseum.org.

8. "Federal Theatre Project, U. S. (1939) Federal Theatre on Treasure Island 'Swing Mikado,' a Cast of 100: Sensational Success; Hot from New York; The Big Hit of the Golden Gate International Exposition," Library of Congress.

9. Lynne Horiuchi and Tanu Sankalia, eds., *Reinventions: San Francisco's Treasure Island* (Honolulu: University of Hawaii Press, 2017), 96.

10. "Not So Golden Gate," *Time*, June 19, 1939, 13.

11. Krystal Messer, "*Dainty Distractions: The Japan Pavilion at the Golden Gate International Exhibition*," UCLA Thinking Gender Papers, January 4, 2014, 2.

12. "Science in the Service of Man," University of California Committee in Cooperation with the Golden Gate International Exhibition, San Francisco, 1939–1940, 65. "Never before seen in nature" is from "Lawrence and the Bomb," American Institute of Physics. Aip.org.

13. Albert Einstein said, "A person who has not made his great contribution to science before the age of 30 will never do so." Source: Zoë Corbyn, "Why Nobel Laureates are Getting Older," Scientific American website. Scientificamerican.com.

3

Gold Comes to Berkeley

On the evening of February 29, in the leap year 1940, golden prizes were awarded at two prominent ceremonies in California. One in Los Angeles at the faux tropical Coconut Grove nightclub in the Ambassador Hotel, where the biggest stars of Hollywood came out for the twelfth annual Academy Awards presentation of the Academy's famous gold statuettes, then only recently dubbed "Oscar."[1] The movie "Gone with the Wind" nearly swept the four major Oscar categories. The other event, the conferral of a heavy gold medal and elaborate diploma for the thirty-eighth Nobel Prize in Physics, took place in the auditorium of the classical revival Wheeler Hall on the campus of the University of California at Berkeley. It was the largest lecture hall on campus and was filled with luminaries of a different type than were at the Coconut Grove that night.

Nobel Prizes for sciences and literature are usually handed out by Swedish royalty during a highly formal ceremony at the Stockholm Konserthuset concert hall followed by a lavish banquet at the Stockholm Stadshus city hall attended by the laureates, their families, and over a thousand other dignitaries. In 1940, however, Europe, if not neutral Sweden, was at war so Sweden's consul-general came to Berkeley to deliver the prize to Ernest Lawrence, the first time a Berkeley professor received a Nobel.[2] Sixty-one years later another Swedish counsel general again took a Nobel Prize medal and diploma to Berkeley. This time to confer them upon Jennifer Doudna, the corecipient of the 2020 Nobel Prize in Chemistry. Due to the COVID pandemic, Doudna's ceremony took place in her backyard in Berkeley attended by a few members of her family. Doudna's was the twenty-sixth Nobel received by a Berkeley professor.

That Berkeley is the home of so many Nobel laureates is due in part to Lawrence. When he won, much of the cutting edge of physics was performed with a pencil, paper, and such apparatus that could fit on a laboratory bench top. And most of that work was done in Europe. One-third of all Noble prizes in physics had gone to German scientists and an American did not win in that category until 1922 and only two more Americans had won the highest prize in physics before Lawrence. His prize was well deserved. In 1929, Lawrence had been toying with the technical problem of how to accelerate positive ions to help him study atomic structure. That year, while paging through a German electrical engineering journal, he found an article written by a Norwegian engineer that described how to more effectively apply high voltage to energize a particle in a linear tube. Lawrence did not read German easily, so he concentrated on the diagrams and photographs and the figures in the article. He quickly grasped the author's general approach to the problem: accelerating positive ions by applying voltages to a series of cylindrical electrodes in line. Paging through the journal, Lawrence realized that this linear accelerator would not be practicable for him to build because it would be "awkwardly long" to fit into his laboratory.[3] Lawrence intuited, however, that speeding positive ions through a circular path would expose them over and over again to the same electric field, increasing the particles' speed with each pass in what Lawrence thought of as a "proton-merry-go-round."[4] Eventually, the energized and accelerated particles would smash into a target element and penetrate the nuclei of its atoms, allowing scientists to probe, study and eventually manipulate the nucleus of an atom.

The first operational cyclotron Lawrence constructed in 1930 was four inches in diameter and made of brass and red sealing wax. It cost about $25 to build.[5] It looked like a kind of toy, but it had powerful progeny. The Large Hadron Collider in Switzerland, which in 2013 discovered the long-sought Higgs boson, is its successor.[6] This happened because Lawrence had a drive to build increasingly powerful cyclotrons that were too big to fit on any lab bench top. To accommodate his work, Lawrence's boss, the head of the Berkeley Physics Department, gave Lawrence use of an old dilapidated two-story wooden building which he named the Radiation Laboratory and was thereafter known as the Rad Lab. Here he built a new 27-inch cyclotron and housed the eighty-ton magnet used to generate the electric field to energize and accelerate the particles within that cyclotron. Each new generation of cyclotron which produced higher and higher energies required bigger vacuum pumps and magnets to create and direct the power. Each generation of cyclotrons also cost almost ten times as much as the prior version.[7]

By September 1932 Lawrence's newest cyclotron was accelerating protons up to 3.6 million electron-volts. The device helped push him into the big leagues of physics in a year crowded with achievement: heavy hydrogen was discovered at Columbia University, the neutron was discovered at the Cavendish Laboratory at the University of Cambridge in England, and the positive electron, or positron, was discovered at the California Institute of Technology. The scientist behind each of these discoveries won a Nobel Prize. By 1939, the year Lawrence won his Nobel, he had developed a colossal 60-inch cyclotron powered by a magnet that weighed 220 tons.[8]

The Nobel Prize award ceremony at Wheeler Hall was opened by the University of California president Robert G. Sproul (rhymes with "owl"). "Extroverted, bluff, with a booming voice and a resonant laugh," Sproul had attended Berkeley where he had been a big man on campus; elected class president, a star athlete and drum major for the Cal band.[9] At Berkeley Sproul received a BS in engineering and struck up a friendship with classmate Earl Warren who we will hear more about later. Sproul was not a scholar, but an indefatigable administrator who rose through the University of California's administrative ranks by virtue of his skills of persuasion, bonhomie, and politics. Before becoming president, he had served as the UC's lobbyist to the legislature.[10] At publicly funded Cal, this was an especially important position. After he became its president, he worked vigorously to advance the university. In the depth of the Depression in 1933, California's governor proposed slashing the university's budget. Sproul took to the parapets and the salons to express his opposition, telling an audience at San Francisco's prestigious Commonwealth Club: "When a nation ceases to encourage and support its universities, it ceases to be a first-rate power. When a state prunes too severely the intellectual life at the top, it produces increasing poverty and despair at the bottom."[11]

Equally adept at glad-handing at a Kiwanis Club lunch or presiding over a fractious academic senate session, Sproul was part Babbitt and part Moses on a mission to build the growing University of California system, which by then included Berkeley, UCLA, and UCSF. His powers as president were limited, the academic senate had to approve his educational choices and the Board of Regents, which could fire him at will, had to approve his policies. Sproul was determined to make the UC system great and with his office and president's house on the Berkeley campus, he grew close to Ernest Lawrence. Lawrence's wife Mary recalled both her husband and Sproul as "big, outgoing, hearty men."[12] The two formed a partnership to bring the Rad Lab the tons of cash it needed to develop ever more powerful (and expensive) cyclotrons apace and exploit them to create new elements. In his opening remarks, Sproul spoke with pride that this was the first time a Nobel Prize had been awarded "for work which was done in its entirety on a campus of the University of

California, and which comes to a man who is a member of its faculty." Sproul further noted that as a public university, Berkeley labored under a handicap that "as soon as a [a faculty member] achieves a position within striking distance of a Nobel Prize, [a prominent private university] can usually offer him such a large salary, or such favorable working arrangements, that he leaves the state university. Fortunately, that has not happened in this instance and we pray that it may never happen."[13]

The next speaker was Raymond T. Birge, the head of Berkeley's physics department and the man who lured Lawrence to Cal. He had done much to advance Lawrence's career. Mary Lawrence, who was the daughter of the dean of Yale Medical School and had an undergraduate degree in bacteriology from Vassar said of Birge, "He was a man of great integrity ... I never saw any sign of a jealous spark in him, and lots of scientists are very jealous of their competitors and other colleagues in their field."[14] In his talk, Birge summarized Lawrence's career to that time and described the specific work that earned Lawrence the prize. He also hinted at the efforts that he and Sproul undertook to hang on to the brilliant experimental physicist, telling the audience that when Lawrence came to Cal, he "already was recognized as one of the most brilliant young physicists in the country," and that "in spite of numerous enticing offers that he has received from elsewhere" he remained at Cal.[15] Indeed Sproul had upset some faculty when he promoted Lawrence to full professor after only two years at Berkeley, becoming the youngest full professor in the history of the university to that time.[16] Birge and Sproul helped fend off lucrative offers tendered to Lawrence including one from Northwestern in 1930, which he was happy to decline but used as leverage for promotion and a salary increase, and Harvard in 1936, which he very nearly accepted, in large part by giving him what resources they could and supporting his own tireless outreach for funding from philanthropies and corporate donors. Birge had once remarked to a professor at another university that Berkeley was becoming less "a university with a cyclotron than a cyclotron with a university attached."[17]

Birge explained why Lawrence was becoming famous, "Now the word 'atom,' as all of you know, means something that cannot be divided, although, as all of you also know, carving up atoms into little bits is at present the favorite pastime of physicists. Indeed, with his cyclotron, Lawrence and his colleagues and students were changing atoms into different elements. This work, Birge said, "requires energy equal to millions ... of volts to bring about, and it is the discovery of a practical method for obtaining by artificial means such high energies that has brought Dr. Lawrence his present fame." He went on to explain why Lawrence deserved his Nobel Prize, "It is doubtful if any scientific instrument invented by man has found more varied and more important applications

... We now know that nearly all of the energy of the universe is locked inside the nuclei of atoms, and we have found recently that even slowly moving neutrons have the ability to cause the nucleus of uranium to explode into two more or less equal parts ... The practical aspects of such an unlocking of nuclear energy, if it is accomplished, are so staggering that some of us shrink even from contemplating them."[18]

The last speaker of the evening was Lawrence. His remarks were brief, generous, pointed, and prescient. He began by honoring his colleagues, telling the audience, "I am mindful that scientific achievement is rooted in the past, is cultivated to full stature by many contemporaries and flourishes only in a favorable environment." Sproul, Birge, and others did much to provide that favorable environment. Lawrence said, "From the beginning of the Radiation Laboratory, I have had the rare good fortune of being in the center of a group of men of high ability, enthusiastic and completely devoted to scientific pursuits." Lawrence was thinking of the many gifted young faculty members and graduate students that he and Birge and their especially compelling colleague, the theoretical physicist J. Robert Oppenheimer, had attracted to Cal. "We have been looking towards the new frontier in the atom," where, "there lies ahead for exploration a territory with treasures transcending anything thus far unearthed."[19]

To get there would require lots of money. Lawrence said, "the difficulties in the way of crossing the next frontier in the atom are no longer in our laboratory. They constitute a very considerable financial problem, which we must hand over to President Sproul." Lawrence explained, "the day when the scientist, no matter how devoted, may make significant progress alone and without material help is past. This fact is most self-evident in our work. Instead of an attic with a few test tubes, bits of wire and odds and ends, the attack on the atomic nucleus has required the development and construction of great instruments on an engineering scale." The promise of increasingly powerful and expensive cyclotrons was spectacular. Lawrence said they would be the instruments, "for finding the key to the almost limitless reservoir of energy in the heart of the atom," bring "a deeper knowledge of the structure of matter" and "constitute a veritable discontinuity in the progress of science."[20] Shifting from that lofty assessment, Lawrence ended on a practical note, telling the audience that the Nobel Prize he received will help him "find the necessarily large funds for the next voyage of exploration farther into the depths of the atom."[21]

NOTES

1. Hilary Lewis, "Oscars: Who Came Up with the Name Oscar?" *The Hollywood Reporter*, February 18, 2015.
2. In a fit of pique after an outspoken critic of the Nazi regime was awarded the 1937 Nobel Peace Prize, Adolf Hitler promulgated a law that prohibited German citizens from accepting any Nobel Prizes. In 1939, the year Lawrence won the prize for physics, two Germans were awarded prizes for chemistry and one German was awarded the prize for physiology or medicine. They had been forced to decline their prizes. One had been briefly imprisoned and thereafter harassed by the Gestapo. The law remained in effect until the fall of the Third Reich. These scientists were later given their Nobel gold medals and diplomas, however, they did not receive the substantial monetary awards because the funds had been returned to the Nobel endowment. For more, see Elisabeth Crawford, "German Scientists and Hitler's Vendetta against the Nobel Prizes," *Historical Studies in the Physical and Biological Sciences* 31, no. 1 (2000): 37–53.
3. Ernest O. Lawrence, "The Evolution of the Cyclotron," Nobel Lecture, December 11, 1951, 431. Nobelprize.org.
4. Deb McCaffrey, "Lawrence and the Cyclotron: the Birth of Big Science," February 26, 2016, Public Library of Science Blogs, ECR Community.
5. $25 from Kat Eschner, "Old Particle Accelerator Tech Might Be Just What the Doctor Ordered," *Smithsonian Magazine*, February 20, 2017.
6. Robert Sanders, "UC's First Nobel Prize Presented in Berkeley 75 Years Ago," February 17, 2015, Berkeley News, Press Release, UC Berkeley.
7. Gregg Herken, *Brotherhood of the Bomb: The Tangled Lives and Loyalties of Robert Oppenheimer, Ernest Lawrence, and Edward Teller* (New York: Henry Holt and Company, 2002), 16.
8. Lynn Yarris, "Ernest Lawrence's Cyclotron: Invention for the Ages," Lawrence Berkeley National Laboratory.
9. Alden Whitman, "Robert G. Sproul, 84, Dies," *New York Times*, September 12, 1975.
10. Whitman, "Robert G. Sproul, 84, Dies."
11. Gray Brechin, "Guttering the Promise of Public Education," UC Berkeley Department of Geography Commencement, May 16, 2009.
12. Suzanne Riess, "Interview with Mary Blumer Lawrence Conducted in 1984," *Robert Gordon Sproul Oral History Project, Volume II*, 865, University of California, Berkeley Bancroft Library Oral History Center.
13. Robert G. Sproul, "Opening Remarks," Nobel Prize in Physics Ceremony in Berkeley, February 29, 1940. Nobelprize.org.
14. Riess, "Interview with Mary Blumer Lawrence Conducted in 1984," 848.
15. R. T. Birge, "Address," Nobel Prize in Physics Ceremony in Berkeley, February 29, 1940. Nobelprize.org.
16. Riess, "Interview with Mary Blumer Lawrence Conducted in 1984," 845.
17. Herbert Childs, *An American Genius: The Life of Ernest Orlando Lawrence* (New York: E. P. Dutton & Co., Inc., 1968), 249.
18. "E.O. Lawrence Wins Nobel Prize in Physics," Lawrence Berkeley National Laboratory. LBL.gov.

19. Ernest Lawrence, "Award Ceremony Speech for the Nobel Prize in Physics, 1939," February 29, 1940. Nobelprize.org.
20. Lawrence, "Award Ceremony Speech for the Nobel Prize in Physics, 1939."
21. Lawrence, "Award Ceremony Speech for the Nobel Prize in Physics, 1939."

4

Making the Desert Bloom

If Lawrence was building the machines to explore the depths of the atom, his friend and colleague J. Robert Oppenheimer was developing the theories that guided their journeys there. The two men were very different in appearance, background and outlook, but they soon became very close friends. Lawrence, "born grown-up" according to his mother, was the happy and expansive middle-class Lutheran son of rural South Dakota.[1] His father was a superintendent of schools and later president of a teacher's college, and his mother had been a high school math teacher before their marriage. Lawrence's childhood had been comfortable but by no means well off. To earn pocket money and save for college, Lawrence sold aluminum pots and pans door to door in high school. He was successful at it and learned interpersonal skills that would serve him later when he was selling funders for his cyclotrons.[2]

Of Norwegian heritage and a strapping six feet tall and 180 pounds for most of his adult life, Lawrence was the leading experimental physicist of his generation by his mid-thirties. It was a mantle he wore easily whether socializing with political and business titans in the woods at the Bohemian Grove or leading a seminar of graduate students. Lawrence had "expressive blue eyes" and the habit of seeming to give whoever he was talking to his complete attention. People who knew him said he had a personal magnetism that everyone felt. He walked with purpose and a spring in his step. He did not have a nickname but when students and colleagues referred to him, he was "E.O.L."[3] His wife Mary "Molly" Blumer Lawrence described him as "genial and outgoing" but added that with people he worked with, he could also be "very impatient and very black and white A person was either a bum or they were terrific. There wasn't too much in between, and he wasn't that willing to make allowances . . . He would get down on somebody because they had behaved in a way that he considered lazy or careless or something like that. He would say, 'Oh, he's just a bum.'"[4]

Oppenheimer, by contrast, was "tall, thin, and awkward, with bushy dark hair and bright blue eyes."[5] His father, Julius, immigrated to the United States from Germany as a teenager and became extremely successful working in a fabric importing business in New York. Despite a lack of formal education, Julius was widely read and loved art. His mother, Ella, had been born in America to parents that had immigrated to America a generation before her birth. She was an artist who had studied in Europe and had her own art students by the time she and Julius met. During their marriage, Julius flourished in business. He and Ella became avid art collectors, owning several important paintings including three Van Goghs, one of which is now in the collection of the Metropolitan Museum of Art.[6] Their son Robert grew up as a young, independently wealthy Manhattanite who was cosmopolitan to his fingertips.

When Lawrence and Oppenheimer arrived at Berkeley, each was on his way to becoming the leading experimental and theoretical physicist, respectively, of his generation. They differed in background, personality, and intellectual strengths. One student of both physicists remembered, Oppenheimer "could always out argue [Lawrence], but logic or not, Ernest was usually right."[7] The two physicists shared traits of curiosity and generosity and became close friends in the 1930s. Lawrence named his son Robert after his friend and colleague.[8]

Chemistry and physics at Berkeley were intellectual kissing cousins and near neighbors. The chemistry department was already distinguished in the first decades of the 1900s. Just before America entered World War I, the state financed the construction of a large and modern building for the department that architect John Galen Howard dressed in a Greek Revival exterior. It provided a beautiful home for an ambitious and already successful department. Physics would be next. Lawrence came to Berkeley in 1928 and Oppenheimer, although hired a few weeks before Lawrence, arrived there the next year.[9] Both men had been highly courted by Raymond Birge, who was not yet chairman of the Physics department, but had been put in charge of building it up. The department had its own new building, LeConte Hall, also designed by Howard in a similar style to Gilman Hall and situated across a small plaza to the west of the chemistry building. Built in 1924 it was one of the largest buildings dedicated to physics of any university in the world and Birge set out to fill it.[10]

LeConte and Gilman Halls were at the center of the campus, overlooked by the Sather Tower campanile that stands over three hundred feet and is visible from across the bay. At that time, Berkeley could not attract established talent from other universities so Birge decided to hire "scientific prodigies on their way up."[11] In the small worlds of experimental and theoretical physics, Lawrence and Oppenheimer stood out. Lawrence had completed his PhD at Yale and had been offered a position as an assistant professor at the prestigious university. Birge countered with flattery, more money than Yale offered, a promised lighter teaching load to allow more time for research and publishing, and a permanent tenure track position as an associate professor at Berkeley. "Now I have an idea that you will like California and California will like you," Birge wrote Lawrence.[12] Perhaps believing that Lawrence would not leave Yale's ivied gothic towers to move out west, the university refused to counter Birge's offer. For the tradition-bound Yale, the associate professorship and not salary was the bigger sticking point. Lawrence telegrammed Birge to accept his offer.

Where Yale would not deviate from established practice to offer Lawrence an associate professorship right away, Birge and Sproul at Berkeley were willing to get creative to attract the best young talent. This was also true when they set out to woo Robert Oppenheimer. Only twenty-five years old, he had breezed through Harvard in three years, majoring in chemistry but gorging himself in classes in physics, literature, and languages. He went on to graduate work in physics at the two pinnacles of the discipline at that time, beginning at the Cavendish Laboratory at the University of Cambridge in England, and ultimately received his PhD in physics from University of Göttingen in Germany in only two years, in 1927.[13] Along the way he picked up a nickname. While briefly studying at the University of Leiden in the Netherlands (where he taught himself enough Dutch in six weeks to give a lecture in the language), colleagues began to refer to him as "Opje," a diminutive of "Oppenheimer" he liked and that stuck, later often anglicized as "Oppie."[14] Already, the newly minted PhD was a recognized member of a rarified group of theoretical physicists leading the revolutionary quantum theory that sought to understand the nature and behavior of matter and energy at the level of the atom and even subatomic level. Berkeley's physics department, "like those in most American universities at the time, was weak in theoretical physics and had no one familiar with the new quantum mechanics" that tried to describe the properties of atoms and their components, which could be counter-intuitive or downright strange to what was described by Newtonian physics.[15] The terms quantum mechanics and quantum theory are often used interchangeably. Quantum theory or mechanics deals with the behavior of matter and light on atomic and subatomic scales. It seeks to describe the properties of molecules and atoms and the electrons, protons, and neutrons that constitute them. At these minute levels, quantum particles do not obey the classical laws of physics and their behavior is difficult to predict. Even Albert Einstein ridiculed some aspects of quantum mechanics calling it "spooky action at a distance" in a gentle dis to his friend the physicist Niels Bohr, one of the founders of quantum theory.[16]

Birge wanted to bring this new learning to Berkeley. In the spring of 1928, he courted Oppenheimer. Birge had to wait in a long line. Oppenheimer later recalled, "I . . . had many invitations to university positions, one or two in Europe, and perhaps ten in the United States."[17] One of those offers was from his alma mater, Harvard, which offered him a light teaching load of only two courses a year, the same teaching commitment Birge promised to Lawrence. Oppenheimer said, "I visited Berkeley and I thought I'd like to go to Berkeley because it was a desert. There was no theoretical physics and I thought it would be nice to try to start something. I also thought it would be dangerous because I'd be too far out of touch [with cutting edge theoretical physics]." Oppenheimer hedged his gamble on Berkeley with a unique dual appointment to the California Institute of Technology, even then a distinguished research university and popularly known as Caltech, where he had done some post-doctoral teaching, "so I kept the connection with Cal Tech . . . it was a place where I could be checked if I got too far off base and where I would learn of things that might not be adequately reflected in the published literature."[18]

Caltech was satisfied to have Oppenheimer spend his time on that campus, participating in seminars and adding to the intellectual atmosphere at the Pasadena, California, campus. It was at Berkeley where he did most of his teaching and where he made its theoretical physics "desert" bloom. At Berkeley, Oppenheimer said, "I started really as a propagator of [quantum] theory which I loved, about which I continued to learn more, and which was not well understood and which was very rich." He proselytized quantum theory, he said, "explaining [it] first to faculty, staff, and colleagues and then to anyone who would listen, what this was about, what had been learned, what the unsolved problems were."[19]

During this time, Oppenheimer grew close to Lawrence and other experimental physicists at Berkeley. The symbiosis of theory and experiment, as historians Alice Kimball Smith and Charles Weiner write, "was characteristic of American universities" where both were housed in a single physics department; "in most European institutions, theoretical and experimental physics were generally done in separate institutes."[20] Oppenheimer initiated a graduate level course on quantum theory "which had not been given before . . . [and] varied in content but was always alright for someone who had had some background in classical physics and preferably at least a qualitative introduction to atomic theory." This was decidedly graduate level material and Oppenheimer "very rarely" worked with undergraduates. He speculated that Berkeley's Physics Department "didn't think I'd be any good for them and it didn't occur to me to ask to teach freshman physics or anything like that."[21]

As Lawrence and Oppenheimer established themselves at Cal, they developed a mutual respect that grew into a deep friendship. Still, they saw each other's professional weaknesses clearly. Referring to a time in the early 1930s before his Nobel Prize when Lawrence had been too quick to promote a dubious pet theory he formulated to explain surprising results from an experiment that turned out to have been contaminated and was proven wrong, Oppenheimer confided to his younger brother, the physicist Frank Oppenheimer, "for all this sketchiness, and the highly questionable character of what he reports, Lawrence is a marvelous physicist."[22] For his part, Lawrence was not blinded by the aura that attended Oppenheimer from the beginning of his academic career. Supporting his friend's promotion to full professor in 1936 at the young age of thirty-two, a promotion Lawrence received extraordinarily early in 1930 at the age of twenty-nine, Lawrence wrote, "[Oppenheimer] has all along been a valued partner," despite his awareness of the theoretical physicist's notorious sloppiness in math. As Oppenheimer's student Robert Serber later noted, "His physics [is] good, but his arithmetic is awful."[23] Their respective professional flaws might have stemmed from being young men facing a frontier and in a hurry to make their marks.

They were making their marks by the mid-1930s and shaping physics, first at Berkeley, then around the world. In recommending Oppenheimer to promotion to full professor, Raymond Birge wrote, "He is a perfect team-mate for Professor Lawrence ... the success of the Radiation Laboratory is due jointly to [Lawrence's] experimental genius and [Oppenheimer's] brilliant theoretical suggestions."[24] These teammates began to attract some of the best physics graduate students in the country. Lawrence involved his graduate students in developing ever bigger cyclotrons, the most important device at that time for studying atomic matter. The Radiation Laboratory, "centered on the cyclotron, focused almost exclusively on experiment. Their machines compiled the physical data around which theories could be built and tested the predictions of theory. In contrast, a theoretician like Albert Einstein did his work with a pencil; he worked out his theory of relativity based on knowledge, intuition, and mathematics."[25] While Lawrence was building ever more powerful cyclotrons, Oppenheimer was "building what would become known as the American school of physics."[26]

As a theoretical physicist, Oppenheimer did not work with expensive equipment and create important research positions that employed numerous graduate students as Lawrence had at his Rad Lab. Instead, Oppenheimer offered his own attractions. Graduate student Robert Serber remembered that by 1934, "Oppenheimer's course in quantum mechanics was well established. Oppie (as he was known to his Berkeley students and colleagues) was quick, impatient, and had a sharp tongue. In his early years as a teacher, he was reputed to have terrorized the students." Now, after five years of experience, "he had mellowed . . . His course was an inspirational, as well as educational, achievement. He transmitted . . . a feeling of the beauty of the logical structure of physics and an excitement in the development of the science. Almost everyone [took] the course more than once, and Oppie occasionally had difficulty in dissuading students from [enrolling in it] a third or fourth time."[27] Serber thought of him as the "Pied Piper of theoretical physics" noting that of the five National Research Council fellows in theoretical physics that year in the whole country, three had followed Oppenheimer to Berkeley to become junior faculty members. (Lawrence and Oppenheimer had both been NRC fellows.) Serber said, "By 1934, Oppie had the liveliest school of theoretical physics in the country."[28]

Another student at the time remembers Oppenheimer in the classroom, "He just ripped across the blackboard and just writing all the time, and also smoking a cigarette at the same time. The whole room was filled with Oppenheimer's smoke . . . He'd puff and write on the board and puff and write on the board. Then, he'd come to the end of his cigarette, and he would somehow manage to get another one lit before he started, and off he'd go."[29] Oppenheimer had a sharp side. "If you asked him questions in class, he would do his best to explain. But his empathy for what people were thinking or how they were feeling was not very good. As a result, he frequently did not really understand the point of what . . . was bothering [the] student. If the student persisted, he could get pretty caustic and sarcastic. The result was that people were afraid to ask him questions after a while."[30] Still, students flocked to Oppenheimer, "he had a lot of students. I should say that he probably had on the order of fifteen to twenty students at any one time. It was fantastic. And there were other people in his group who were people who had come who had already had PhDs, and would come to sort of work there. So that it was not possible for him to personally be working, really, with all these people at one time."[31]

Students and junior faculty alike were attracted to Oppenheimer's brain and personality. Serber remembered that Oppenheimer's mind "was so quick and his speech so fluid that he dominated nearly every gathering. He was generous and could be very charming."[32] Oppenheimer's students adopted his speech patterns and personal mannerisms. They also received from him "a cultural education as well as instruction in physics" as he generously shared with them his tastes for fine food, impressionist art, and music, especially Bach, Mozart, Beethoven, and string quartets.[33] Harold Cherniss, a close friend who was earning a doctorate at Cal in Greek, Latin, and Sanskrit, confirms that people were attracted to

Oppenheimer. "He was terrifically attractive . . . when he wanted to be. He could also be very cruel in his remarks. He did not suffer fools gladly, of course. Being intellectually sharp as he was, keen, or seeing the point of things almost immediately, he tended to irritate people who were more on his level. He was always very, very kind and considerate to anybody below him, if I may use that term. But not at all to people who might be considered his intellectual equals. This, of course, irritated people, made people very angry, made enemies."[34] Surprisingly, for a man who had lived his life to that time in cloistered ivory towers, Oppenheimer "was always eager to take people out. He had a large motorcar, which he didn't know how to drive very well. These were the days of Prohibition, you know. He knew all of best restaurants and speakeasies in San Francisco. We would go with him to these places."[35]

It was a heady time in experimental and theoretical physics and few researchers added as much effervescence to their fields as Lawrence and Oppenheimer. The year 1932, when they had been on campus only a few years, is considered an annus mirabilis among historians of science because of the far-reaching significance for physics of events that took place that year, including "the discovery of the neutron, which put nuclear physics on a sound footing for the first time; the discovery of the positron, the first evidence of antimatter; the publication of Werner Heisenberg's seminal papers consolidating the theory of the nucleus; and the key breakthroughs in the development of particle accelerators."[36] By 1934, "some of the most important theoretical work in exploring the vast new world opened up by these events was taking place at [Berkeley] around . . . Oppenheimer."[37]

While his branch of physics was blooming, Oppenheimer took time to explore other areas of learning, especially poetry and literature. It was Harold Cherniss who introduced Oppenheimer to Berkeley's noted Sanskrit scholar Arthur Ryder. The physicist began studying that ancient language under his tutelage. It seemed natural to Cherniss that Oppenheimer would be interested in Sanskrit, "if you get a taste of it, you can't help but get interested in it." Cherniss said, "probably Arthur Ryder had more of an influence on him in this respect than say some other Sanskritist may have had, because Ryder was a very remarkable man himself. Through him, Oppenheimer was introduced to the Vedas and things like that" which appealed to Oppenheimer, who Cherniss observes was inclined to the "mystical and cryptic . . . he liked things that were difficult."[38]

Oppenheimer would join Cherniss and his wife for dinners at the couple's house, "he was always proceeded by a large bouquet of flowers" for the hostess.[39] Other times, Oppenheimer would show up and cook dinner for the couple, one time introducing them to an Indonesian dish called nasi goreng, which his friends called "nasty gory." Oppenheimer brought over all the ingredients he needed and spent over an hour chopping and cooking. Cherniss remembers, "Finally, when he said it was done, ready, he turned to my wife and asked her whether she had some eggs. Because he said he'd like a couple of soft-boiled eggs, because he didn't eat this stuff. Anyway, it was brought in in a large tureen. Robert had his eggs. My wife took one taste of it and said she'd get herself some eggs, too. I ate the rest of it myself, terrifically hot, and I liked hot things. But they couldn't eat any of it . . . I thought it was good."[40]

In 1936, Harvard, which failed to try hard enough to attract Lawrence and Oppenheimer when they were looking for their first academic jobs, made a concerted effort to attract the two scientists after their initial successes at Cal, dangling huge pay raises if they would leave the San Francisco Bay for the Charles River. In the middle of the Depression, Harvard offered to quadruple Lawrence's salary, to between $10,000 and $12,000 per year and double Oppenheimer's to $6,000. Oppenheimer, independently wealthy and thoroughly enjoying his work and life at both Cal and Caltech was not tempted. Lawrence, keenly aware of the costs of the kind of "Big Science" he was developing, took the offer to Sproul.

Unable to match Harvard's salary offers, Sproul did increase funding and, more importantly to Lawrence, increased the scientist's autonomy by making the lab where he and his team worked, the so-called Radiation Laboratory, a separate entity from the physics department, and agreed to have the university pay $20,000 per year toward the Rad Lab's staff costs and expenses. Further, Sproul worked with Lawrence to tap outside donors, like the banker William Crocker who ponied up $75,000 to keep Lawrence and further his research. A Rad Lab building was named the Crocker Laboratory and its grateful staff referred to the next cyclotron they developed as the "Crocker Cracker," a distinctive honor in a time before every lecture hall, park bench, drinking fountain, and dry-erase board on a college campus was graced by a donor's name. Like the giant magnets that powered cyclotrons, Lawrence attracted talented young physicists and funds from philanthropies and government sources, both of which were rare at that time. Lawrence did not feather his own nest. As director of the Rad Lab, he made a salary of $2,000 per year. His assistant director earned $3,000 and post-doctoral research associates earned a minimum of $1,000. Lawrence also valued nonscientific talent. He estimated that the work performed by his extremely able secretary and assistant, Helen Griggs, was worth a salary of $1,200 per year. Sproul refused to raise any secretary's pay to that level, so Lawrence "augmented her salary [using] sources outside the University's control."[41]

A good part of the success Berkeley achieved in nuclear sciences at this time was due to the symbiosis between chemistry and physics and between the two houses of physics: experimental and theoretical. At

Berkeley, these groups were accustomed to interacting with each other.[42] Lawrence leading the experimentalists and Oppenheimer the theorists "complemented each other perfectly" and there was no rivalry between them of the kind "that often complicates such relationships at universities and research laboratories."[43] Among the talented graduate students attracted to Berkeley at that time was Glenn T. Seaborg, a young man who had grown up in the Watts section of Los Angeles and worked his way through UCLA as an undergraduate. He came to Berkeley for a PhD in chemistry and would soon change the world. "For me," Seaborg said, "Berkeley was Wonderland. And it was a wonderful time in the field of nuclear science."[44] At Cal, Seaborg rated the chemistry department, "top notch," holding its own with the newly prominent physics department. He especially appreciated that the disciplines worked unusually well together at Berkeley. By 1934, Seaborg recalled, "The mood of the scientific world was one of great excitement, and of all the places in that world, Berkeley had the most potential—the chemistry department was the best in the United States, and the physics department had the country's most advanced laboratory."[45] Berkeley's chemistry department was run by the cantankerous Gilbert N. Lewis, according to Seaborg, "the greatest physical chemist of his day."[46] Lewis had an eye for talent, and of the five chemistry junior faculty members hired under his direction in the 1930s, three would win Nobel Prizes. Seaborg would be one of those three.

Under Lewis, graduate students focused on research and seminars. Seaborg remembers there being little classwork in his program. Grad students like Seaborg interacted regularly with Lewis and the other great chemists at Berkeley and with the physicists too. "I was thrilled to sit at the same table with these great men. The intellectual stimulation was continual. It's hard to convey the excitement of just being around these people, but for months I walked around almost in a trance." Seaborg recalls, "The seminars were ongoing and open to anyone."[47] Seaborg remembered, "The week started with the Monday evening physics journal club, the only time the Rad Lab cleared out. Ernest Lawrence presided, and he never announced in advance the topic to be discussed. You had to show up to find out whether the presentation that week could be by a world authority or by a graduate student. This approach spurred attendance and added to the anticipation, as did the extraordinary nature of the physics department."[48] Participants got a ringside seat to the integration of experimental and theoretical physics. Seaborg said, "When Lawrence's experimentalists ran into roadblocks and conundrums, they would bring their problems to Oppie and his theorists at the seminars. There was perhaps no other institution with such a confluence of experimentalists and theorists, and their Monday evening exchanges were fascinating."[49] Although he was a graduate student in chemistry, Seaborg's PhD thesis "had nothing to do with chemistry; the subject was entirely within the domain of physics." No one on the review committee "was so crass" to point it out because "Berkeley was unconcerned about such crossovers."[50] Indeed, Gilbert Lewis was known to joke "that the only way to tell the difference between chemistry and physics at Berkeley was to ask in which building [Gilman or LeConte] work was going on."[51]

While a new world of nuclear science was being pried open by Lawrence's cyclotrons and Oppenheimer's theories, the country and most of the world was stuck in the Great Depression. Money was hard to come by, which is why it was necessary for Lawrence to work so hard to find funding for his costly Rad Lab. Oppenheimer, whose work mostly only used a blackboard and chalk, had lived his life in great affluence, his father becoming wealthy in the fabric trade. Unusual for somebody never accustomed to thinking about money, Oppenheimer was sensitive to the deprivations of the penurious grad students and junior faculty he worked with. Robert Serber recalls, "After seminars Oppie would often take the whole bunch out to a good and expensive restaurant in San Francisco, usually Jack's, [a big] occasion for us who were living through the Depression hand-to-mouth."[52] Jack's, a venerable favorite in San Francisco's financial district even then was old, colorful, and expensive. At the end of one group dinner there attended by the participants in a joint seminar with researchers from Berkeley and Stanford, Oppenheimer's friend and contemporary, the Stanford physicist Felix Bloch, feeling magnanimous, "leaned over and picked up the check. He looked at it, blinked, and put it back down."[53] When Oppenheimer came into his inheritance after the death of his father in1937, he made a will leaving the money to the University of California for fellowships to graduate students.[54]

NOTES

1. Lynn Yarris, "Ernest Orlando Lawrence—The Man, His Lab, His Legacy," Science Beat, Lawrence Berkeley National Laboratory, LBL.gov. Lawrence's religious affiliation is from: Stephane Groueff, "Interview of Eleanor Irvine Davisson Conducted on February 8, 1965, at Berkeley, CA." Voices of the Manhattan Project, Atomic Heritage Foundation. Manhattanprojectvoices.org.

2. Childs, *An American Genius: The Life of Ernest Orlando Lawrence*, 42.

3. Groueff, "Interview of Eleanor Irvine Davisson Conducted on February 8, 1965, at Berkeley, CA."

4. Suzanne Riess, "Interview with Mary Blumer Lawrence Conducted in 1984," 860.

5. Robert Serber with Robert P. Crease, *Peace and War Reminiscences of a Life on the Frontiers of Science* (New York: Columbia University Press, 1998), 25.

6. Jeremy Bernstein, "Oppenheimer's Beginnings," *New England Review* 25, no. 1/2, 39.

7. Lynn Yarris, "Ernest Orlando Lawrence—The Man, His Lab, His Legacy," Science Beat, Lawrence Berkeley National Laboratory. LBL.gov.

8. Luis W. Alvarez, *Adventures of a Physicist* (New York: Basic Books, 1987), 77.

9. Nuel Pharr Davis, *Lawrence and Oppenheimer* (New York: Simon and Schuster, 1968), 16.

10. Gray Brechin, *Imperial San Francisco* (Berkeley: University of California Press, 2006), 307.

11. Michael Hiltzik, *Big Science: Ernest Lawrence and the Invention That Launched the Military-Industrial Complex* (New York: Simon and Schuster Paperbacks, 2015), 41.

12. Hiltzik, *Big Science: Ernest Lawrence and the Invention That Launched the Military-Industrial Complex*, 42.

13. H. A. Bethe, "J. Robert Oppenheimer: 1904–1967," *Biographical Memoirs of Fellows of the Royal Society* 14 (November 1968): 392.

14. Dutch in six weeks is from Kai Bird and Martin J. Sherwin, *American Prometheus, The Triumph and Tragedy of J. Robert Oppenheimer* (New York: Vintage Paperback, 2006), 74. Source of Opje/Oppie nickname for Oppenheimer is Serber with Crease, *Peace and War: Reminiscences of a Life on the Frontiers of Science*, 28.

15. Alice Kimball Smith and Charles Weiner, eds., *Robert Oppenheimer: Letters and Recollections* (Cambridge: Harvard University Press, 1980), 130.

16. "Einstein's 'Spooky Action at a Distance' Paradox Older Than Thought," *MIT Technology Review*, March 8, 2012.

17. Smith and Weiner, *Robert Oppenheimer: Letters and Recollections*, 114.

18. Smith and Weiner, *Robert Oppenheimer: Letters and Recollections*, 114.

19. Smith and Weiner, *Robert Oppenheimer: Letters and Recollections*, 131.

20. Smith and Weiner, *Robert Oppenheimer: Letters and Recollections*, 131.

21. Smith and Weiner, *Robert Oppenheimer: Letters and Recollections*, 131.

22. Smith and Weiner, *Robert Oppenheimer: Letters and Recollections*, 171.

23. J. L. Heilbron and Robert W. Seidel, *Lawrence and His Laboratory: A History of the Lawrence Berkeley Laboratory*, volume 1 (Berkeley: University of California Press, 1989), 256.

24. David C. Cassidy, *J. Robert Oppenheimer and the American Century* (New York: Pearson, 2005), 161.

25. Glenn T. Seaborg with Eric Seaborg, *Adventures in the Atomic Age: From Watts to Washington* (New York: Farrar, Straus and Giroux, 2001), 25.

26. Seaborg with Seaborg, *Adventures in the Atomic Age: From Watts to Washington*, 25.

27. Serber with Crease, *Peace and War Reminiscences of a Life on the Frontiers of Science*, 149.

28. Serber with Crease, *Peace and War Reminiscences of a Life on the Frontiers of Science*, 28.

29. Cindy Kelly, "Interview with Edward Gerjuoy Conducted on April 13, 2008." Voices of the Manhattan Project, The Atomic Heritage Foundation. Mahattanprojectvoices.org.

30. Cindy Kelly, "Interview with Edward Gerjuoy Conducted on April 13, 2008."
31. Cindy Kelly, "Interview with Edward Gerjuoy Conducted on April 13, 2008."
32. Serber with Crease, *Peace and War Reminiscences of a Life on the Frontiers of Science*, 25.
33. Serber with Crease, *Peace and War Reminiscences of a Life on the Frontiers of Science*, 29.
34. Martin J. Sherwin, "Interview with Harold Cherniss, Part 1, Conducted on May 23, 1979." Voices of the Manhattan Project, The Atomic Heritage Foundation. Manhattanprojectvoices.org.
35. Martin J. Sherwin, "Interview with Harold Cherniss, Part 1, Conducted on May 23, 1979."
36. Serber with Crease, *Peace and War Reminiscences of a Life on the Frontiers of Science*, ix–x.
37. Serber with Crease, *Peace and War Reminiscences of a Life on the Frontiers of Science*, x.
38. Martin J. Sherwin, "Interview with Harold Cherniss, Part 1, Conducted on May 23, 1979."
39. Martin J. Sherwin, "Interview with Harold Cherniss, Part 1, Conducted on May 23, 1979."
40. Martin J. Sherwin, "Interview with Harold Cherniss, Part 1, Conducted on May 23, 1979."
41. Smith and Weiner, *Robert Oppenheimer: Letters and Recollections*, 213, footnote 10. Salary data is on page 228.
42. "Physicists differentiate between experimentalists and theoreticians. Few scientists manage to bridge this gap, but the Berkeley physics department had an extraordinary complementarity." Source: Seaborg with Seaborg, *Adventures in the Atomic Age: From Watts to Washington*, 25.
43. Seaborg with Seaborg, *Adventures in the Atomic Age: From Watts to Washington*, 50.
44. Seaborg with Seaborg, *Adventures in the Atomic Age: From Watts to Washington*, 23.
45. Seaborg with Seaborg, *Adventures in the Atomic Age: From Watts to Washington*, 24.
46. Seaborg with Seaborg, *Adventures in the Atomic Age: From Watts to Washington*, 24.
47. Seaborg with Seaborg, *Adventures in the Atomic Age: From Watts to Washington*, 25.
48. Seaborg with Seaborg, *Adventures in the Atomic Age: From Watts to Washington*, 25.
49. Seaborg with Seaborg, *Adventures in the Atomic Age: From Watts to Washington*, 26.
50. Seaborg with Seaborg, *Adventures in the Atomic Age: From Watts to Washington*, 40.

51. Brechin, *Imperial San Francisco*, 307.

52. Serber with Crease, *Peace and War Reminiscences of a Life on the Frontiers of Science*, 29.

53. Serber with Crease, *Peace and War Reminiscences of a Life on the Frontiers of Science*, 31.

54. Smith and Weiner, *Robert Oppenheimer: Letters and Recollections*, 8–9.

5

A Hit on Treasure Island

If times were hard for graduate students, they were far harder for the unemployed that President Franklin Roosevelt's various work programs were designed to help. Skilled and unskilled workers of all kinds found wage paying jobs with an alphabet soup of agencies created by the federal government: CCC, FSA, TVA, WPA, and more that employed people thrown out of work, in some cases for years, by the Great Depression. Artists too found work in these programs, including painters Mark Rothko and Jackson Pollock, writers including Saul Bellow, John Cheever, Ralph Ellison, and Richard Wright, and photographers including Walker Evans, Dorothea, Lange Carl Mydans, and Marion Post Wolcott, all of whom produced sometimes significant work for WPA wages. Asked why artists should be included in the government's work relief projects, FDR's closes advisor Harry Hopkins said, "Hell, they've got to eat just like other people."[1]

One artist who benefitted was a Black actor and baritone named Joseph Henry James. Born in 1910 in Philadelphia, James was left fatherless at the age of three. He and his mother moved in with his uncle, a fireman in Camden, New Jersey. James's mother and uncle were musically gifted: his uncle possessed "a wonderful bass voice," his mother was an alto, and James's much older sister sang with the outstanding Philadelphia contralto Marion Anderson, who later gained fame singing before a crowd of seventy-five thousand people at the Lincoln Memorial.[2] The site had been arranged by Eleanor Roosevelt after Anderson had been denied use of the Daughters of the American Revolution Hall in segregated Washington, DC, because she was Black. James said, "life wasn't soft for Negro kids with nothing but the streets to play in . . . my mother could see that from a little innocent window breaking I'd soon enough be hitting the big time, so a year after she died [ca. 1918] I was packed off to Princess Ann Academy, a negro boarding school in Maryland."[3] James earned his tuition singing in the school's quartet.

After graduation, James and three classmates he sang with looked for a Black college willing to recruit the group. They enrolled at Claflin College in South Carolina. His train ride to college was James's first experience with the overt Jim Crow regime of the south. He remembered, "Us moving into that Jim Crow car when the train hit Norfolk was something of a shock. I got out of the grimy rattletrap during a stopover to get a bite to eat, they wouldn't serve us in the diner, and I went to an all-night restaurant. As I opened the door, the negro janitor frantically waved me away. I didn't dig until he yelled for me to go around back. There was a little window in the back of the restaurant, something like the door of a dog house, where they'd throw food at you. It kind of took my appetite away—and that's some kind of trick for an 18-year-old kid still growing."[4] Claflin College was serious about music the way some colleges today are serious about sports. James said, "We sang two years at Claflin, but did not see much of the place—they sent us all over the country singing to raise funds for the college. Once in a while we would get a few dollars for ourselves and sometimes the college would throw a benefit so we could buy some clothes."[5] On tour in Boston, James decided to leave the group and the school. He supported himself singing on live radio and looked to further his education in music.

James was accepted into the Boston University College of Music. He studied there two years until he could no longer support himself. It became a question of "eat or study music."[6] Looking for paid professional jobs, he landed a baritone part in a Boston theatrical company's performance of Paul Green's *Potter's Field*. The show, with James in the cast, made it to Broadway in New York, but closed after only three days. Some of the chronology of his career is a little uncertain after nine decades. One noted music scholar thinks James performed and traveled with the Hall Johnson Choir, coming with them to Los Angeles in 1932. Hall Johnson was an arranger-composer-musician especially noted for his work in Black spirituals. He composed the successful folk opera *Run, Little Chillun* that opened on Broadway in 1933 and toured the country under the sponsorship of the Federal Theatre and Music Projects divisions of the WPA. James performed in the show *Brother Moses* in the title role during its runs in Los Angeles, San Diego, and San Francisco.[7]

He also found work in Hollywood as he recalled, "mostly running around like a savage in a G-string, feeling pretty silly . . . and dubbing in for actors who couldn't sing."[8] Music scholar Leta Miller thinks that James later joined the touring choir of Eva Jessye, a choral conductor who gained fame during the Harlem Renaissance. James said, "That was a weird trip, almost 20 of us jammed into two seven passenger sedans covered with suitcases and trunks. We covered 6,000 of the most agonizing miles I have ever traveled—breaking down all the way. We'd crawl out from under the car we were trying to patch together to go on stage and sing as if nothing had happened."[9] When James returned to New York he found work for a time as a singing waiter at the Hotel New Yorker, and in 1935 got a part in *Porgy and Bess* in Boston and New York.[10] Three years later, James returned to Los Angeles for a revival of *Porgy and Bess*, again as a member of the chorus. The show moved to the Curran Theater in San Francisco for a three-week run at the start of what had promised to be a lucrative tour. In San Francisco the show was "an artistic success but a financial failure," perhaps due to heavy rains and flooding during the last week of the engagement that kept away theatergoers.[11] The show's producer canceled the tour. James remained in San Francisco.

Although this production of *Porgy and Bess* did not thrive in San Francisco in 1938, the earlier success of Hall Johnson's folk opera *Run, Little Chillun* "provided the impetus" for staging *Swing Mikado*, a reimagination of Gilbert and Sullivan's comic opera, *The Mikado*.[12] The most popular Gilbert and Sullivan production in the United States, *The Mikado*, one of few G&S productions that still can "reliably fill theaters today," is a two-act comic operetta, set in Edo-era Japan.[13] It is a "satire of Victorian culture masquerading as a convoluted and kitschy love story."[14] The characters, with faux-Japanese names like Nanki-Poo, Pish-Tush, Ko-Ko, Pooh-Bah, and Yum-Yum were typically performed by White actors costumed in caricatures of traditional Japanese garb and kabuki-style makeup. The *Swing Mikado* moves the setting to a fictionalized kingdom ("a coral island in the Pacific") obviously still based on Japan; adds musical swing arrangements by Elmer Keeton, an Oakland, California–based music teacher and director of the Bay Area Negro Chorus; and arranger Gentry Warden, a Black musician from the Federal Music Project, a sister organization to the FTP. The show originated in Chicago in 1938 with an all-Black cast and had been a success.

The San Francisco production used many of the same performers that appeared in *Chillun*, including Joseph James in the role of Pooh-Bah.[15] The show was supported by the Federal Theater Project, who hired the (White) director from *Chillun* to codirect this production with the singer and Black actor Jester Hairston, billed as associate director and also playing the role of Ko-Ko.[16] Music scholar Leta Miller notes that casting the all-black troupe "carried a subtle subtext about the relationship between African Americans and the Japanese. In fact, admiration for Japan among Black Americans had a long and very public history dating back to the Japanese victory over the Russian fleet in 1905."[17] Its Asian-Pacific setting fit into the Pacific theme of the Golden Gate International Exhibition with its theme of "Pageant of the Pacific."

The show opened at the Federal Theatre on Treasure Island at the Golden Gate International Exposition in June 1939 to a rave review from John Hobart, the theater critic for the *San Francisco Chronicle*. The production featured fifteen soloists, more than sixty men and women in the singing chorus and almost twenty performers in the dancing chorus.[18] The show kept the original music but made small changes to some lyrics to "omit racists references and adapt to the change in geographical setting."[19] There was "really magnificent" singing throughout. Hobart said, "it was wonderous to hear this huge crowd of singers with full-bodied voices." Hobart noted the production preserved much of the original G&S songs but added new rhythms into the score "working subtle and unexpected changes with the familiar music" that pleased both swing aficionados and fans of conventional Gilbert & Sullivan shows. Hobart specifically complimented the performances of Jester Hairston and Joseph James. With the show's "zest and originality," Hobart predicted "packed houses from now on."[20]

After only two weeks, the show closed on Treasure Island. The show's backer, the Federal Theater Project, was an agency of the Works Progress Administration, which had done so much to provide jobs, wages, and dignity to millions of Americans during the worst of the Depression. In a gambit to win approval of a compromise relief bill in the US Congress, funding to the FTP was slashed which led to numerous show closures. As a result, over four hundred performers were put out of work in the San Francisco area, including the cast of *The Swing Mikado*. It was a blow to officials at the GGIE, which lost a prime attraction to a fair that struggled to meet attendance expectations. The show found private funding and carried on at the Geary Theater in San Francisco, and with that Joseph James and his wife Alberta, herself a pianist, continued to make their home in the city. When the show closed, the Jameses sometimes performed together on radio and in concerts.[21]

NOTES

1. Jerry Adler, "1934: The Art of the New Deal," *Smithsonian Magazine*, June 2009.
2. Pele Edises, "Joe James Is a Busy Man," *People's World Daily*, January 6, 1945.
3. Edises, "Joe James Is a Busy Man."
4. Edises, "Joe James Is a Busy Man."
5. Edises, "Joe James Is a Busy Man."
6. Edises, "Joe James Is a Busy Man"
7. Dana Whitson and Larry Clinton, "Joseph James, Entertainer," Sausalito Historical Society, February 13, 2019. Sausalitohistoricalsociety.com.
8. Edises, "Joe James Is a Busy Man."
9. Edises, "Joe James Is a Busy Man."

10. Leta E. Miller, *Music and Politics in San Francisco* (Berkeley: University of California Press, 2012), 260 and footnote 52 on page 312.

11. Miller, *Music and Politics in San Francisco*, 260.

12. Miller, *Music and Politics in San Francisco*, 260.

13. E. Tammy Kim, "An Asian-American Reimagining of Gilbert and Sullivan's 'The Mikado,'" *The New Yorker*, December 27, 2016.

14. Kim, "An Asian-American Reimagining of Gilbert and Sullivan's 'The Mikado.'"

15. Description of Gentry Warden from Leta E. Miller, "Elmer Keeton and His Bay Area Negro Chorus: Creating an Artistic Identity in Depression-Era San Francisco," *Black Music Research Journal* 30, no. 2 (Fall 2010): 125.

16. "Gordon Lange, Co-director of 'Swing Mikado' Has Been Around," *San Francisco Chronicle*, September 1, 1939, 10. See Program for the "Swing" Mikado at the Federal Theatre, Golden Gate International Exhibition, June 1939, Library of Congress.

17. Miller, *Music and Politics in San Francisco*, 262.

18. Program for the "Swing" Mikado.

19. Leta E. Miller, "Elmer Keeton and His Bay Area Negro Chorus: Creating an Artistic Identity in Depression-Era San Francisco," *Black Music Research Journal* 30, no. 2 (Fall 2010): 107.

20. John Hobart, "'The Swing Mikado' Makes Hit, 'De Punishment Fits De Crime,'" *San Francisco Chronicle*, June 16, 1939, 6.

21. Edises, "Joe James Is a Busy Man."

6

Fission from the Old World

By the time the fair at Treasure Island ended its first season in late October 1939, Europe was at war. In early September of that year, Hitler's Germany invaded Poland, compelling Britain, with its colonies and dominions, and its ally France to declare war on Germany. Unlike World War I, this war did not come as a surprise. Germany's militaristic expansion had been underway for several years and went hand in glove with increasing anti-Semitism in the country. When the Nazi party came into power in 1933, through the beginning of World War II, Germany enacted hundreds of laws and decrees that restricted all aspects of public and private life for Jews. In 1933 Jews were excluded from the civil service and the number of Jewish students at German schools and universities was severely reduced. Jewish participation in the medical and legal professions was restricted. The next year Jewish actors were forbidden to perform on stage or screen. Later, Jews were required to register their property and assets in a clear prelude to the eventual expropriation of this wealth by the state. By late 1938, Jewish students and professors alike were expelled from public schools and universities altogether.

German Jewish scientists were quick to see where Germany's ratcheting anti-Semitic laws were heading. Some of them emigrated before German law prohibited them from doing so, leaving behind members of their families who lacked the rare and desirable educations that made the scientists welcome in countries otherwise that severely restricted immigration. German law also required emigrating Jews to leave behind most of their personal property, making them penniless refugees. Edith Frank, the mother of Holocaust diarist Anne Frank, wrote in a letter at the end of

1937: "I think that all the German Jews are searching the world today and there is no room for them anymore."[1] In 1939, the United States's combined quota for annual immigration from Germany and Austria (27,370 people) was filled for the first time during the Nazi era.[2] More than a thousand German Jewish scientists, perhaps a quarter of all the scientists working in Germany at the time, came to the United States before the war to escape Nazi persecution.[3]

For decades Germany had been a world leader in the sciences and especially in physics. Many German Jewish physicists enjoyed international reputations. The already world-famous Albert Einstein left Germany in 1933, making a new home in the United States. Over the next few years some of Germany's best physicists including Hans Bethe, John von Neumann, Leo Szilard, Edward Teller, Stanislaw Ulam, and many others emigrated, most coming to the United States. Italian physicist Enrico Fermi, whose wife was Jewish, left fascist Italy in 1938 when that country began to pass anti-Semitic racial laws. He and his wife and children immigrated to America; a move financed by the money that came with the Nobel Prize in Physics he won that year. By this time Oppenheimer and his "American School" of theoretical physicists and Ernest Lawrence and his "cyclotroneers" were becoming leaders in their fields, even as the influx of top scientists emigrating to the United States added to the power of physics in America.

After the neutron was discovered 1932 at the Cavendish Laboratory in Cambridge, scientists discovered it would make a good probe of the atomic nucleus. This spurred an especially exciting time in nuclear physics in the established capitals of the science, like Cambridge University in England and in Germany at the University of Göttingen, and the Kaiser Wilhelm Institute near Berlin, as well as at the upstart Rad Lab. Cambridge's distinguished Cavendish Lab, designed and initially run by the great Scottish mathematician James Clark Maxwell, had been the home of several giants in physics. The classicist campus at the University of Göttingen attracted some of the best minds in Europe for over two hundred years. The Kaiser Wilhelm Institute in bucolic Dahlem, outside of Berlin, was a classic historicist campus, dubbed the "German Oxford," purpose-built in 1912 to maintain Germany's superiority in chemistry and physics.[4]

Ernest Lawrence's Rad Lab, by contrast, was not impressive to behold. It was an old wooden building that had been abandoned by the engineering department. The white exterior paint was peeling in places. But it contained something new that would come to be associated with California's Silicon Valley a generation later: flat hierarchy. Physicist Luis Alverez, when he was one of the top graduate students at the University of Chicago, stopped by the Rad Lab for a visit in the mid-1930s. He remembered, "Inside, it was the most exciting place I had ever seen."[5] It was not the décor that excited Alvarez, but the culture. At Chicago, "we enjoyed fine camaraderie in the halls. But it was considered a serious breach of etiquette for anyone to suggest how a friend's experiment might be improved. By contrast, everyone at the Radiation Laboratory was encouraged to offer constructive criticism of the experiments his colleagues were performing." Alvarez noticed that at the Rad Lab, "everyone shared . . . [there] were no interior doors. Its central focus was the cyclotron, on which everyone worked and which belonged to everyone equally." Alvarez said, "Ernest Lawrence's greatest invention was doing physics in cooperative teams."[6]

The old world was not yet ready to cede leadership. In the rush to develop more powerful cyclotrons, the Rad Lab suffered some near misses. One important discovery they could have made but did not was artificial radioactivity. The Rad Lab was supremely positioned to look for it but failed to do so. Instead that discovery was made in 1934 by Irène Joliot Curie, the daughter of Pierre and Marie Curie, and her husband Frédéric Joliot. This was the same time that Lawrence was conceding defeat on his mistaken hypothesis that deuteron—a proton and neutron joined to form the nucleus of heavy hydrogen—is unstable. His theory had been roundly criticized by scientists elsewhere. Lawrence's error was found to be the result of contamination of the cyclotron by stray deuterons. Admitting his error in 1934, Lawrence was sanguine, saying, "We would be eternally miserable if our errors worried us too much because as we push forward we will make plenty more."[7] Lawrence did not mope over mistakes, but like a start-up that grows more professional as it quickly matures, the Rad Lab did pull up its socks and became more careful in conducting experiments. There was lots of room to grow. Glenn Seaborg remembered, "Our knowledge of the nucleus was so rudimentary at this point that many experiments consisted simply of bombarding an element to study what kinds of nuclear reactions would take place and what kinds of new isotopes might be formed." One of Seaborg's Rad Lab colleagues called it a "wonderful time. Radioactive elements fell in our laps as though we were shaking apples off a tree."[8] The same apple tree simile was used by German physicist Otto Hahn, called "the father of nuclear chemistry," to describe the successful work he and the Austrian Jewish physicist Lise Meitner performed together. Hahn said, "new elements fell like apples when you shook the tree."[9]

In 1934 Enrico Fermi bombarded neutrons at uranium, producing what he thought were the first elements heavier than uranium. It was not understood what was happening in these processes until late 1938. It took the collaboration of chemistry and physics to figure it out.

Following Fermi's work, Meitner and Hahn, along with German chemist Fritz Strassmann, all with the Kaiser Wilhelm Institute near Berlin, similarly bombarded uranium and other elements with neutrons. They studied the decay products they created; Hahn, a chemist, performing chemical analysis and Meitner, a physicist, explaining the nuclear processes involved. Hahn and Meitner had a long partnership that ended in July 1938 when she, an Austrian Jew, emigrated to Sweden when it was no longer tenable for her to continue working in Germany. She left Berlin with only two suitcases and found refuge, if not a welcome she found warm, in Sweden at the Nobel Institute for Physics. In Sweden, Meitner kept up her correspondence with Hahn, and continued to advise him about their joint research. In December 1938, Hahn and Strassmann, continuing their experiments bombarding uranium with neutrons, found what appeared to be isotopes of barium among the decay products. This puzzled them because they believed that a tiny neutron could not cause the nucleus to split in two to produce much lighter elements. Hahn sent a letter to Meitner describing the strange finding.[10] This was perhaps the biggest "apple" to fall anywhere to date, only Hahn did not realize it yet.

In December 1938, over Christmas vacation, Meitner and her nephew, Otto Frisch, a physicist in Denmark, discussed Hahn's letter to Meitner. Meitner and Frisch realized that something previously thought impossible was actually happening: that a uranium nucleus had split in two. After the holidays, Meitner and Frisch continued to collaborate over long distance phone calls. Meanwhile, Hahn and Strassmann published the results of their experiment in the German journal *Naturwissenschaften* on January 6, 1939. Meitner's work was not acknowledged in this article. (It would have been politically difficult if not impossible in Nazi Germany for Hahn and Strassmann to include her, a Jew in exile, as a coauthor. But Hahn, to his discredit, also subsequently failed to acknowledge his debt to her later when it would have been safe for him to do so.)

Meitner and Frisch published their theoretical interpretation of the results in the British journal *Nature* on February 11. In this article, Frisch coined the word "fission" to describe the process. Both articles were immediately recognized as significant and Meitner and Frisch's article was the starting point for further research into the nature of fission. Ruth Lewin Sime, historian of science and biographer of Lise Meitner writes, "Meitner's exclusion from [Hahn's article] was damaging, not only as an injustice to her and a violation of normal standards of scientific attribution, but also because it separated her and physics from the discovery itself. The separate publications created an artificial divide . . . an artifact of Meitner's forced emigration and the political conditions of the time." Sime continues, "Within weeks, Hahn exploited that division. Politically insecure, hoping that fission would protect him and [the KWI], he began to claim that the discovery belonged only to chemistry and that physics did not contribute to it. Hahn never wavered from this view. . . . Still, the historical record exists, and with it we can understand the remarkable interdependence of physics and chemistry that made this discovery possible."[11]

Before the journal articles reached subscribers, word of fission got out from a "grapevine" of distinguished physicists that included the kind and soft-spoken dean of nuclear physics Niels Bohr, who worked with Frisch at his lab in Denmark, and Enrico Fermi. Both Bohr and Fermi brought word of fission to a theoretical physics conference they attended in late January in Washington DC. Heading to a nearby lab, a group of physicists confirmed Hahn and Strassmann's findings on January 28. It is strange that this grapevine did not extend to Berkeley. Instead, Luis Alvarez, who had recently joined the faculty at Berkeley and worked in the Rad Lab had to read about fission in an article, although that coinage was not yet used, in the *San Francisco Chronicle*.[12] Alvarez recalls, "I remember exactly how I heard about it. I was sitting in the barber chair in Stevens Union having my hair cut, reading the *Chronicle* . . . in the second section, buried away some place, was an announcement that some German chemists had found that the uranium atom split into two pieces when it was bombarded with neutrons . . . I remember telling the barber to stop cutting my hair and I got right out of that barber chair and ran as fast as I could to the Radiation Laboratory."[13] The first person Alvarez saw was Phil Abelson, his graduate student. He told Abelson to lie down as he unloaded his news.

Abelson had been repeating work pioneered by Fermi to bombard uranium with neutrons. This generated what Fermi called the transuranium elements. It was unknown at the time that these were actually products of fission and that the concept of transuranium elements was a wild goose chase, albeit one for which he had been awarded his Nobel Prize. Using equipment that Alvarez and Abelson built by hand, Abelson, bit by bit, began to puzzle out the truth about the so-called transuranium elements. Alvarez says, "when I arrived panting from the Students Union . . . I saw Phil [and] said: 'Phil, I've got something to tell you but want you to lie down first.' So being a good graduate student he lay down on the table right alongside the control room of the cyclotron. 'Phil, what you are looking at are not transuranium elements,' . . . I showed him what was in the *Chronicle*, and of course he was terribly depressed . . . Abelson . . . had been working very hard to try and find out what transuranium elements were produced when neutrons hit uranium; he was so close to discovering fission that it was almost pitiful. He would have been there, guaranteed, in another few weeks."[14]

Leaving Abelson dejected, Alvarez went to find Oppenheimer, who was "working with his entourage in his bullpen in LeConte Hall." Oppenheimer "instantly pronounced the reaction impossible and proceeded to prove it mathematically." The next day, Alvarez and a colleague performed an experiment that demonstrated fission to Oppenheimer. Alvarez says, "I would say that in less than 15 minutes Robert had decided that this was indeed a real effect and, more importantly, he had decided that some neutrons would probably boil off in the reaction, and that you could make bombs and generate power, all inside of a few minutes . . . But it was amazing to see how rapidly his mind worked, and he came to the right conclusions."[15] If Hahn and Strassmann, and Meitner and Frisch were the first to realize there was a genie out of its bottle, within a few short years and with the industrial might of the most powerful nation on earth behind him, spending $2 billion in the effort, Oppenheimer would bend that genie to his will.

Although fission was undeniably significant, some of the best physicists in the world did not think it would be possible to make a bomb from the fission of the uranium nucleus. Oppenheimer told his colleagues at Caltech about fission, but nobody there pursued it. As late as April, Niels Bohr thought a uranium bomb was impossible to build because it was "preposterous" to expect to separate enough uranium-235.[16] "It would take the entire efforts of a country to make a bomb," Bohr noted. Oppenheimer was more optimistic, in a letter to colleagues he wrote less than a week after Alvarez demonstrated fusion to him, Oppenheimer speculated that a ten centimeter "cube of uranium deuteride . . . might very well blow itself to hell."[17] By April 29, the German government had established a conference to study uranium fission. As a result, the government decided to obtain all uranium stocks in Germany and banned the export of uranium compounds from Czechoslovakia, which Germany controlled after it invaded that country a month earlier. German scientists told the government that a uranium bomb was possible. By the summer of 1939, the German army, the *Wehrmacht*, established an office for nuclear research in Berlin. When the war began in Europe in September 1939, only Germany had a military effort devoted solely to exploring the military uses of nuclear fission.[18] The governments of the United Kingdom, Japan, and the Soviet Union were also exploring ways to make a fission weapon.

Berlin had an inchoate plan to research an atomic bomb. In large measure, America's riposte was being born at Berkeley where the powerful cyclotrons developed by the Rad Lab and the close collaboration between chemistry and physics and experiment and theory, embodied by the friendship and partnership between Lawrence and Oppenheimer, pointed the way to an American atomic bomb project.

NOTES

1. Gertjan Broek, "The (Im)possibilities of Escaping. Jewish Emigration 1933–1942," Anne Frank House. Annefrank.org

2. "Jewish Emigration from Germany," The US Holocaust Memorial Museum. Ushmm.org.

3. David Nachmansohn, *German-Jewish Pioneers in Science, 1900–1933* (New York Springer-Verlag, 1979), 119.

4. "Architecture and Environs: The Historic Research Campus in Dahlem, Berlin," Harnack House, Conference Venue of the Max Planck Society. Harnack-haus-berlin.mpg.de.

5. Luis W. Alvarez, *Adventures of a Physicist* (New York: Basic Books, 1987), 35.

6. Alvarez, *Adventures of a Physicist*, 36.

7. "Big Science, Neptunium," American Institute of Physics. Aip.org.

8. Seaborg with Seaborg, *Adventures in the Atomic Age: From Watts to Washington*, 33.

9. Richard Rhodes, *The Making of the Atomic Bomb* (New York: Simon and Schuster, 1986), 234.

10. Ernie Tretkoff, "December 1938: Discovery of Nuclear Fission," This Month in Physics History, American Physical Society News, December 2007, volume 16, number 11. Aps.org.

11. Ruth Lewin Sime, "Science and Politics: The Discovery of Nuclear Fission 75 Years Ago," *Annalen der Physik* (Berlin) 526, no. 3–4, (2014): A27–A31.

12. "200 Million Volts of Energy Created by Atom Explosions," *San Francisco Chronicle*, January 31, 1939, 2.

13. Charles Weiner and Barry Richman, "Luis W. Alvarez Oral History Conducted on February 14, 1967," Niels Bohr Library and Archives, American Institute of Physics. Aip.org.

14. Weiner and Richman, "Luis W. Alvarez Oral History Conducted on February 14, 1967."

15. Weiner and Richman, "Luis W. Alvarez Oral History Conducted on February 14, 1967."

16. Lawrence Badash, Elizabeth Hodes, and Adolph Tiddens, "Nuclear Fission: Reaction to the Discovery in 1939," *Proceedings of the American Philosophical Society* 130, no. 2 (June 1986): 213.

17. Badash, Hodes, and Tiddens, "Nuclear Fission: Reaction to the Discovery in 1939." In the uranium bomb "Little Boy" that destroyed Hiroshima only 1.09 kg of the 64 kg of uranium used was converted into energy. It was the equivalent of detonating 15,000 tons of TNT, according to Los Alamos National Laboratory calculations. Known as a gun-type fission device, it fires a mass of uranium into another to create a supercritical mass. Source: Marc Lallanilla, "The First Atomic Bombs: Hiroshima and Nagasaki," Live Science, March 11, 2022. Livescience.com.

18. Badash, Hodes, and Tiddens, "Nuclear Fission: Reaction to the Discovery in 1939," 215.

7

Panic in California

When airplanes and submarines of the Japanese Imperial Navy bombed and strafed the US naval base at Pearl Harbor in Oahu, Hawaii, on the morning of December 7, 1941, the immediate victims were the sailors, soldiers and civilians killed or injured in what President Roosevelt called the "dastardly attack." More proximal victims were Japanese Americans who, for no reason other than their race, were subject to an atrocious violation of their civil rights when they were effectively stripped of their property and liberty, rounded up and forced into internment far away from their homes. This happened because they were not White and had no political clout.

The first Japanese immigrant known to come to San Francisco arrived in 1860, coincidently, the same year Japan assigned an ambassador to the United States. Seven years later more Japanese settlers came to San Francisco, and by 1870 the government of Japan opened a consulate in the city.[1] Despite the decades long experience of Japanese and Chinese immigrants in California, there was tremendous racial hatred of them in the country and especially in California, where most of them lived. The Immigration Act of 1924 prohibited further immigration to the United States from Japan. It also made the over forty-seven thousand Japanese already in the United States, the Issei, ineligible for naturalization.

In 1940, fewer than 127,000 people of Japanese descent lived in the continental United States. Over ninety thousand, almost three out of every four, lived in California. The American born children of Japanese immigrants, called Nisei, were US citizens. There were around eighty thousand Nisei living in the United States when the war began.[2] Issei and Nisei suffered petty apartheid in California where "for years they had experienced all kinds of racial discrimination—laws against intermarriage with whites, legal exclusion from swimming pools and dance halls, extralegal bars to employment and to middle-class housing districts."[3] There were no Japanese American senators, congressmen, or state assembly representatives. Few segments of political or social life in California were sympathetic to the Issei or Nisei. Many otherwise politically progressive leaders, including California governor and later senator Hiram Johnson, were openly antagonistic to Chinese and Japanese immigrants.

Many Issei and their families lived in rural communities. Those who lived in cities usually resided in Japanese communities called *Nihonmachi* (Japanese towns) in Los Angeles and Bay Area cities including San Francisco and Oakland. In San Francisco, the largest numbers of Japanese lived in an area called the Fillmore or Japantown, a "district bounded by California Street on the north, O'Farrell Street on the south, Octavia Street on the east, and Fillmore Street on the west." This was a transitional area that was mostly free from race-based restrictive covenants that discouraged home sales to non-Whites. Here, Japanese and some Black San Franciscans lived side by side. In Oakland, the Japanese community lived mainly in an area "bounded on the north by 10th Street, on the south and west by the estuary, and on the east by Farrell Street." Here people of Japanese, Chinese, Portuguese, and African descent lived together.[4] Although restrictive covenants narrowed the choice of neighborhoods available to Japanese (as well as Black and Chinese) residents, the Nihonmachi did provide residents a common culture and language, which was especially important to Issei residents. As American-born and Americanized Nisei children grew up, they tended to move away from Japan towns to more prosperous neighborhoods. In the Fillmore, as the Nisei moved out, Black San Franciscans tended to move in. Prior to World War II, however, the numbers of both populations in San Francisco were small.

The day after Pearl Harbor was attacked the two largest Japanese language newspapers in San Francisco were closed by the US government. All transportation on the San Francisco Bay Bridge was under close surveillance and cars operated by Issei or Nisei were stopped by the California Highway Patrol and carefully searched for explosives. The army did the same on the Golden Gate Bridge, which is anchored upon military reservations at either end. Officials of United Airlines, American Airlines, and T.W.A. prohibited the transportation of "any person who is a Japanese national or who is suspected of being a Japanese national."[5] The chief law enforcement officer of the federal government, Attorney General Francis Biddle, tried to calm any fear and race-based hatred Americans might feel toward Issei and their American citizen children, the Nisei. He said, "There are in the United States many persons of a Japanese extraction whose loyalty to this country, even in the present emergency, is unquestioned. It would therefore be a serious mistake to take any action against these people. State and local authorities are urged to take no direct action against Japanese in their communities but should consult with representatives of the FBI." California Governor Culbert Olson, to a lesser degree echoed Biddle's statement, saying, "Without doubt, we must separate the sheep from the wolves. All alien enemies should be interned, but we also must make sure that loyal Japanese are protected." At this time, Germany and Italy had not yet declared war against the United States, so the only enemy aliens were Issei or other Japanese nationals. Federal officials emphasized that there would be no mass internment of enemy aliens.

Nevertheless, the Japanese communities in California were nervous and had much to fear. Threats of mob violence spread in the Fillmore. Issei parents crowded the San Francisco health office anxious to get copies of the birth certificates for their American-born children.[6] Issei and Nisei in the Fillmore tried to remain indoors as much as possible to avoid trouble. By contrast, Whites "curious to see the reaction of the Japanese in America, thronged to [Japanese neighborhoods] in such numbers that fifty policemen were called to disperse the crowd. The entire area between Post and Bush Streets and along Buchanan Street was placed under a heavy guard of foot, motorized, and mounted police. The entire district was blocked off."[7]

In the first weeks of the war, there was relatively little violence reported against Issei or Nisei. The US Treasury Department closed all alien Japanese businesses "until further notice" and froze all alien funds. Enemy aliens, which included the Issei, and by this time German and Italian aliens after Germany and Italy declared war on the US, faced travel restrictions. Hundreds of citizens of Germany, Italy, and Japan, now considered enemy aliens, were picked up by federal agents. "By the second week of the war the Treasury Department unfroze some of the alien funds; businesses reopened; and travel restrictions were relaxed. The populace was still calm."[8] The FBI continued to apprehend suspect enemy aliens, and by the end of the month it was reported that 1,291 Japanese had been taken into custody.[9] On December 27, 1941, Biddle issued the first general order towards enemy aliens, declaring all short wave radios, cameras, and firearms contraband for them. German, Italian, and Japanese enemy aliens were required to turn in these items to officials by December 29. "Scores of aliens thronged to the police stations with their contraband. In Berkeley by noon on the 29th, 50 cameras, 5 guns, 26 radios and a 4-foot samurai sword were turned in. In Oakland over 800 pieces of equipment were turned in, most of them from Japanese. Alameda's large Japanese population turned in 215 cameras, 71 radios, and 35 guns. In San Francisco over 1,000 radios were turned in, most of them from Japanese. The United States Attorney in San Francisco explained that the articles were not being confiscated but that they were merely being held until the end of the emergency."[10]

On New Year's Day in 1942, the Justice Department announced very restrictive travel bans for all enemy aliens. These were eased a week later. At about this time, Attorney General Biddle announced the registration of all German, Italian, and Japanese aliens over the age of fourteen. They were photographed, fingerprinted, and each was issued with an identification card bearing the person's photograph.[11] At the same time, President Roosevelt and Biddle decried the growing animosity directed against Japanese communities along the West Coast, where, among other injustices, Issei and even Nisei were being dismissed from their jobs. Roosevelt said at the time, "It is one thing to safeguard American industry, and particularly defense industry, against sabotage, but it is very much another to throw out of work honest and loyal people who are sincerely patriotic. Such a policy is stupid and unjust."[12] Biddle called the anti Issei and Nisei actions "stupid and un-American." A few days later, Biddle elaborated, "The Federal Government is fully aware of the dangers from disloyal aliens as well as disloyal citizens and it has control of their activities." Biddle asked that the people of California take no action against the children, families, or relatives of axis nationals. "Let us not subject them to the fears that people living in Axis countries have, for those are the fears we are fighting against. Let us set a good example of what we mean by the American way in our own neighborhoods."[13] In Los Angeles, Mayor Fletcher Bowron tried to calm the anti-Japanese sentiment he saw growing by urging, "all residents of Los Angeles continue to treat both aliens and native-born Japanese with courtesy and respect and that no advantage of any kind be taken of the Japanese people."[14]

Still, the prejudice worsened, especially against the Issei and Nisei. Much of this was encouraged by racist city and state political leaders and local and state law enforcement. Indeed, San Francisco Mayor Angelo Rossi, the son of Italian immigrants, was quick to turn against Japanese Americans, and Bowron in Los Angeles soon abandoned his initial support for them too. It is a sad litany described by Berkeley student Tamotsu Shibutani in a research paper he wrote in 1942 when these events were still very fresh. On January 28, 1942, the mayor of Los Angeles "in one of the first moves affecting Nisei, announced that 39 American-born Japanese [municipal employees] had been given a 'leave of absence' for the duration of the war, and that Nisei on the waiting list [for city jobs] had been suspended." The Mayor assured the workers that they would be given back their jobs at the end of the war but pointed out that he was forced to discharge them because he had no way of determining their status as 'full' citizens of the United States. On the same day, the Los Angeles County supervisors unanimously adopted a resolution urging the Federal government to remove the county's 13,391 alien Japanese from the defense areas and began consideration of a step like that of Mayor Bowron. "On the following day, the California State Personnel Board took drastic action against the employment of persons who are the immediate descendants of persons from countries at war against the United States."[15]

On the same day William Randolph Hearst's *San Francisco Examiner* printed one of the most vicious articles written since the outbreak of the war, urging the evacuation of all Japanese from the coastal area. Hearst's syndicated columnist and part time actor Henry McLemore wrote in his regular column titled, "The Lighter Side," mixing garden variety nastiness, "[Japanese] get ahead of you in the stamp line at the post office" with lies packaged as fact, "Everywhere that the Japanese have attacked to date, the Japanese population has risen to aid the attackers" citing incorrect stories that local Issei and Nisei participated in that attack at Pearl Harbor. McLemore advocates for the "immediate removal of every Japanese on the West Coast to a point deep in the interior, "If making 1,000,000 innocent Japanese uncomfortable would prevent one scheming Japanese from costing the life of an American boy, then let 1,000,000 innocents suffer." Now thoroughly wound up, he concludes, "Personally, I hate the Japanese. And that goes for all of them. Let's stop worrying about hurting the enemy's feelings and start doing it."[16]

On January 30, the San Francisco Board of Supervisors passed a resolution like that of the one passed in Los Angeles County requesting the Federal government to transfer inland all alien Japanese.[17] It was in this kind of nervous atmosphere that the members of the San Francisco Polo Club took their mounts through the beaches of San Francisco in search of invaders from Japan.[18] By the end of January, the West Coast was increasingly gripped by anti-Japanese hysteria at first aimed at Issei and then growing to include Nisei American citizens too. By February 21, President Roosevelt placed the army in charge of security on the West Coast. Shibutani writes, "Once the army was in [control] the populace seemed more at ease, but the tension continued to be high until the first week in March, when the army announced that all Japanese (citizens as well as aliens) would be evacuated. As the various communities began to evacuate, the high feeling began gradually to decline once more."[19]

It is difficult to overstate the panic that gripped people, civilian and military alike, on the West Coast immediately following Pearl Harbor. Only four army divisions and one Marine Corps division, about one hundred thousand men in all, thinly spread from Puget Sound to San Diego were stationed to defend the vast coastline. Many of these soldiers and Marines were only half trained, all were ill equipped.[20] America's defense planners had relied on the US Navy's Pacific fleet, based in Hawaii, to protect the West Coast of the continental United States against serious attack. After the disastrous losses that fleet suffered at Pearl Harbor it seemed that the entire 1,300-mile length of Pacific Ocean coastline was open to attack by the Japanese. This left vulnerable nearly half of the American military aircraft production (and almost all of the heavy bomber output) that came from eight aircraft plants in the Los Angeles area.[21] All of those plants were within range of naval guns should Japanese destroyers appear off the coast.[22] Also vulnerable were the many naval yards, ship terminals and vital ports, like those in Los Angeles and San Francisco, and the California oil industry, all of which were essential to the war America entered after Pearl Harbor.

The military on the West Coast was under the over-all leadership of Lieutenant General John L. DeWitt, the three-star general in command of the Fourth Army. The senior tactical commander in California was Major General Joseph Warren Stilwell. This two-star general was "imaginative and unorthodox" and rated the best of the nine corps commanders in the army.[23] He was known as "Vinegar Joe" because he did not hide is disregard at incompetence or pompousness, of which there was plenty of in the small, cliquish peacetime army. When Japan attacked Pearl Harbor, it was up to Stilwell to figure out how to defend the entire West Coast. He had little to work with. America's army during the Depression had been small and underequipped. When World War II started in Europe, America's army was only the seventeenth largest in the world, behind Romania.[24]

With war on the horizon, Congress initiated a peacetime draft in September 1940. When Pearl Harbor was attacked, the army's ranks had swollen with recent enlistees and draftees. Officers and enlisted personnel all had a lot to learn about keeping a cool head in an emergency. Within hours of the attack in Hawaii, Stilwell's phone at his home base at Fort Ord in Monterey, California, was ringing with panicked reports of the Japanese fleet within miles of the California coast. He was told periscopes had been seen off Cliff House in San Francisco and off Point Lobos in picturesque Carmel. We know what Stilwell was thinking and feeling at this time because throughout his army career he kept notebooks and diaries that he used to, as he described, "vent his bile." Some days there were only short entries, other days longer ones. Stilwell never intended for his diaries to be published, even writing on the flyleaf of the pocket diary for 1906, "this little book contains none of your damn business!"[25] They make very interesting reading and give valuable insight to what Stilwell experienced as it happened.

In his diary Stilwell describes the confusion that sent him up and down the California coast from San Francisco to San Diego and inland to San Bernardino meeting with local civilian and military officials. Stilwell did not believe the West Coast was at risk of a serious attack and reading his diary entries for these days you can feel his frustration with the panicked soldiers and civilians. On December 8, while at the command headquarters of the army's Southern Sector in San Bernardino, Stilwell reported to the War Department about the lack of ammunition in the area, he had "almost a hatful" of bullets and shells. Inevitably, "rumors begin" that spread panic throughout the state, including a "Sunday night 'air raid' at San Francisco. Two blackouts in San Francisco. Second on account of Navy patrol. Fourth Army kind of jittery. Much depressed. Blackout on. Calmed 'em down."[26] One man remembers that blackout. Young Berkeley chemist Glenn T. Seaborg was going to have a very big impact on the war, but on that day after Pearl Harbor he was just another nervous civilian. "I had dinner with some friends across the bay in San Francisco," Seaborg writes, "The city was completely blacked out. After hearing a radio report of an air-raid alarm, we sought refuge in the basement of their apartment building. Huddling in the basement while straining to hear the hum of incoming bombers was a frightening experience that brought the reality of war home in dramatic fashion."[27]

The next day Stilwell was on an inspection trip when he received news that a Japanese attack, if not invasion, was imminent: "Fleet of thirty-four [Japanese] ships between San Francisco and Los Angeles [was reported]. Later [confirmed to be]—not authentic." Stilwell confided to his diary that day, "(Sinking feeling is growing.) More threats of raids and landings."[28] Those "34 Japanese warships" had been 14 fishing trawlers that were returning to their slips in Monterey. The "sinking feeling" Stilwell experienced was inspired by panicking soldiers and sailors, and not by the threat of the Japanese Imperial Navy. Nerves were jangled by the news on the next day, December 10, of an authentic and significant disaster to Allied forces: Japanese aircraft, in an attack lasting only two hours, sunk Britain's newest battleship, the *Prince of Wales* and the battle cruiser *Repulse* off the coast of Malaya, losing the esteemed Royal Navy command of the seas in that area. America's war planners had relied on Great Britain's Royal Navy to defend allied interests in the Far East. Of this news, Stilwell writes, "My God, worse and worse."[29]

Four days after Pearl Harbor, on December 11, Germany and Italy, at the request of Japan, declared war on the United States. The day saw Stilwell at a command post in San Diego when he was handed the phone to hear this report from the Fourth Army Headquarters in San Francisco: "'The main Japanese battle fleet is 164 miles off San Francisco. General alert of all units.'" Stilwell chastised himself, "I believed it, like a damn fool, and walked around the room trying to figure out what to do." Stilwell writes, "I imagined a wild rush up to Frisco with all available troops." Most of these troops were newly recruited Marines from the Camp Elliott training grounds in San Diego, five hundred miles away, a very long distance in the days before the interstate highway system. Stilwell continued, "the first thing to do seemed to be to inform the marines at Camp Elliott . . . General Vogel . . . agreed to play ball."[30]

Stilwell grew more expansive in his diary entry this day, "The first reaction to that news is like a kick in the stomach—the unthinkable realization that our defenses were down, the enemy at hand, and that we not only had nothing to defend ourselves with, that time was against us. We could not ship the ammunition in time, nor could we evacuate the three million people in this area. Had the Japs only known, they could have landed anywhere on the coast, and after our handful of ammunition was gone, they could have shot us like pigs in a pen. (We had about ten million caliber 30 [rifle bullets], a few hundred 75s, and 266 155s. No trench mortars at all." The rumors were not true and no Japanese fleet was amassing off the coast of San Francisco. Stilwell writes, "Of course [the 4th] Army passed the buck on this report. They had it from a 'usually absolutely reliable source,' but they never should have put it out without check."[31]

On December 13, Stilwell spilled more vinegar on the Fourth Army. He writes, "Not content with the above blah, [the 4th] Army pulled another at ten-thirty today. 'Reliable information that attack on Los Angeles is imminent. A general alarm being considered.' The old sinking feeling again." Buoyed by a small improvement in his ammunition stores and the impending arrival of an additional regiment, Stilwell writes he, "Got what hope I could from that, and then decided to disbelieve the report. Of course, the attack never materialized, but a 'general alarm' would have been just as serious. The plain truth is that it is not possible to evacuate three million people east, over waterless desert, and there would have been frightful casualties if a general exodus had started. What jackass would sound a 'general alarm' under the circumstances? The [Fourth] Army G-2 is just another amateur, like all the rest of the staff. Nothing should go out unconfirmed. Nothing is ever as bad as it seems at first." But the West Coast was far from girded for war. Stilwell only had six tanks that worked at his home base at Fort Ord, he confided in his diary, "(The others won't run.)"[32]

California did suffer some enemy action. Amid reports of sightings of Japanese submarines, on December 23, the captain of the oil tanker *S.S. Montebello* resigned his post rather than take out the ship. Command fell to the first mate, who along with the crew, decided to face the danger and set out for their destination, Vancouver, British Columbia. Four hours into the trip, two seamen on watch reported to the captain that they were being stalked by what they took to be a Japanese submarine. Their suspicions were soon confirmed when they spotted in the early morning darkness a Japanese I-21 submarine following behind on the Montebello's port quarter. The submarine loosed a single torpedo, which stuck the ship. Luckily, it hit the only compartment not filled with oil or gasoline. Within five minutes of the initial sighting, the acting captain gave the order to abandon ship. The Japanese sub opened fire with its deck gun, raking the blazing ship with machine-gun fire. All thirty-eight members of the crew and their captain loaded into four lifeboats and watched as the submarine submerged and their ship burned. It sank in less than an hour. The crew rowed for six hours, finally reaching the southern coast of Cambria, California. All hands survived.[33]

Exactly two months later, on February 23, 1942, George Washington's birthday and coincidentally while a Roosevelt fireside chat "On the Progress of the War,"[34] was broadcast in California, a Japanese I-17 submarine shelled an oil refinery at Goleta, near Santa Barbara, in a fusillade lasting twenty minutes. It was the first attack on the American mainland in the war.[35] There were no injuries, but these attacks did stoke the fears of civilians and the military. The next night began the "Battle of Los Angeles" where reports of unidentified aircraft precipitated a blackout in the city. Antiaircraft artillery began to fire shortly after three o'clock in the morning, probably spurred by a weather balloon over Santa Monica. During the next hour, the guns fired some 1,400 rounds of 3-inch antiaircraft ammunition against a variety of "targets" in the Los Angeles area. Nobody could agree on what had caused the reports of enemy activity, and luckily only pride was hurt: the army concluded that there had been from one to five unidentified planes that touched off the "battle" whereas the navy decided that there had been no excuse for the firing.[36]

If the US Fourth Army was in a tizzy, there was one old woman in Oakland who kept calm. Mostly of German descent, but perhaps one-eighth Black and married to a dark-skinned West Indian, which in America at that time made her Black too, she was in California for a few months to help her daughter care for her two grandchildren. Her granddaughter a 13-year-old Black girl named Marguerite Johnson remembers, "World War II started on a Sunday afternoon when I was on my way to the movies. People in the streets shouted, 'We're at war. We've declared war on Japan.' I ran all the way home. Not too sure I wouldn't be bombed before I reached [my brother] and Mother. Grandmother . . . calmed my anxiety by explaining that America would not be bombed, not as long as Franklin Delano Roosevelt was President. He was, after all, a politician's politician and he knew what he was doing."[37] Unfortunately, many military, law enforcement, and political leaders were not so calm.

NOTES

1. Tamotsu Shibutani, "The Initial Impact of the War on the Japanese Communities in the San Francisco Bay Region—A Preliminary Report," 42. bk0014b1h0t-FID1.pdf. Japanese American Evacuation and Resettlement Records, University of California, Berkeley Bancroft Library.

2. There were about eighty thousand Nisei and their children Sansei at the time of internment. Most of the Sansei were babies or very young children at that time. The Nisei themselves mostly were teenagers or young adults because their immigrant parents, struggling against poverty, had tended to postpone marriage. As a consequence there was a missing generation among Japanese Americans. In 1942 the median age of Issei males was fifty-six; the median age of female Issei forty-seven. The median age of Nisei was only eighteen. Source: John Morton Blum, *V Was for Victory: Politics and American Culture during World War II* (San Diego: Harcourt, Brace & Company, 1976), 156.

3. Blum, *V Was for Victory: Politics and American Culture during World War II*, 156.

4. Tamotsu Shibutani, "The Initial Impact of the War on the Japanese Communities in the San Francisco Bay Region – A Preliminary Report," bk0014b1h0t-FID1.pdf, 41, Japanese American Evacuation and Resettlement Records, University of California, Berkeley Bancroft Library.

5. "Quick Jap Roundup Starts Here," *San Francisco Examiner*, 10. "SF Bridges under Guard for Sabotage," *San Francisco Examiner*, December 8, 1941, 10.

6. Shibutani, "The Initial Impact of the War on the Japanese Communities in the San Francisco Bay Region—A Preliminary Report," 59.

7. Shibutani, "The Initial Impact of the War on the Japanese Communities in the San Francisco Bay Region—A Preliminary Report," 59.

8. Shibutani, "The Initial Impact of the War on the Japanese Communities in the San Francisco Bay Region—A Preliminary Report," 60.

9. Shibutani, "The Initial Impact of the War on the Japanese Communities in the San Francisco Bay Region—A Preliminary Report," 60.

10. Shibutani, "The Initial Impact of the War on the Japanese Communities in the San Francisco Bay Region—A Preliminary Report," 61.

11. Shibutani, "The Initial Impact of the War on the Japanese Communities in the San Francisco Bay Region—A Preliminary Report," 62.

12. Lawson Fusao Inada, *Only What We Could Carry* (Berkeley: Heyday Books, 2000), 14.

13. Shibutani, "The Initial Impact of the War on the Japanese Communities in the San Francisco Bay Region—A Preliminary Report," 62.

14. Inada, *Only What We Could Carry*, 16.

15. Shibutani, "The Initial Impact of the War on the Japanese Communities in the San Francisco Bay Region—A Preliminary Report," 67.

16. Henry McLemore, "The Lighter Side," *The San Francisco Examiner*, January 29, 1942.

17. Shibutani, "The Initial Impact of the War on the Japanese Communities in the San Francisco Bay Region—A Preliminary Report," 67.

18. Roger W. Lotchin, *The Bad City in the Good War* (Bloomington: Indiana University Press, 2003), 1.

19. Shibutani, "The Initial Impact of the War on the Japanese Communities in the San Francisco Bay Region—A Preliminary Report," 65.

20. Joseph W. Stilwell arranged and edited by Theodore H. White, *The Stilwell Papers* (New York: Shocken Books, 1972), 1.

21. Stetson Conn, Rose C. Engelman, and Byron Fairchild, *Guarding the United States and Its Outposts*, Office of Military History, Department of the Army, Washington, DC, 1964, 82.

22. Barbara W. Tuchman, *Stilwell and the American Experience in China, 1911–1945* (New York: Grove Press, 1985), 230.

23. John K. Fairbank in his introduction to Tuchman, *Stilwell*, v.

24. Rick Atkinson, "Ten Things Every American History Student Should Know about Our Army in World War II," Foreign Policy Research Institute, May 28, 2009. Fpri.org.

25. Tuchman, *Stilwell and the American Experience in China, 1911–1945*, xii.

26. Stilwell arranged and White, "*The Stilwell Papers*," 3.

27. Seaborg with Seaborg, *Adventures in the Atomic Age: From Watts to Washington*, 82.

28. Stilwell and White, *The Stilwell Papers*, 3. NB: Insertions in brackets or parentheses are Stilwell's.

29. Tuchman, *Stilwell and the American Experience in China, 1911–1945*, 230.

30. Stilwell and White, *The Stilwell Papers*, 4. NB: Insertions in brackets or parentheses are Stilwell's.

31. Stilwell and White, *The Stilwell Papers*, 4–5. NB: Insertions in brackets or parentheses are Stilwell's.

32. Stilwell and White, *The Stilwell Papers*, 5. NB: Insertions in brackets or parentheses are Stilwell's.

33. "Sinking," California Department of Fish and Wildlife. Wildlife.ca.gov.

34. Presidential Speeches, "Franklin D. Roosevelt, February 23, 1942: Fireside Chat 20: On the Progress of the War," Miller Center, University of Virginia. Millercetner.org.

35. "Sub Shells Santa Barbara Coast," *The San Diego Union*, February 24, 1942, 1.

36. Conn, Engelman, and Fairchild, *Guarding the United States and Its Outposts*, 87–88.

37. Angelou, *I Know Why the Caged Bird Sings*, 208.

8

Drumbeat to Internment

After war was declared, citizens of Germany, Italy, and Japan living in the United States were deemed enemy aliens and investigated. At the time of Pearl Harbor, there were about 127,000 people of Japanese ancestry living in the United States. Almost three-quarters were American-born citizens of the United States, only about one-quarter were Issei, who had been denied citizenship by law. In California alone, however, there were almost 52,000 Italian aliens—more than the total of Japanese aliens in the entire United States—and almost 20,000 German aliens. Except for refugees escaping Mussolini and Hitler and a few latecomers, the Italians and Germans living in this country were aliens by choice because there was no law preventing them from seeking citizenship. In Los Angeles, where the largest concentration of Japanese in the United States lived, there were 17,528 German-born alien residents compared to only 8,726 Issei.[1]

The FBI rounded up a few thousand German, Italian, and Japanese citizens living in the United States that they considered suspicious. More than a thousand were arrested on December 7 and 8.[2] In the case of people of Japanese ancestry, suspicion extended to American-born citizens too. This was never the case with German Americans or Italian Americans. It started out of simple fear stoked by racism. Unlike German Americans and Italian Americans who had political clout in Congress and formed important voting blocs, "Japanese-Americans were not white and had no political importance."[3] Because of the Immigration Act of 1924, the Issei, immigrants born in Japan, almost a quarter of the total Japanese American population, were prevented from becoming US citizens.[4] Their children born in the United States, known as Nisei, were American citizens.

Issei and Nisei alike faced increasing suspicions from some White citizens in the West Coast states, but the worst xenophobia was fueled by officials. Some were just scared, others were bigoted, but most surprising were the responses of leaders then or later famous for their moral principles, rectitude, and even liberalism. For them, their actions following Pearl Harbor were the worst moments of their careers.

In the days immediately following the attack at Pearl Harbor, there were reports of enemy ships off the West Coast. These reports were all false, but they unnerved military and civilian leaders and the public. On December 10, army authorities received a report from "an agent of the Treasury Department" that "an estimated 20,000 Japanese in the San Francisco metropolitan area were ready for organized action." The jittery Ninth Corps Area army staff failed to investigate the rumor and hurriedly completed a plan for a large-scale evacuation of potential Japanese uprisers that was approved by the corps area commander. Only then did the army staff contact the local FBI head who "scoffed at the whole affair as the wild imaginings of a discharged former FBI man."[5] The army reported the rumor and their plan for removal of Japanese from San Francisco to Washington hoping that "it may have the effect of arousing the War Department to some action looking to the establishment of an area or areas for the detention of aliens."[6]

Spurred by this activity—all based on an erroneous rumor that had been dismissed by the FBI—on December 19, General DeWitt, head of the Western Defense Command, recommended to his superiors "that action be initiated at the earliest practicable date to collect all alien subjects fourteen years of age and over, of enemy nations and remove them to the Zone of the Interior." At this time, DeWitt was against removing American citizens. DeWitt remarked to the commander of the army's provost marshal general that "he had just been visited by a representative of the Los Angeles Chamber of Commerce, who had asked for a roundup of all Japanese in the Los Angeles area." DeWitt told the man,

> if we go ahead and arrest the 93,000 Japanese, native born and foreign born, we are going to have an awful job on our hands and are very liable to alienate the loyal Japanese from disloyal . . . I'm very doubtful that it would be common sense procedure to try and intern or to intern 117,000 Japanese in this theater. . . . I told the governors of all the states that those people should be watched better if they were watched by the police and people of the community in which they live and have been living for years . . . and then inform the F.B.I. or the military authorities of any suspicious action so we could take necessary steps to handle it . . . rather than try to intern all those people, men, women and children, and hold them under military control and under guard. I don't think it's a sensible thing to do . . . I'd rather go along the way we are now . . . rather than attempt any wholesale internment. . . .

An American citizen, after all, is an American citizen. And while they all may not be loyal, I think we can weed the disloyal out of the loyal and lock them up if necessary.[7]

His counterpart agreed.

The US Attorney General Francis Biddle remembers that General DeWitt, "kept his head at first and resisted suggestions that the Japanese be herded out of the coastal territory, which was his jurisdiction."[8] But pressure from California political and law enforcement authorities increased, especially from some California congressional delegations and the state's governor, Culbert Olson, and Attorney General Earl Warren. The actions of Earl Warren in this episode are especially surprising given his later championing of liberalism during his time as chief justice of the Supreme Court. Looking at Warren's actions at this time, we see the man grappling with his worst instincts. When nervous authorities launched several air raid warnings in the Bay Area in the weeks following Pearl Harbor, each one a false alarm, not all citizens were as sanguine about the threat as Marguerite Johnson's grandmother. One air raid warning in early 1942 drove Earl Warren, along with his wife and children, to spend two evenings in the basement of their home in Oakland, eating sandwiches and sleeping in sleeping bags, while keeping one ear open for the sounds of an attack.[9] Still, Warren strenuously objected in early 1942 when the California State Personnel Board moved to prevent Japanese Americans from taking civil service exams. But Warren was beginning to lose his perspective and in his mind the distinction between potentially dangerous Japanese enemy aliens and loyal Japanese American citizens began to erode from the frictions of bias and fear. Meanwhile, General DeWitt, according to Biddle, "was apt to waver under popular pressure, a characteristic arising from this tendency to reflect the views of the last man to whom he talked. He had convictions—but again they did not stick when the final test case."[10]

In early January 1942, representatives from the Department of Justice, which Biddle headed, and the War Department, both civilians and military, met to discuss the security situation on the West Coast. Soon after, the army designated eighty-six "Category A" zones in California from which DeWitt wanted enemy aliens excluded, plus eight "Category B" zones in which enemy aliens could remain only by special permission. The first two Category A zones included the San Francisco waterfront and the area around the Los Angeles Municipal Airport.[11] Only 40 percent of aliens in those areas would have been Japanese, the majority would have been Italians.

Roosevelt's representative for all matters relating to the defense of the nation, including the issue of Japanese Americans living on the West Coast was Henry L. Stimson. He was a deeply experienced member of

FDR's cabinet. With the global war in Europe and Asia already underway, Democrat FDR asked Stimson, a Republican lawyer, to serve as secretary of war (the cabinet position retitled secretary of defense in 1947). Stimson had served as secretary of state under President Hoover and had been secretary of war under President Taft. In his cabinet, Roosevelt respected and usually deferred to Stimson's judgment on matters of defense. In the wake of Pearl Harbor, Stimson felt great urgency to deal with the threat he perceived coming from Issei and Nisei in California. This was probably due to his misunderstanding of the security situation on the West Coast resulting from misinformation he received from his deputies and from General DeWitt. Attorney General Biddle writes that Stimson informed him: "As late as yesterday, 24 January, [DeWitt] stated over the telephone that shore-to-ship and ship-to shore radio communications, undoubtedly coordinated by intelligent enemy control were continually operating. A few days ago it was reported by military observers on the Pacific coast that not a single ship had sailed from our Pacific ports without being subsequently attacked. General DeWitt's apprehensions have been confirmed by recent visits of military observers from the War Department to the Pacific coast. The alarming and dangerous situation just described, in my opinion, calls for immediate and stringent action."[12] Stimson had been grossly misinformed by some of the same jittery military authorities that distressed General Stilwell. No Japanese submarines or surface ships came anywhere near the West Coast in December and the FBI and others had disproved all claims of hostile shore-to-ship and ship-to shore communications, "they were phantoms like the imaginary enemy aircraft that set off the 'Battle of Los Angeles.'"[13]

Stimson's assessment of the threat posed by Issei and Nisei was further clouded by his unfamiliarity with such people and his misconceptions about them that were common at that time. In the lead up to the war and during the years of fighting, Stimson's judgment and deliberation were vital to the country. Unfortunately, those qualities left him in this instance. Stimson kept a diary that gives invaluable insight into his perceptions of the many great events in which he participated. Of the Issei and Nisei, Stimson writes, "The continued pressure of a large, unassimilated, tightly knit racial group, bound to an enemy nation by strong ties of race, culture, custom and religion along a frontier vulnerable to attack, constituted a menace which had to be dealt with."[14] He was not thinking of the German aliens or Italian aliens, who could have fit this description, only the Japanese aliens and Japanese American citizens. Secretary of the Treasury Henry Morgenthau Jr., in his memoir written after the war, writes, "deep-rooted hostility to the Japanese generated frequent rumors about espionage and subversion and frightened demands for repressive treatment not only of local Japanese residents but also of Nisei, American citizens of Japanese descent."[15]

If the soldiers hitting the air raid sirens in California were jumpy, the senior most military leadership in Washington had a more considered view about the threat to the West Coast. On February 4, 1942, General Mark W. Clark of the army general headquarters and Admiral Harold R. Stark, chief of naval operations, testified before two congressional subcommittees considering strengthening defenses along the West Coast, and the threat of sabotage. General Clark said that he thought the Pacific states were unduly alarmed. While both he and Admiral Stark agreed the West Coast defenses were not adequate to prevent the enemy from attacking, they also agreed that the chance of any sustained attack or of an invasion was as General Clark put it—nil.[16] The FBI agreed. At around this time, J. Edgar Hoover, the director of the Federal Bureau of Investigation, who later would not enjoy a reputation for always being judicious in matters of security against real or imagined enemies of the United States, in a memorandum to his boss Attorney General Biddle, "denied the existence of any information showing that the attacks on ships leaving the West Coast ports were associated with espionage activity ashore. Every complaint of signaling," he added, had been investigated; but in no case had "any information been obtained which would substantiate the allegation that there had been signaling from shore-to-ship since the beginning of the war."[17]

Fear was stirred up by nationally syndicated newspaper columnists, who in that age of newspapers, wielded tremendous power to influence readers all over the country and in turn the municipal, state, and national politicians who governed them. One immensely popular columnist was Westbrook Pegler, a Pulitzer Prize winner whose strident opinions often went against FDR and organized labor and whose columns leaned toward rabble-rousing populism. In 1941 Pegler polled just behind Roosevelt and Josef Stalin in reader nominations for *Time's* "Man of the Year." In February 1942 Pegler wrote in his column, "the Japanese in California should be under armed guard . . . to hell with habeas corpus until the danger is over."[18] Pegler's columns ran in 174 newspapers with a combined ten million subscribers.[19] Walter Lippmann, a more temperate columnist considered the "dean of American political journalism"[20] had a readership similar in size to Pegler.[21] On February 13, 1942, he published a piece titled "Fifth Column," equating Japanese Americans with spies. Lippmann wrote:

> The enemy alien problem on the Pacific Coast, or much more accurately the Fifth Column problem, is very serious and it is very special . . . The peculiar danger of the Pacific Coast is in a Japanese raid accompanied by enemy

action inside American territory . . . For while the striking power of Japan from the sea and air might not in itself be overwhelming at any one point just now, Japan could strike a blow which might do irreparable damage if it were accompanied by the kind of organized sabotage to which this part of the country is especially vulnerable.[22]

Lippman then uses a curious kind of logic to suggest because there had been no sabotage from Issei or Nisei in America up to that time, there must be something brewing. Lippman writes, "From what we know about Hawaii and about the Fifth Column in Europe this is not, as some have liked to think, a sign that there is nothing to be feared. It is a sign that the blow is well-organized and that it is held back until it can be struck with maximum effect."[23] Except for the popular nationally syndicated columnist Ernie Pyle, who went on to greater fame as a beloved war correspondent killed by a Japanese machine gun on an island near Okinawa, and a series of articles by political writer Chester Rowell in the *San Francisco Chronicle*, no national or local newspaper columnists of note opposed the internment of their fellow citizens.[24]

Despite this feverishness in the first months of the war, there were few vigilante acts of violence against Issei or Nisei. As the journalist Jim Newton writes, "California politicians . . . later blamed the public for what happened next, but that was false. It was not the public that led this descent. It was the work of leaders."[25] What happened next was a drumbeat to intern American citizens for no reason other than their race. It was a tragic episode that was rooted in xenophobia. In the first weeks after Pearl Harbor, there was no serious suggestion to intern or move the Japanese and Japanese Americans off the West Coast. Francis Biddle, who had become attorney general of the United States in early September 1941 was soon thrust into a terrible constitutional crisis over the fate of Japanese in America and particularly Japanese Americans. Biddle remembers, "By the third week in January [1942] members of the congressional delegation from California were pressing me to move out the Japanese from the West Coast. Particularly insistent was Representative Leland Ford, of California, who made it clear that he wished to include American citizens [i.e., American-born citizens of Japanese descent, Nisei]. On January 24 I wrote him that unless the writ of habeas corpus were suspended, I did not know any way in which Japanese born in this country could be interned."[26]

A report issued by the Commission on Pearl Harbor, headed by Justice Owen Roberts of the US Supreme Court, was released on January 25, 1942. The report concluded that there had been widespread espionage in Hawaii before Pearl Harbor, both by Japanese consular agents and by Japanese residents of Oahu who had "no open relations with the Japanese foreign service." The latter inflammatory charge was later proven false, but the report had a large and immediate effect, both on public opinion and on government action. The report contained no references to sabotage, as Biddle noted, "But it did enumerate in detail the espionage activities of Japanese residents in Hawaii and helped turn the tide in favor of stricter measures to prevent sabotage and espionage."[27]

On January 27, General DeWitt spoke at length with Governor Culbert L. Olson of California and afterward reported: "There's a tremendous volume of public opinion now developing against the Japanese of all classes, that is aliens and non-aliens, to get them off the land, and in Southern California around Los Angeles—in that area too—they want and they are bringing pressure on the government to move all the Japanese out. As a matter of fact, it's not being instigated or developed by people who are not thinking but by the best people of California. Since the publication of the Roberts Report they feel that they are living in the midst of a lot of enemies. They don't trust the Japanese, none of them."[28] Two days later, DeWitt spoke with California Attorney General Earl Warren. Warren told DeWitt, "He was in thorough agreement with Governor Olson that the Japanese population should be removed from the state of California." DeWitt now agreed with Olson and Warren and said he would be willing "to accept responsibility for the enemy alien program if it were transferred to him."[29]

DeWitt also changed his mind about the ability of the FBI to handle any domestic threat posed by Japanese Americans or Issei. On 30 January he wrote in an unsigned memo: "As a matter of fact, the steps now being taken . . . through the F.B.I. will do nothing more than exercise a controlling influence and preventive action against sabotage; it will not, in my opinion, be able to stop it. The only positive answer to this question is evacuation of all enemy aliens from the West Coast and resettlement or internment under positive control, military or otherwise." DeWitt told his aide he "wanted the removal of German and Italian aliens as well as all Japanese residents and he wanted all evacuees from any one particular area to be moved at the same time."[30]

Now, DeWitt who had been careful to make a distinction between Japanese American citizens (usually Nisei or the fewer in number Kibei, Japanese Americans born in America but reared and educated in Japan) and Japanese aliens (usually Issei) lumped together all people of Japanese descent, as warranting removal from areas deemed sensitive to defense interests. He continued, however, to observe the distinction between alien Germans and Italians and Americans who had descended from those countries. DeWitt learned a little about the racism that was prevalent in California at that time. He explained in a memo to colleagues, "what the California authorities proposed to do was to move both citizen and alien Japanese . . . from urban areas and from along the coast to agricultural areas within the state. They wanted to do this in particular in order to avoid having to replace the Japanese with Mexican and Negro laborers who might otherwise have to be brought into California in considerable numbers."³¹

In a phone call with his aide, DeWitt described the pressure he was getting from "some of the best people" in California. He said,

> You see, the situation is this: I have never on my own initiative recommended a mass evacuation, or the removal of any man, any Jap, other than an alien. In other words, I have made no distinction between an alien as to whether he is Jap, Italian, or German—that they must all get out of [prescribed regions]. The agitation to move all the Japanese away from the coast, and some suggestions, out of California entirely—is within the State, the population of the State, which has been espoused by the Governor. I have never been a [party] to that, but I have said, if you do that, and can solve that problem, it will be a positive step toward the protection of the coast . . . But I have never said, "You've got to do it, in order to protect the coast"; I can take such measures as are necessary from a military standpoint to control the American Jap if he is going to cause trouble within those restricted areas.³²

Anti-Japanese sentiment increased, first from California state officials and later more broadly among the people. Sentiment against aliens from Italy and Japan, never that heated in the first place, abated. As late as February 17, DeWitt remained "opposed to any preferential treatment to any alien irrespective of race" and wanted German and Italian aliens included in any removal orders. The War Department, however, did make distinctions for White aliens. As the army's official history of these events states, "There was to be no evacuation of Italians without the express permission of the Secretary of War except on an individual basis. Although the War Department plan ostensibly provided that German aliens were to be treated in the same manner as the Japanese, it qualified this intention by providing for the exemption of 'bona fide' German refugees. This qualification automatically stayed the evacuation of German aliens until General DeWitt could determine who among them were genuine refugees."³³

A congressional committee also investigated the possible removal of Japanese aliens and Japanese Americans from the West Coast. Called the Tolan Committee after its chairman, Representative John Tolan, a Democrat from Oakland, California. The committee held hearings in San Francisco; Portland, Oregon; and Seattle, Washington, to discuss the issue of Japanese internment. The hearings opened in San Francisco on February 21, 1942. The testimony of witnesses, speaking under oath, shows the mindset of those who had General DeWitt's ear. San Francisco Mayor Angelo J. Rossi, a first generation American from Italian parents, was the first to speak. Rossi pointed out the "seriousness of having alien enemies in our midst." He continued reading from his prepared statement, "The Japanese situation should be given immediate attention. It admits no delay. The activities of the Japanese saboteurs and fifth columnists in Honolulu and the battle fronts of the Pacific have forced me to the conclusion that every Japanese aliens should be removed from this community. I am also strongly of the conviction that Japanese who are American citizens should be subjected to a more detailed and all-encompassing investigation. After investigation, if it is found that these citizens are not loyal to this country, they, too, should be removed from the community."[34]

Earl Warren was the next principal witness. His testimony illustrates what he had been telling General DeWitt:

> I want to say that the consensus of opinion among the law-enforcement officers of this state is that there is more potential danger among the group of Japanese who are born in this country than from the alien Japanese who were born in Japan . . . We believe that when we are dealing with the Caucasian race we have methods that will test the loyalty of them, and we believe that we can, in dealing with the Germans and the Italians, arrive at some fairly sound conclusions because of our knowledge of the way they live in the community and have lived for many years. But when we deal with the Japanese we are in an entirely different field and we cannot form any opinion that we believe to be sound.[35]

This was very similar to the beliefs about Japanese Americans that Secretary of War Stimson shared in his memoir.

The Tolan Committee was a sideshow. Separately, the drumbeat to intern Japanese aliens and Japanese Americans developed its own momentum spurred by the prejudice of California political leaders including Governor Olson and Attorney General Warren, opinion leaders like influential national columnists, and General DeWitt and his staff who had been tasked with defending the West Coast. President Roosevelt deferred to his trusted and experienced Secretary of War Stimson, who, in turn, deferred to General DeWitt, who, as we have seen, was influenced by Olson and Warren. By the time Warren testified to the Tolan Committee, President Roosevelt had already signed Executive Order 9066 which authorized the evacuation of people deemed a threat to national security from the West Coast to relocation centers further inland. Although it applied to "any or all persons" in practice it was used against only people of Japanese ancestry. The United States was not alone in making this grievous error. On December 30, 1941, the commander of the Canadian army's Pacific forces had recommended removal of all persons of Japanese descent, whether or not citizens, from the coastal areas; the evacuation there began the following February and was completed by October.[36]

At the time he testified to the Tolan Committee, Angelo Rossi did not appear to see the irony in his stance as a first-generation Italian American, whose heritage from what had become an enemy country, against Japanese Americans. Others did notice. In mid-1942 controversy had been generated over Rossi's loyalty to America. The San Francisco Board of Supervisors had to pass a resolution of support for the mayor in order to overcome the "hysteria and prejudices with which the human mind may be pervaded, particularly in war times."[37] At the time the board decried hysteria and prejudice, the Issei and Nisei of the Fillmore and across the West Coast already had been rounded up and taken away.

Many have wondered why Roosevelt, a liberal champion, would sign such an order. Biddle writes,

> I do not think [Roosevelt] was much concerned with the gravity or implications of this step. He was never theoretical about things. What must be done to defend the country must be done. The decision was for his Secretary of War, not for the Attorney General, not even for J. Edgar Hoover, whose judgement [FDR] greatly respected. The military might be wrong. But they were fighting the war. Public opinion was on their side, so that there was no question of any substantial opposition, which might tend toward the disunity that at all costs he must avoid. Nor do I think that the constitutional difficulty plagued him—the Constitution has never greatly bothered any wartime President. That was a question of law, which ultimately the Supreme Court must decide. And meanwhile—probably a long meanwhile—we must get on with the war.[38]

Biddle, who always had been against relocation, admits he could have done more, specifically, he could have more forcefully urged Stimson, who very much disliked the racial element that had crept into the issue of alien relocation, to reconsider. But, Biddle writes, "I was new to the Cabinet, and disinclined to insist on my view to an elder statesman [Stimson] whose wisdom and integrity I greatly respected."[39]

NOTES

1. Conn, Engelman, and Fairchild, *Guarding the United States and Its Outposts*, 116.
2. Jim Newton, *Justice for All, Earl Warren and the Nation He Made* (New York: Riverhead Books, 2006), 122.
3. Blum, *V Was for Victory: Politics and American Culture during World War II*, 156.
4. Issei and other Asians excluded from citizenship who served in World War I became eligible for citizenship in 1935 after Congress passed the Nye-Lea Act. The powerful veterans lobby, the American Legion, supported the legislation.
5. Conn, Engelman, and Fairchild, *Guarding the United States and Its Outposts*, 117.

6. Conn, Engelman, and Fairchild, *Guarding the United States and Its Outposts*, 117–118.

7. Conn, Engelman, and Fairchild, *Guarding the United States and Its Outposts*, 117–118.

8. Francis Biddle, *In Brief Authority* (New York: Doubleday & Company, 1962), 215.

9. Newton, *Justice for All, Earl Warren and the Nation He Made*, 123.

10. Biddle, *In Brief Authority*, 215. DeWitt changed his mind. By 1943, long after his command had uprooted every last Japanese from their homes in California and the western half of Oregon and Washington and shipped them off to inland concentration camps, he had achieved a 180-degree turn in his beliefs. He was able to appear before a congressional committee and utter these infamous words to justify his action: "A Jap's a Jap. They are a dangerous element . . . There is no way to determine their loyalty. . . . It makes no difference whether he is an American citizen; theoretically he is still a Japanese, and you can't change him . . . You can't change him by giving him a piece of paper." (The first sentence, "A Jap's a Jap," does not appear in the official edited record of his testimony. However, it was played up in stories written by newspapers and the wire service that covered the hearing. Biddle, 260.)

11. Biddle, *In Brief Authority*, 263.

12. Conn, Engelman, and Fairchild, *Guarding the United States and Its Outposts*, 120.

13. Conn, Engelman, and Fairchild, *Guarding the United States and Its Outposts*, 120.

14. Blum, *V Was for Victory: Politics and American Culture during World War II*, 159–160.

15. John Morton Blum, ed., *From the Morgenthau Diaries, Years of War, 1941–1945* (Boston: Houghton Mifflin, 1967), 243–244.

16. Conn, Engelman, and Fairchild, *Guarding the United States and Its Outposts*, 126.

17. Biddle, *In Brief Authority*, 222–223.

18. Blum, *V Was for Victory: Politics and American Culture during World War II*, 155.

19. David Witwer, "Who Was Westbrook Pegler?" *Humanities* 33, no. 2 (March/April 2012).

20. Jack Goodman, editor, *While You Were Gone* (New York: Simon and Schuster, 1946), 367–368.

21. Source of "dean of American political journalism": Alden Whitman, "Walter Lippmann, Political Analyst, Is Dead at 85," *New York Times*, December 15, 1974, 1.

22. Walter Lippmann, "The Fifth Column," *Los Angeles Times*, February 13, 1942.

23. Lippmann, "The Fifth Column."

24. Morton Grodzins, *Americans Betrayed, Politics and the Japanese Evacuation* (Chicago: University of Chicago Press, 1949), 265.

25. Newton, *Justice for All, Earl Warren and the Nation He Made*, 123.

26. Biddle, *In Brief Authority*, 215.

27. Biddle, *In Brief Authority*, 215–216.

28. Conn, Engelman, and Fairchild, *Guarding the United States and Its Outposts*, 122.

29. Conn, Engelman, and Fairchild, *Guarding the United States and Its Outposts*, 122.

30. Conn, Engelman, and Fairchild, *Guarding the United States and Its Outposts*, 123.

31. Conn, Engelman, and Fairchild, *Guarding the United States and Its Outposts*, 125.

32. Conn, Engelman, and Fairchild, *Guarding the United States and Its Outposts*, 126.

33. Conn, Engelman, and Fairchild, *Guarding the United States and Its Outposts*, 136–137.

34. Angelo Rossi, "Testimony to the Select Committee Investigating National Defense Migration," House of Representatives, Seventy-Seventh Congress, February 21, 1942.

35. Earl Warren, "Testimony to the Select Committee Investigating National Defense Migration," House of Representatives, Seventy-Seventh Congress, February 21 and 23, 1942.

36. Biddle, *In Brief Authority*, 217.

37. San Francisco Board of Supervisors, Journal of the Proceedings 37, June 8, 1942, 1376.

38. Biddle, *In Brief Authority*, 226.

39. Biddle, *In Brief Authority*, 226.

9

Developing the Means

Like most Americans, Oppenheimer and Lawrence felt great urgency about supporting their country in the war. Both had seen friends and colleagues who were Jewish physicists escape Nazi Germany by finding support from foundations and universities to research and teach in the United States. Some escaped in the nick of time.[1] In the front of their minds was the fact that fission was first discovered by German chemists Otto Hahn and Fritz Strassmann in December 1938. This was the earth-shattering discovery reported in the *San Francisco Chronicle* that had Berkeley physicist Luis Alvarez leaping out of the barber chair because his student had been weeks away from making this discovery himself. It took physicist Lise Meitner, in exile in Sweden, and her nephew, physicist Otto Frisch in Denmark, to complete the fission puzzle, but nobody doubted the depth of talent in nuclear research that remained in Nazi Germany. After the United States entered World War II, both Lawrence and Oppenheimer put themselves fully at the service of the US government. Lawrence, one of only four Americans to hold a Nobel Prize in Physics, and already considered the dean of experimental physics in the country, was readily accepted and given a role mobilizing scientists and his cyclotron for the war effort. At first he had to fight to convince the government to take his friend Oppie.

Once fission was proved, it was clear to many scientists that it might become possible to harness nuclear energy to create a wholly new type of weapon. Germany was the first nation to establish a program with that aim but Britain was close on its heels, starting its own committee in the spring of 1940. America's nuclear program started as the result of a letter to President Roosevelt written by Albert Einstein, at the behest and with the help of his friend and colleague the émigré Hungarian physicist Leo Szilard. In a two-page typewritten letter dated August 2, 1939, Einstein laid out the pertinent recent discoveries and stated that "it may become possible to set up a nuclear chain reaction in a large mass of uranium, by which vast amounts of power . . . would be generated." Einstein went on to explain that this "phenomenon would also lead to the construction of . . . extremely powerful bombs of a new type . . . A single bomb of this type, carried by boat and exploded in a port, might very well destroy the whole port together with some of the surrounding territory." On the second page, Einstein goes on to suggest that the president create a trusted liaison with the key physicists working on nuclear science and warns that so far in this country the only work in this area was being done "within the limits of the budgets of University laboratories."[2] The weight of the government was behind atomic research in Germany and Britain. In the United States, university coffers and private organizations like the Rockefeller Foundation paid for most of the work in atomic research done until the war. Szilard and Einstein, like Lawrence, Oppenheimer, and their colleagues, some fresh from Germany, worried that America lagged Nazi atomic weapons research.

With the German invasion of Poland and the war in Europe underway, it took Roosevelt a little over two months to act on Einstein's letter. On October 11, 1939, Roosevelt met with his longtime friend and kitchen cabinet member Alexander Sachs, a Wall Street economist to discuss the matter. Sachs had been briefed on the letter by Szilard and was prepared to urge Roosevelt to act on it. Initially Roosevelt "was noncommittal and expressed concern over locating the necessary funds, but at a second meeting with Sachs over breakfast the next morning Roosevelt became convinced of the value of exploring atomic energy." Roosevelt wrote Einstein back on October 19, 1939, informing the physicist that he had set up a committee consisting of civilian and military representatives to study uranium. At first, the so-called Uranium Committee proceeded at a leisurely pace that was at odds with the urgency of the situation and did little to improve the shoestring budgets or attempt to coordinate research. This left a leadership vacuum that key physicists like Lawrence and others took it upon themselves to fill.

The slow pace of research was especially frustrating for Ernest Lawrence who was sure the United States would become involved in the war, probably since the time in late 1939 when his younger brother, Dr. John Lawrence, a physician who used Rad Lab cyclotrons to pioneer nuclear medicine at Berkeley and San Francisco, survived being torpedoed by a German U-boat while traveling aboard the British passenger ship *Athenia* that set sail on the eve that England and Germany went to war. Ninety-three passengers, eighty-five of them women and children and nineteen crew members, were killed in the German attack on the passenger liner.[3] These would be among the first American and British civilian casualties of the war. Many of the American survivors were taken to Glasgow, Scotland where they awaited another ship to take them home.

That so many Americans had been onboard and that some had been killed grabbed attention in the United States. The US ambassador to the Court of St. James, Joseph P. Kennedy, unable to make it to Glasgow, sent one of his sons to represent him. This was twenty-two-year-old Jack Kennedy, who was with his family in England on a break from studies at Harvard. This would not be the last time John F. Kennedy would represent the US government.[4] At Glasgow, Kennedy met with some of the ship's survivors. One journalist on the scene wrote, "Ambassador of mercy—Jack Kennedy, son of America's ambassador, Joseph P. Kennedy, spent one of the busiest days of his young life today, going from hotels to hospitals in Glasgow, visiting the *Athenia*'s American survivors. His boyish charm and natural kindliness persuaded those who he had come to comfort that America was indeed keeping a benevolent and watchful eye on them." Others were not easily comforted by what they called the "schoolboy diplomat" shouting "demands for a convoy of ships to accompany them and guarantee safe passage back to the US." Already cool under pressure, it was said that the young Kennedy, "displayed a wisdom and sympathy of a man twice his age."[5]

With war in Europe underway, Lawrence led his researchers at the Rad Lab with redoubled urgency. It was an urgency every physicist there shared. "Even in our corner of the war—work on the bomb—we believed we were behind the Germans and in danger of losing the race." Seaborg writes, "Hahn and Strassman, the discoverers of fission, had a two-year head start on us. People like Robert Oppenheimer had studied physics in Europe because it had the leading physics schools. German engineering was the most respected in the world, especially when it came to arms; those Panzers rolling across Europe in the blitzkrieg seemed unstoppable."[6] Also, there was an undeniable appeal for physicists to exercise the full use of their powers along the lines of excellence, a pursuit that John F. Kennedy when he was president would sometimes cite as the ancient Greek definition of happiness. Discovering new elements "was exhilarating" for any physicist or chemist.[7] None was more exhilarated by the challenge of this work at the frontiers of physics and chemistry than Glenn Seaborg who was working to create a new fissionable element that could complement or maybe supplant uranium-235. It could be "a big prize." Seaborg writes, "a fissile [element] 94 might be more useful than U-235 for two reasons. First, element 94 could be separated chemically from uranium, while we knew of no reliable way to separate isotopes of the same element from each other . . . Second, U-235 is rare, making up less than 1 percent of uranium. The rest is U-238. So less than 1 percent of the uranium stock, which seemed to be an exceedingly rare element, was usable. If we could transform U-238 into a fissionable material, we could increase the amount of usable material a hundredfold."[8] This had been the research interest pursued by Seaborg's colleague and fellow resident of the university's faculty club, physicist Edwin McMillan, who later married Lawrence's wife's sister. McMillan worked first with U-238 and had made some strides, but he had to abandon this research when he went to MIT to work on radar, a top priority of wartime scientific research on a par with the Manhattan project.

With McMillan's blessing, Seaborg and his team at Berkeley took on the project collaborating with McMillan long distance. In a few months of work using the Rad Lab's newest cyclotron, the team had success. On February 23, 1941, working in room 307 of Gilman Hall, the team proved they created a new element with the atomic number of 94. In normal times, they would have rushed to publish their work to establish their claim to have been the first to create the yet unnamed element 94. But it was not normal times. Many scientists had already agreed among themselves to embargo their papers describing cutting edge atomic research to prevent helping the German bomb researchers. Later, all publications regarding nuclear research was stopped by law in the United States. Instead, Seaborg and McMillan and their collaborators reported their discovery to the sleepy Uranium Committee and wrote a confidential report to the editor of the prestigious journal *The Physical Review*, which withheld publication of the report, but established their priority to the discovery of element 94.

But what to name the newest element in the world? For a time, Seaborg and the team simply called it 94, "But even this revealed too much for casual conversations around the Faculty Club or lab" where informed listeners could easily guess what they were talking about. The team considered naming it "extremium" or "ultimium" because it was so rare and difficult to make. The prior two man-made elements had been named after planets (uranium and neptunium, the latter cocreated in 1940 at Berkeley by McMillan) so the team opted to name their element after the next planet in order, Pluto. (This was before it had been demoted to the status of dwarf planet, much to the chagrin of fictional Caltech theoretical physicist Sheldon Cooper.) The team briefly considered the name plutium, but plutonium sounded better. It also set up a not very subtle joke for generations of chemistry students. On the periodic table, where each element has a one- or two-letter abbreviation, plutonium should be abbreviated PL. Seaborg instead chose to abbreviate the new element PU. "We thought our little joke might come under criticism," he writes, "but it was hardly noticed."[9] The world would not learn of the existence of plutonium until the second atomic bomb, "Fat Man," a plutonium-based nuclear weapon, exploded 1,650 feet over Nagasaki four years later.[10] In 1951, McMillan and Seaborg equally shared the Nobel Prize in Chemistry.

At the time that American physics was girding for war, the country was suffering significant defeats in the Pacific. The main battleline of America's Pacific fleet had been sunk or neutralized in the Japanese attack at Pearl Harbor. American army and navy bases in the Philippines were overrun when Japanese forces invaded those islands the day after Pearl Harbor. America's ally Great Britain, whose mighty Royal Navy the United States relied upon to control the seas in the Far East, also suffered devastating naval losses to Japanese forces that pushed Britain's navy and army out of Hong Kong and Singapore. For Americans, the war news was bleak. The US Navy was licking its wounds, the army was building up, and the country's industries were rapidly converting to war production. Until that happened, there was little that the United States could do to take the war to the enemy. To bolster American morale, President Roosevelt wanted US forces to bomb the Japanese mainland as soon as possible. The navy and the army air force developed the idea to use an aircraft carrier strike force to carry bombers within flying range of Japan. They tasked an extraordinary aeronautical engineer, test pilot, former military pilot, and onetime Berkeley student named James H. Doolittle to plan and lead the attack. Doolittle received the highest priority to recruit and train a hand selected team of air crews to fly their land-based bombers off the short, heaving deck of an aircraft carrier far away in enemy waters.

On March 23, 1942, with the order "Tell Jimmy To Get On His Horse," Lt. Col. James H. Doolittle learned that the navy was ready to transport his flight of B-25 twin-engine bombers to bring the war to Japan, if only for one bombing mission.[11] Two days later, these airplanes were lifted by crane and lashed onto the deck of the brand new Yorktown-class carrier, *USS Hornet* fresh from its shakedown cruise and which had just arrived at the Naval Air Station at Alameda, California. On April Fool's Day the carrier, with the bombers lashed on the deck in plain sight, moved to anchor in the middle of San Francisco Bay. Doolittle gave his aircrew a last evening of shore leave. Like other servicemen finding themselves in the city, many went to the Top of the Mark, the popular bar at the top of the Mark Hopkins Hotel on San Francisco's Nob Hill.[12] The next day, a few minutes before noon the *USS Hornet*, one of only four aircraft carriers the US Navy had in the Pacific, passed under the Golden Gate Bridge with its complement of twin-engine bombers crowding its deck to join the other ships in its taskforce headed toward Japan.[13] Doolittle would use conventional weapons to execute his audacious mission. Three and a half years later, another ship would sail under the Golden Gate Bridge carrying a most unconventional weapon, one sketched on a chalkboard by Robert Oppenheimer in an office in LeConte Hall in Berkeley in the summer of 1942.

For much of 1941, America's nuclear efforts were directed by committees that were shifting as the country fully engaged in the war. The Uranium Committee moved under a newly created group called the National Defense Research Committee (NDRC) led by Vannevar Bush, the president of the Carnegie Institution and former engineering dean at the Massachusetts Institute of Technology. This group coordinated the country's scientific research for the war effort, but was independent of the military and lacked the authority and the funds to carry research forward into development and production.[14] To give the NDRC additional support, President Roosevelt created the Office of Scientific Research and Development (OSRD) as an independent entity within the Office for Emergency Management. Bush was appointed director of the OSRD and given the authority and budget to fund research. James B. Conant, president of Harvard University, replaced Bush as chairman of the NDRC, which remained in charge of government support of work in nuclear fission. Bush and Conant worked well together.

Another oar in the water was provided by Arthur Compton, a physicist from the University of Chicago who had won a share of the 1927 Nobel Prize in Physics when he was thirty-five years old. Compton was chairman of the committee of the National Academy of Science that had been charged with advising the government regarding the military usefulness of atomic energy. Although a sense of urgency animated each of these leaders, it was not clear that a fission weapon could be created, and there were many urgent demands for scarce scientific resources for research into areas that were critically important for the war effort and far less speculative, including radar.

It was not until September 1941 that both Lawrence and Oppenheimer were figuratively grabbed by their lapels by Mark Oliphant, a distinguished Australian physicist working in England who was visiting the Rad Lab. Oliphant confided to Lawrence and Oppenheimer the results of the secret work toward developing a fission weapon being done in England. Oppenheimer remembers Oliphant said to him, "it was terrible that Fermi and [Oppenheimer] were not involved in this."[15] Oliphant convinced Lawrence that a fission bomb was possible; that Germany had a project well underway to develop such a weapon; and that Oppenheimer should be part of any program that America put together to develop a fission weapon. Oliphant probably also shared his dismay at the slow work of the Uranium Committee to date. Now hot with purpose, Lawrence did not express his concerns through official channels, instead, in his usual fashion, he directly buttonholed his fellow Nobel laureate, Arthur Compton. Compton, in turn, arranged for Conant and Lawrence to discuss the matter at his home when both Conant and Lawrence were due to receive honorary degrees at the University of Chicago, where Compton was a member of the physics faculty.

Compton says that Conant was inclined to drop support of nuclear research during the war in favor of projects that were also very important and more certain in their outcomes, and that Compton and Lawrence convinced him to change his mind. In their meeting in Compton's living room, Lawrence described the state of research in England that he had learned from Mark Oliphant, which was ahead of the United States but quickly exhausting its resources. Lawrence also described Seaborg's recent work creating a new element and indicated that a bomb could be made with either uranium-235 or the element that Seaborg and his colleagues created, still unnamed at that time. Lawrence outlined for Conant how "using an atomic chain reaction [uranium-238] would be converted into plutonium of mass 239, and by chemical methods the new element would be extracted from the uranium."[16] Together, Compton and Lawrence got Conant to change his mind and support work for a fission weapon. Conant understood it would be a massive undertaking and that there was no way the United States could build such a bomb "unless we get into it with everything we got." As Conant knew, that included the vast industrial might of the United States and the intellectual power of the best experimental and theoretical physicists in the country.

Conant said to Lawrence, "Ernest, you say you are convinced of the importance of these fission bombs. Are you ready to devote the next several years of your life to getting them made?" Compton writes, "the question brought up Lawrence with a start. I can still recall the expression in his eyes as he sat there with his mouth half open. Here was a serious personal decision." Lawrence's work making bigger and ever more powerful cyclotrons was by far the most important pursuit in his professional life. Through persuasion and constant effort, he convinced funders to finance him and the most talented young talent in the country to come to him to Berkeley to pursue this vision. Compton says Lawrence "hesitated only a moment" before telling Conant, "If you tell me this is my job, I'll do it."[17]

In the meantime, Oppenheimer began some secret chalkboard work, "to look at it, some reasonable ideas about the possible range of critical masses" and possible ways of assembling a fission weapon.[18] Seven decades later, one of Oppenheimer's students remembered these heady days. Edward Gerjuoy was in some ways typical of the kind of scrappy, talented students Oppenheimer attracted. The son of Jewish immigrants, he entered City College of New York at the age of fifteen. This school is famous for educating poor but very smart kids, especially immigrants and first-generation Americans like two of its notable graduates: former Intel Chairman Andy Grove who immigrated to America at the age of twenty, escaping communist Hungary; and former US Secretary of State General Colin Powell, who was born in Harlem to parents who immigrated from Jamaica. The school has produced ten Nobel laureates and counting. As

Gerjuoy somewhat jokingly remembers about CCNY, "the teachers were terrible and the students fantastic." He majored in physics and mathematics until the chair of the math department told him he would never find a job at a university as a mathematician because he was Jewish. At CCNY, Gerjuoy briefly had been a member of the Young Communists League "but was expelled for laughing during meetings."

For graduate school, he made his way to Berkeley because it was one of the few places in the country he could study quantum mechanics.[19] Oppenheimer was making that desert bloom at Cal. Gerjuoy remembers that even in the months before Pearl Harbor, Oppenheimer was engaged in secret work at LeConte Hall and invited Gerjuoy to participate. This would have been the work calculating critical mass and assembly of a potential fission weapon. Being inclined to pacifism and not wanting to be involved with what he knew was likely weapons work of some kind, Gerjuoy declined. After Pearl Harbor, Oppenheimer quickly cleared Gerjuoy for his doctorate, which meant the end of his teaching assistanceship at Cal. Gerjuoy, whose draft board classified him as 1-A (available for military service), had to find a suitable research position or get drafted. With his new PhD in hand, Gerjuoy approached Oppenheimer, telling him he had changed his mind and would like to join him. Oppenheimer replied, "With your attitude, I do not want you."[20] Gerjuoy left Cal to work at a nearby shipyard and later did research in sonar during the war. He never made it to Los Alamos.

At this time, Oppenheimer was not officially a part of the Uranium Committee, which became known as the S-1 Committee and under the leadership of Bush and Conant acted with increased urgency and purpose toward researching and developing a fission weapon. "Although I realized that there was a job to do, I did not think it was mine or recognize that it was mine." Oppenheimer continued, "But that changed in the spring of [1942] and I first found out" that the effort to that date was suffering "from terrible lack of communication, misconceived ideas of secrecy, and from inadequate theoretical guidance."[21]

Lawrence worked behind the scenes to speed research and funding, tasks at which he was especially adept. When the first director of the Uranium Committee had been moving too slowly for Lawrence's taste, he maneuvered to get appointed as an advisor to the director and in that role shifted funding to Berkeley for plutonium research and to labs at other universities that shared his sense of urgency. Developments continued to the point where on November 6, 1941, Bush reported to President Roosevelt that research suggested enough fissionable uranium (uranium-235) could, in theory, be produced, at a cost of $50 million to $100 million. In the intervening weeks, the United States was attacked by Japan, declared war on that country and had war declared on it by both Germany and Italy. Roosevelt found time on January 19, 1942, to reply to Vannevar Bush in a handwritten note on White House stationery: "V. B. OK—returned—I think you had best keep this in your own safe FDR."[22] After dithering for two and a half years, the United States was throwing its industrial and intellectual might into developing an atomic weapon.

Lawrence was named one of three program chiefs and was the first to receive large-scale funding to advance his research into an electromagnetic process for developing quantities of fissionable uranium and plutonium. To move fast, he wanted and needed his friend Oppenheimer. Lawrence needed all his influence to make that happen. Oppenheimer was already being watched by the FBI. The bureau had opened its first file on him in March 1941. A confidential informant, whose identity was deleted in the declassified file released decades later, told an FBI agent that Oppenheimer was known to Communists in the Bay Area. Physicist Hans Bethe who knew Oppenheimer very well describes him differently. Bethe recalls that "Most of the time [Oppenheimer] was indifferent to the events around him; he never read a newspaper, he had no radio or telephone, he learned of the stock market crash in 1929 only long after the event. His interest in politics began in 1936. He had been much disturbed by the treatment of the Jews in Germany, including some of his relatives. He saw the effect of the American depression on his students, and had great compassion with them and others who could not find any jobs. In these days, Oppie's sympathies were quite left-wing. He contributed to a strike fund of the Longshoremen's Union and to various committees helping the Spanish Loyalists in the Civil War." In 1940 Oppenheimer married Katherine Harrison. She was a Communist as were his brother, experimental physicist Frank Oppenheimer, and Frank's wife Jackie. Oppenheimer, Bethe writes, "apparently never joined. As far as I can tell, he moved away from the party in 1939 and 1940. He was disgusted by the pact between Stalin and Hitler which permitted Hitler to start the Second World War. He was deeply distressed by the fall of France in 1940. I saw him shortly thereafter at an evening party when he spoke long and eloquently about the terrible tragedy."[23]

NOTES

1. Oppenheimer sponsored family members and settled them in Berkeley, sparing them the death camps that awaited most Jews in Germany.

2. "Einstein Letter," The Manhattan Project, an interactive history, US Department of Energy, Office of History and Heritage Resources. Osti.gov.

3. Evan Mawdsley, "Sinking the SS Athenia," August 4, 2020. Yalebooks.yale.edu.

4. For materials regarding the sinking of the USS *Athenia* see: John F. Kennedy Presidential Library and Museum, John F. Kennedy Personal Papers, JFKPP-004-019.

5. Lesley Roberts, "JFK in Scotland: Former US President Began Journey to White House with Public Speech in Scottish Hotel in 1939," *Daily Record*, September 8, 2013.

6. Seaborg with Seaborg, *Adventures in the Atomic Age: From Watts to Washington*, 87.

7. Seaborg with Seaborg, *Adventures in the Atomic Age: From Watts to Washington*, 68.

8. "Big prize" is Seaborg with Seaborg, 68. Quote is Seaborg with Seaborg, 69.

9. Seaborg with Seaborg, *Adventures in the Atomic Age: From Watts to Washington*, 72.

10. Owen Summerscale, "A History of Plutonium," *Actinide Research Quarterly*, September 21, 2022, Los Alamos National Laboratory. Discoverlanl.gov.

11. Carroll V. Glines, *The Doolittle Raid* (New York: Orion, 1988), 37, 40.

12. Glines, *The Doolittle Raid*, 47.

13. Lotchin, *The Bad City in the Good War*, 17.

14. Development of ODRD, The Office of Scientific Research and Development (OSRD) Collection, Library of Congress. Loc.gov.

15. Stephane Groueff, "Interview with J. Robert Oppenheimer Conducted on September 12, 1965." Voices of the Manhattan Project, Atomic Heritage Foundation. Manhattanprojectvoices.org.

16. Arthur Holly Compton, *Atomic Quest* (New York: Oxford University Press, 1956), 7.

17. Compton, *Atomic Quest*, 8.

18. Groueff, "Interview with J. Robert Oppenheimer Conducted on September 12, 1965."

19. Arthur B. Kosowsky, "Edward Gerjuoy," *Physics Today*, March 31, 2018.

20. Cindy Kelly, "Interview with Edward Gerjuoy Conducted on April 13, 2008." Voices of the Manhattan Project, The Atomic Heritage Foundation. Manhattanprojectvoices.org.

21. Groueff, "Interview with J. Robert Oppenheimer Conducted on September 12, 1965."

22. "President Franklin Roosevelt's note to Vannevar Bush giving Bush the tentative go-ahead to build the atomic bomb, January 19, 1942," The Manhattan Project Interactive History, US Department of Energy. Osti.gov.

23. Bethe, "J. Robert Oppenheimer, 1904–1967," *Biographical Memoirs of Fellows of the Royal Society* 14, 397.

Figure 1. Golden Gate Bridge Anchored upon stunning and storied terrain, the Golden Gate Bridge was designed for beauty and meant for adventure. *Source:* Hiller, Chas. M. Golden Gate Bridge E4. San Francisco California Golden Gate Bridge, 1934. Photograph. https://www.loc.gov/item/99403559/.

Figure 2. San Francisco-Oakland Bay Bridge. That the San Francisco–Oakland Bay Bridge was built for practical considerations shows in its design. Feeding automobile and rail traffic into San Francisco's Embarcadero lined with busy ports, this bridge was meant for commerce.

Work on both bridges began in 1933 in the depths of the Depression that gripped the country. By the time they were completed a few years later the world was dramatically changing. These two bridges would link the future Marinship ship yard and Berkeley to San Francisco and help tighten the San Francisco Nexus. *Source:* Birds' eye view of S.F.-Oakland Bay Bridge / Piggett Photo. San Francisco Oakland California San Francisco Bay Area Oakland Bay Bridge, ca. 1936. Photograph. https://www.loc.gov/item/2001695057/.

Figure 3. San Francisco General Strike. San Francisco's industrial waterfront was the site of a general strike lasting four days in July 1934. Violence between San Francisco police, strikers, and "punchers" hired by labor and management alike to add muscle to their chosen sides led to bloodshed and a few deaths. The California National Guard was called out to support police. They brought with them tanks and machine guns. *Source:* San Francisco History Center, San Francisco Public Library.

Figure 4. Japanese American Internment. In the wake of Executive Order 9066, Japanese American citizens, known as Nisei, and their parents who had been prohibited by law from becoming citizens because they were Asian (Issei), were rounded up by soldiers at rifle point and sent to internment camps for the duration of the war. April 1942.

The celebrated San Francisco photographer Dorothea Lange documented the internment of Japanese Americans for the War Relocation Authority. Lange writes in her original caption for this photograph, "A crowd of onlookers on the first day of evacuation from the Japanese quarter in San Francisco, who themselves will be evacuated within three days." *Source:* Dorothea Lange, San Francisco, California, April 1942. National Archives and Records Administration, Records of the War Relocation Authority. (210-GC-426)

Figure 5. Tanforan Assembly Center. These horse stalls served as accommodations for internees at the Tanforan Racetrack near San Francisco. The racetrack grounds was hastily converted into an assembly center where internees were imprisoned until camps could be constructed in remote areas of the western states. 1942. *Source:* Dorothea Lange, San Bruno, California, 1942. Courtesy of the National Archives and Records Administration.

Figure 6. Ernest Lawrence. Experimental physicist Ernest O. Lawrence was Berkeley's first Nobel laureate. Inventor of a series of increasingly powerful and expensive cyclotron particle accelerators, he is considered the father of "Big Science" in which applied research in physics required costly infrastructure affordable only by very large institutions and governments. Circa 1932. *Source:* Photo courtesy of Lawrence Berkeley National Laboratory. © 2010 The Regents of the University of California, Lawrence Berkeley National Laboratory.

Figure 7. Robert Oppenheimer. Theoretical physicist J. Robert Oppenheimer more than any other American scientist was responsible for proselytizing quantum mechanics in the United States during the 1930s. Serving as the scientific director of the Manhattan Project, he is considered by many to be the father of the atomic bomb. Circa 1930s.

The two men joined the physics faculty at Cal when it was a "desert" and together shifted the center of gravity of that science from Europe to Berkeley. Contemporaries and close friends for a decade and a half, they are seen here at the height of their creative powers, before their sad falling out in the years following the war. *Source:* Photo courtesy of Lawrence Berkeley National Laboratory. © 2010 The Regents of the University of California, Lawrence Berkeley National Laboratory.

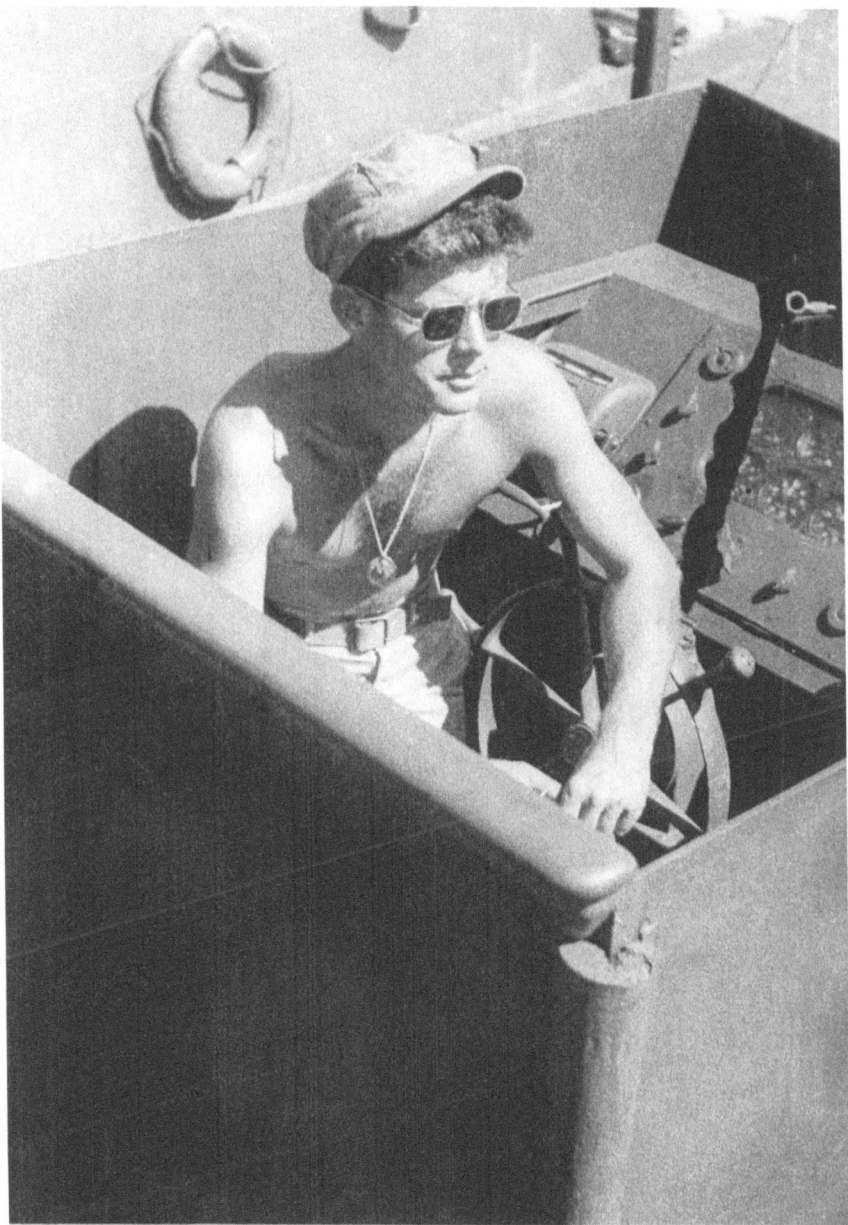

Figure 8. John F. Kennedy. John F. Kennedy registered for the draft while auditing classes at Stanford University. Pictured here in 1943, Kennedy sits in the cockpit of the Motor Torpedo Boat PT-109 he commanded. After seeing combat and suffering from ill health, Kennedy returned home as a decorated war hero to recuperate and contemplate what to do with his life. Briefly considering a career in journalism, his father arranged a position for him as a columnist with the Hearst news syndicate reporting from the United Nations Conference on International Organization in San Francisco in 1945. During the conference, Kennedy wrestled in print with issues of global war and peace while having fun in boomtown San Francisco. *Source:* Copyright John F. Kennedy Library Foundation. Kennedy Family Collection. John F. Kennedy Presidential Library and Museum, Boston.

Figure 9. Joseph James. Singer, actor, welder, labor leader and civil rights activist Joseph James is seen here in 1945. James fought the practice of segregated auxiliary union chapters that required Black workers to pay the same union dues as their White colleagues but receive dramatically unequal union representation and support. With the help of the NAACP's Thurgood Marshall and two local attorneys, James sued the union, taking *James v. Marinship* to the California Supreme Court. He emerged victorious and helped break Jim Crow union auxiliaries in the United States. *Source:* San Francisco History Center, San Francisco Public Library.

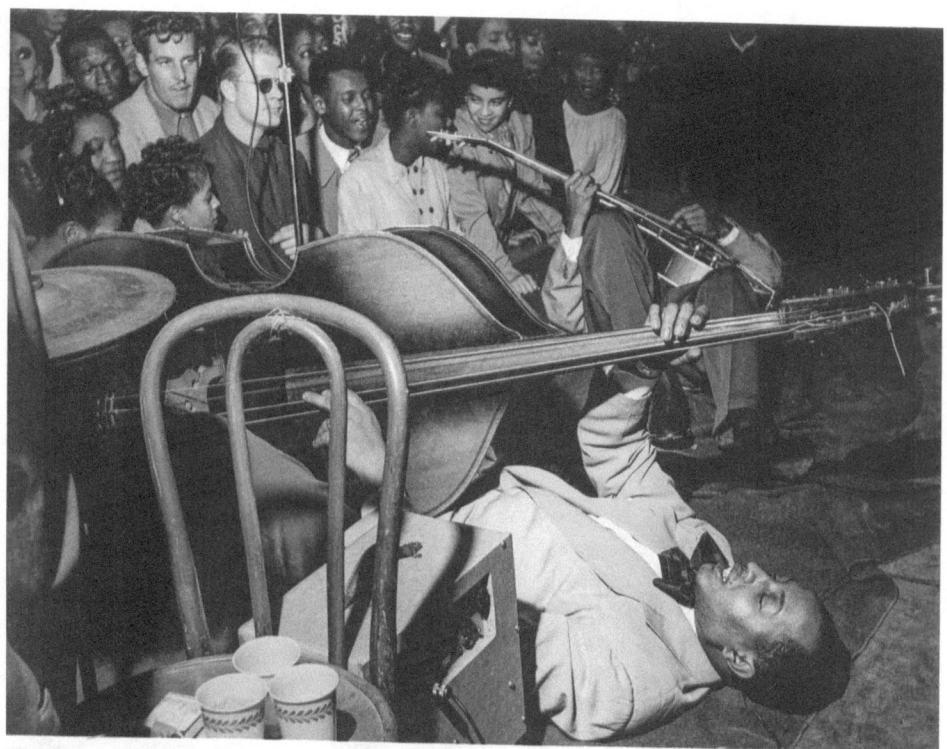

Figure 10. Vernon Alley. Bass player Vernon Alley at the Primalon Ballroom in the Fillmore. A popular musician before the war, Alley enlisted in the US Navy in 1942 and served as a musician with "The Jive Bombers", a navy band. After the war, Alley resumed his successful musical career in San Francisco and was a key figure in the small but infinitely cool world of Fillmore District jazz. Later, Alley served as a labor leader and arts activist and became one of the first Black members of the Bohemian Club.

This photo was taken circa 1948 by David Johnson who grew up in Depression-era Florida cotton fields and joined the navy during the war. Seeing San Francisco for the first time before shipping out to the Pacific, he survived the war and returned to the city to study photography under Ansel Adams. Johnson operated a photo studio in the Fillmore and worked as a photographer with the *Sun-Reporter*, a newspaper serving the Black community in the city, while holding other jobs and becoming a community leader. *Source:* Bass player Vernon Alley, 1948, David Johnson Photograph Archive, BANC PIC 2017.001. © The Regents of the University of California, The Bancroft Library, University of California, Berkeley.

Figure 11. Top of the Mark. Service members, officers and enlisted alike, rubbed elbows with civilians and enjoyed the panoramic views at the storied Top of the Mark, the rooftop bar at the Mark Hopkins Hotel on the summit of Nob Hill. During World War II the tradition of squadron bottles was born here in which GIs flush with cash bought bottles of liquor that they left in the care of the bartenders at the Top of the Mark for subsequent patrons from their branch of service to enjoy for free. For thousands of soldiers, sailors, and airmen, this bar provided the quintessential San Francisco experience that they longed to relive. Open daily, the Top of the Mark was closed for business only twice during the war—the day President Roosevelt died and the day Japan surrendered. *Source:* San Francisco History Center, San Francisco Public Library.

10

✣

Sketching the Atomic Bomb

In September 1942, the army engineer who led the construction of the recently completed massive pentagon-shaped headquarters of the War Department near Washington DC, Colonel Leslie R. Groves, was put in charge of the operation to create a fission weapon, code-named the Manhattan District but known to history as the Manhattan Project. Famous in army circles for his critical and stubborn attitude, egotism, intelligence, and drive to succeed, Groves, newly promoted to general, set off to visit the three main sites of nuclear research in America at that time: Columbia University, the University of Chicago, and Cal to get a sense of where the state of the art rested. He was also in search of a scientific director to oversee the design of the weapon. When Groves got to Cal and met Oppenheimer, he was immediately impressed. Oppenheimer remembers meeting Groves at the house of University of California President Robert Sproul on the Berkeley campus. Sproul hosted a lunch for Groves, and Oppenheimer attended. Oppenheimer remembers: "after lunch, I said, 'This thing will never get on the rails unless there is a place where people can talk to each other and work together on the problems of the bomb ... there has got to be a place where people are free to discuss what they know and what they do not know and to find out what they can.' And that made an impression on him."[1]

The two men could not have been more dissimilar, but they hit it off. Groves recognized that Oppenheimer knew nothing about administration, industrial organization, or the realities of the way the US government works. "But very few college professors [in physics] had much knowledge of these things," Groves said. It was the depth of Oppenheimer's knowledge of everything else that impressed Groves, who graduating fourth in his class at US Military Academy at West Point, keenly appreciated education and intelligence.[2] "Oppenheimer's great mental capacity impressed me. . . . He learned Sanskrit for the fun of it."[3] Oppenheimer, probably with an eye to joining the Manhattan Project, made himself available to Groves as an unofficial advisor. After spending time traversing the country in the close quarters of train compartments of the 20th Century Limited with Oppenheimer and two of Groves's assistants discussing the challenges of the project, Groves was adamant that he wanted Oppenheimer as his scientific director. "There was nobody else."

Groves remembers Oppenheimer was not a popular choice with Bush or Conant or some of the other key physicists. Interestingly, looking back after more than twenty years, Groves remembers his choice also "did not meet with the approval of Ernest Lawrence." The problem that the key physicists had with Oppenheimer, Groves thought, was that Oppenheimer was not a Nobel laureate. This did not bother the general. Oppenheimer was a theoretical physicist and Groves thought the Nobel Prize committee favored experimentalists. "He had not [won a Nobel] and that was held against him." Groves also noted that Oppenheimer had been less influential than Lawrence and viewed as an "upstart . . . although he was not much younger than Lawrence, he had always been a lesser figure at Berkeley than Lawrence. There was a certain amount of jealousy I think between Lawrence and Oppenheimer, it was sort of natural. They were competitors and very young." Groves also sensed the intense focus that Oppenheimer developed on the theoretical problem of developing an atomic weapon. Oppenheimer, Groves said, "may not [appear] to you as being aggressive, but he always had his eye right on the ball . . . I do not think he ever failed to realize that, 'Here is where I should be moving to.'"[4] Groves surmised, "Every contact I had with Oppenheimer increased my respect for his intelligence. He's a real genius. While Lawrence is very bright he's not a genius, just a good hard worker."[5]

According to Groves, Lawrence thought the general was wrong to put much focus on the design of the bomb at this early stage of the Manhattan Project. Lawrence preferred putting all the talent and other resources toward creating fissionable material which was going to be a massive scientific and industrial undertaking that had never before been accomplished. Groves said, "[Lawrence] told me, 'Thirty scientists in three months could design this bomb.' Well they probably could have, but they would not have been ready and it would not have been the best bomb and we would not have known what the strength was. We would not have known a lot of things."[6] Groves trusted Oppenheimer to lead a group of scientists to answer those questions and design an atomic bomb before Germany or Japan created one. Groves got his way and got his man in Oppenheimer.

The FBI objected. Not because Oppenheimer did not have a Nobel but because they thought he was a security risk. Groves read what the FBI had on Oppenheimer and overruled the Bureau and his own security personnel who were also against using the scientist in any way. Groves said, "I merely wrote an order to our security people citing that Dr. Oppenheimer was cleared. He could not have been cleared in any possible way excepting by some such drastic action as that; you could not justify the clearance."[7]

Groves trusted his judgment about Oppenheimer. Aside from the blossoming respect Groves felt for Oppenheimer, the general was pragmatic. "[Oppenheimer] knew everything at that time ... He knew so much I did not want him out."[8] Also, Groves had a far more subtle understanding of the appeal of left wing politics during the Depression and the rise of fascism than did the FBI or his own army security personnel. "Well, there was no reason to suspect that there was anything wrong [with Oppenheimer's loyalty and risk to project security] ... During the Depression years, and during the Spanish War, all the liberals in this country and almost everybody ... [was] in favor of the Spanish Communists winning ... Everybody who was in college at that time was infected by the idea of socialism."[9] Groves thought Oppenheimer was politically naïve and he knew that Oppenheimer was surrounded by communists. "His wife had had this terrible experience [her second husband, an ardent communist, had been killed fighting fascists in Spain during that country's revolution]; she had been befriended by the Communists afterwards. His sister-in-law was an ardent Communist ... His brother [Frank Oppenheimer] was a card-carrying Communist," and Groves did not hold that against him. Oppenheimer "had attended a number of meetings, he had associated with people that were wrapped up in it, but so had everybody else in the academic world ... I do not think that was ever proven or suggested that he was [a communist]."[10]

With this nuanced view of the appeal of left wing politics, what worried Groves about security with Oppenheimer was the risk of the scientist stumbling into a honeytrap set by communists. "I was always afraid about [extortion] on Oppenheimer because I did not know."[11] Groves worried that Oppenheimer could have been targeted by communists. He tells an interviewer a story related to him by one of his security people about a young male scientist in San Francisco who had been targeted by a rich, female "red-hot Commie." The scientist is a music fan and the femme fatale invites him to her house where she and friends are having a group in for chamber music. After about an hour, as Groves tells it, "Some girl yelled above the hubbub and said, 'It is about time for some fun.' Somebody turned out all the lights and they proceeded to match up on the floor, maybe twenty or thirty people ... A real orgy ... The purpose was to entrap young men that they thought would go places."[12] There is no known record of Oppenheimer being lured to any such honeytraps, but he tended to create his own problems.

As early as March 28, 1941, the FBI became interested in Oppenheimer. Their voluminous files on him begin on this date with a letter and report concerning him sent from the San Francisco field office to FBI headquarters in Washington DC.[13] He was already a prominent physicist, not as widely famous as Lawrence, but preeminent in the small but increasingly important world of theoretical physics. Of course it wasn't Oppenheimer's physics that attracted the FBI's attention, but his politics. At this distance, after the atrocities of Stalin had been revealed, and the failure and fall of the Soviet Union is decades in the past, it is difficult to remember the hold the Red Scare had on people in America. The Communist Party was not illegal in the United States, but its members were suspect and subject to discrimination and investigation. If many people harbored sympathy with some of the equality goals of communism (these were referred to as "Fellow Travelers"), few were willing to risk opprobrium by actually joining the party. Some of those who did join were hardcore communists who remained committed. More often, casual party members in America drifted away from the party, growing tired of the party line claptrap and increasing blindness that American Communist Party officials showed toward Stalin's bloody purges in the Soviet Union and his pacts with Nazi Germany until Hitler invaded Russia. Robert Oppenheimer denied that he was ever a member of the Party. This may or may not be true. Certainly he had distanced himself from the party as did his brother Frank and his wife Kitty.

By May 1941, the FBI selected Oppenheimer as a candidate for "custodial detention," presumably in the event of a communist upheaval in the country. They based this decision on their conclusion that he had communist "tendencies," supported by evidence including his membership in the executive committee of the American Civil Liberties Union, which the bureau described as a Communist Party front, and a report by the university police chief at Berkeley that Oppenheimer subscribed to the Communist newspaper, *People's World*. The FBI noted that in 1940 Oppenheimer attended a meeting of local communist officials at the home of his close friend, Berkeley professor of French literature, Haakon Chevalier, who the FBI believed was a Communist Party advisor. Historian Barton J. Bernstein writes,

> The FBI continued to investigate Oppenheimer. A secret report from the Bureau's San Francisco field office stated that Oppenheimer, unlike some others then under FBI scrutiny, had been "more discreet in exhibiting his Party connections but they, nevertheless, are known to exist." It also cited a confidential informant who said that Oppenheimer had donated $100 to

the Communist party. The San Francisco FBI chief was so suspicious that he wanted to establish "technical surveillance" (a wiretap) on one of Oppenheimer's associates in order to gather more information on that associate, on Oppenheimer, on Chevalier, and on a few others who were described as being part of a small web.

Bernstein reports that, "Hoover was outraged that the agent had violated regulations by putting this request on paper, rather than doing it by telephone. Hoover rejected the request and scolded the agent."[14]

Lawrence knew of his close friend Oppenheimer's left-leaning tendencies and considered them to be only a foible. He convinced the program head, Arthur Compton, to include Oppenheimer in preliminary work on the atomic bomb stating correctly, "Oppenheimer has important new ideas, I have a great deal of confidence in Oppenheimer."[15] Oppenheimer drifted away from any political activity as he grew more consumed with the bomb project. Oppenheimer, as Lawrence knew, was a vital member of an extremely small community of theoretical physicists conversant with the very latest developments in fission research. Lawrence needed Oppenheimer to drive the theoretical work that underpinned the Rad Lab's experimental efforts, most of which were being directed to the problems with creating fissionable material for atomic weapons. Oppenheimer threw himself into the challenge. He was appointed head of the group assigned to study "neutron diffusion in an atomic bomb and the energy yield obtainable from it," in other words, how explosive an atomic bomb could be.[16] The work consumed him and he had to abandon his commitments at Caltech to focus on the preliminary theoretical underpinnings of an atomic bomb.

In the summer of 1942, Oppenheimer took room 325 LeConte Hall, the office of Edwin McMillian who was away at MIT doing work in radar, and turned it into the first organizing center of the scientific effort behind the Manhattan Project. Oppenheimer cherry-picked a handful of young but already prominent theoretical physicists to brainstorm with him that summer. In a nod to security, the door was fitted with a new lock with a single key issued to Oppenheimer. The office's windows and balcony door had been covered with wire mesh.[17] The small group of physicists included the German émigré Hans Bethe, the Hungarian émigré theoretical physicist Edward Teller, and Oppenheimer's former student and teaching assistant Robert Serber and a few of Oppenheimer's graduate students. Bethe thought "it would be a very simple thing to figure out this problem," but soon realized, "how wrong we were."[18] Some members of the group, under the leadership of Serber, did calculations on the topic at hand—the explosiveness of an atomic bomb. The rest, especially Teller, Oppenheimer, and Bethe, indulged "in a far-off project—namely, the question of whether and how an atomic bomb could be used to trigger an [even more powerful Hydrogen] H-bomb."[19]

Of this peculiar summer school, Oppenheimer said, "We had an adventurous time. We spent much of the summer of 1942 in Berkeley in a joint study that for the first time really came to grips with the physical problems of atomic bombs, atomic explosions, and the possibility of using fission explosions to initiate thermo-nuclear reactions."[20] Serber and Teller both attributed the success of the group to Oppenheimer's personal leadership. Teller said, "As Chairman, Oppenheimer showed a refined, sure, informal touch. I don't know how he acquired this facility for handling people. Those who knew him well were really surprised. I suppose it is the kind of knowledge a politician or administrator has to pick up somewhere."[21] For his part, Teller would never lose his focus on the possibility of an even more powerful bomb that fused hydrogen isotopes, and later became known as the father of the hydrogen bomb, which ten years later would lead him to turn against the man he admired so much. Bethe was also invigorated by the sessions at Berkeley. He writes, "Grim as the subject was, it was a most exciting enterprise. We were forever inventing new tricks, finding ways to calculate, and rejecting most of the tricks on the basis of the calculations. Now I could see at first-hand the tremendous intellectual power of Oppenheimer who was the unquestioned leader of our group."[22] Oppenheimer was becoming a compelling leader; all except one of the scientists he worked with that summer joined him the next year in his top-secret high dessert lab.[23]

At the end of the summer, "there was little doubt that a potentially world-shattering undertaking lay ahead," Oppenheimer said. The group could clearly imagine the explosions of a uranium or plutonium bomb and the even greater explosion of a hydrogen bomb. But the physicists could also envision "how rough, difficult, challenging and unpredictable this job might turn out to be."[24] Oppenheimer's summer conference concluded that a fission bomb was feasible but would require "a major scientific and technical effort."[25] At one point in their work, figures seemed to indicate that an atomic explosion might generate temperatures high enough to ignite the hydrogen in the atmosphere and oceans and thus destroy the world. Oppenheimer immediately pursued Arthur Compton who was on vacation at his cottage on a remote lake in northern Michigan to warn him that such an event seemed theoretically possible. The two agreed that Oppenheimer's Berkeley group of theorists must continue their calculations and if their work failed to prove that an atomic explosion could be contained, the bomb project must stop. "Better to accept the slavery of the Nazis," Compton later writes, "than to run a chance of drawing the final curtain on mankind!"[26] Further theoretical work from the group at LeConte Hall satisfied Oppenheimer and Compton that an atomic bomb blast would not blow up the world.[27] Unknown to the team at Berkeley, three months earlier the German physicists Werner Heisenberg and Robert Döpel had built rudimentary prototype atomic reactors that sustained nuclear fission and achieved the beginnings of a chain reaction that Enrico Fermi would later fully achieve in Chicago. At this time, the Germans were ahead in the race to build an atomic bomb.

As Niels Bohr speculated back in 1940, it would indeed take the industrial power of a nation to produce an atomic bomb. It would also take more intellectual resources than fit in an office in LeConte Hall. Oppenheimer said,

> In later summer, after a review of the experimental work, I became convinced, as did others, that a major change was called for in the work on the bomb itself. We needed a central laboratory devoted wholly to this purpose, where people could talk freely with each other, where theoretical ideas and experimental findings could affect each other, where the waste and frustration and error of the many compartmentalized experimental studies could be eliminated, where we could begin to come to grips with chemical, metallurgical, engineering and ordnance problems that had so far received no consideration. We therefore sought to establish this laboratory for a direct attack on all the problems inherent in the most rapid possible development and production of atomic bombs.[28]

Oppenheimer had in mind replicating the success of the close collaboration of theoretical and experimental physics that was embodied with LeConte Hall, with chemists at Gilman Hall and the cyclotroneers in Lawrence's Rad Lab and personified by close personal and working relationship he and Lawrence shared.

Set amid a forest of tall redwood trees seventy miles north of San Francisco near Monte Rio in Sonoma County is an encampment called the Bohemian Grove. It is the retreat of the San Francisco Bohemian Club, where business leaders, artists, and selected academics, all male because it is a men-only club, meet each summer to cast aside cares, participate in and enjoy camp shows and take in nature. It is forbidden to discuss business in the grove. This rule was cast aside for two days in September 1942 when Bohemian Club member Ernest Lawrence invited a small group of scientists and advisors to pick up where Oppenheimer's summer work at LeConte left off. These included the so-called S-1 Committee comprised of the six key scientists who led the initial core group of America's fission bomb project and other scientists and advisors, including Oppenheimer.

Of the nine scientists planning the bomb at this early stage, four were from Berkeley, showing the importance of the physics juggernaut that Lawrence and Oppenheimer had created in just over ten years. It was at the Bohemian Groves's two-story, shingled clubhouse on a rise above the Russian River that that the S-1 Committee sketched the industrial framework for the huge undertaking to create fissionable material and outlined the bespoke process for research and development for design of the bomb and its eventual construction and final testing. The building had been searched for listening devices so the men could relax and enjoy the beautiful but rustic ambience of their surroundings including a large stone fireplace and long communal table for meals.[29] One of the S-1 Committee members later writes, "The California redwoods that surrounded us in the Bohemian Grove included some that had been growing for thousands of years . . . would they be able to stand against the changes that man was bringing?"[30] It was here that the group decided that of the four uranium separation processes then under consideration, only the one advocated by Lawrence would be pursued in the Manhattan Project. As one physicist not in the S-1 Committee observed, "Lawrence was a promoter par excellence."

In the autumn of 1942, General Leslie R. Groves assumed charge of the Manhattan Engineer District, the effort to design and build an atomic bomb that became known as the Manhattan Project. This was to be the highest priority and most complex technological undertaking in the war. It was going to be led by an army general, but its scientific leaders were decidedly unmilitary. For a moment, there was thought of making the Manhattan Project physicists commissioned officers. In a sign of his enthusiasm, Oppenheimer even reported to the Presidio army base in San Francisco for the purpose of beginning officer's training. Luckily, he reconsidered pursuing an army commission. Most of his fellow physicists, who were independent-minded at best and often downright otherworldly, objected outright to joining the US Army as physicists. Oppenheimer said, "After a good deal of discussion with the personnel who would be needed at Los Alamos and with General Groves and his advisers, it was decided that the Laboratory should, at least initially, be a civilian establishment in a military post."[31] It was during this time, while the army considered turning Manhattan Project scientists into "90-day wonders" that Oppenheimer showed General Groves Los Alamos. The general immediately acquired the site for Oppenheimer's work.

NOTES

1. Groueff, "Interview with J. Robert Oppenheimer Conducted on September 12, 1965."

2. Stephane Groueff, *Manhattan Project: The Untold Story of the Making of the Atomic Bomb* (Lincoln, NE: iUniverse, 2000), 5.

3. Stephane Groueff, "Interview with General Leslie Groves Conducted on January 5, 1965, Part 6." Voices of the Manhattan Project, Atomic Heritage Foundation. Manhattanprojectvoices.org.

4. Groueff, "Interview with General Leslie Groves Conducted on January 5, 1965, Part 6."

5. Groueff, "Interview with General Leslie Groves Conducted on January 5, 1965, Part 6."

6. Groueff, "Interview with General Leslie Groves Conducted on January 5, 1965, Part 6."
7. Groueff, "Interview with General Leslie Groves Conducted on January 5, 1965, Part 6."
8. Groueff, "Interview with General Leslie Groves Conducted on January 5, 1965, Part 6."
9. Interview with General Leslie Groves conducted by Stephane Groueff on January 5, 1965, Part 6. Voices of the Manhattan Project, Atomic Heritage Foundation. Manhattanprojectvoices.org.
10. Groueff, "Interview with General Leslie Groves Conducted on January 5, 1965, Part 6."
11. Groueff, "Interview with General Leslie Groves Conducted on January 5, 1965, Part 6." In this interview, Groves adds disturbingly, "Ernest Lawrence . . . said that 'The average Jew had no moral principles on a lot of scores.' He said, particularly with respect to sex life . . . 'You cannot trust them at all.' He said, 'You take somebody that you think has been happily married for thirty years and you find him in bed with his stenographer.' That was a shock to me, but I learned to agree that that was so." Although anti-Semitism was rife in society and in academic quarters at that time, I have seen no other references to any anti-Semitism on the part of Lawrence. Groves might be adding an anti-Semitic element to Lawrence's objection to Oppenheimer's possibly adulterous relationship with Ruth Tolman, the wife of distinguished Caltech physicist and chemist Richard Tolman who was a close colleague of Oppenheimer's.
12. Groueff, "Interview with General Leslie Groves Conducted on January 5, 1965, Part 6."
13. "J. Robert Oppenheimer, Part 01 of 13," The Federal Bureau of Investigation. Vault.fbe.gov.
14. Barton J. Bernstein, "The Oppenheimer Loyalty-Security Case Reconsidered," *Stanford Law Review* 42, no. 6 (July 1990): 1392.
15. Letter from E. O. Lawrence to A. H. Compton dated October 14, 1941, Ernest O. Lawrence Papers, University of California, Berkeley Bancroft Library.
16. Bethe, "J. Robert Oppenheimer, 1904–1967," *Biographical Memoirs of Fellows of the Royal Society*, 398.
17. Peter Goodchild, *J. Robert Oppenheimer: Shatterer of Worlds* (Boston: Houghton Mifflin, 1981), 51.
18. Hans Bethe, "Testimony to the United States Atomic Energy Commission," in The Matter of J. Robert Oppenheimer, Vol. 6, April 18, 1954, 1048.
19. Bethe, "J. Robert Oppenheimer, 1904–1967," *Biographical Memoirs of Fellows of the Royal Society*, 398.
20. J. Robert Oppenheimer, "Testimony to the United States Atomic Energy Commission," in The Matter of J. Robert Oppenheimer, Vol. 1, April 12, 1954, 32.
21. Goodchild, *J. Robert Oppenheimer: Shatterer of Worlds*, 52–53.
22. Bethe, "J. Robert Oppenheimer, 1904–1967," *Biographical Memoirs of Fellows of the Royal Society*, 398.
23. Smith and Weiner, *Robert Oppenheimer: Letters and Recollections*, 227.
24. Oppenheimer, "Testimony to the United States Atomic Energy Commission," 32.

25. Smith and Weiner, *Robert Oppenheimer: Letters and Recollections*, 227.
26. Compton, *Atomic Quest*, 128.
27. Smith and Weiner, *Robert Oppenheimer: Letters and Recollections*, 227.
28. Oppenheimer, "Testimony to the United States Atomic Energy Commission," 32–33.
29. Description of the clubhouse from John Van Der Zee, *The Greatest Men's Party on Earth: Inside the Bohemian Grove* (New York: Harcourt Brace Jovanovich, 1974), 120.
30. Compton, *Atomic Quest*, 154.
31. Oppenheimer, "Testimony to the United States Atomic Energy Commission," 33.

11

✣

A National Disgrace

On February 19, 1942, two months after the Japanese bombing of Pearl Harbor, President Roosevelt signed Executive Order 9066, leading to the forced assembly and relocation of over 127,000 people of Japanese ancestry, US citizens and non-citizens alike, on the West Coast.[1] It was a gross violation of civil rights of US citizens caused by executive order and upheld by the Supreme Court. This did not happen because of any genuine national security threat presented by Issei or Nisei to the war effort or to protect them from a groundswell of vigilante threats. The momentum for this order came from key political leaders including California Governor Culbert Olson and Attorney General Earl Warren, who had an uneasy relationship with each other because Warren was a rising star who was expected to run against Olson for the governorship later in 1942; flatly racist congressmen, mayors, and other civic and law enforcement leaders; as well as some maybe racist and certainly greedy agricultural interests that had sway in California where agriculture was a significant industry. Most directly, it was the result of misinformation about Japanese attacks in California believed and propagated by General DeWitt, the misunderstanding and prejudice of Japanese Americans held by Secretary of War Henry Stimson, and the sad acquiescence of President Roosevelt. Because the Issei and Nisei populations in the country were so small and had no political clout, there was no political support at the national level in Congress or within the western states to counteract the momentum to strip them of their civil rights.

In the weeks leading up to Roosevelt's Executive Order 9066, Japanese Americans were left in a tense limbo subject to ill-defined restrictions on their lives. Togo W. Tanaka, the twenty-six-year-old editor of the bilingual English and Japanese newspaper *Rafu Shimpo* in Los Angeles writes of the uncertainties and indignities his readers in the Japanese community faced daily at this time: Issei had to seek and receive police permission to travel to a weekly doctor's appointment and a group of seven archery enthusiasts were advised to seek permission to hold their regular practices. The families of some Issei and Nisei men, taken into custody by the FBI, were left destitute as breadwinners because they were taken away suddenly and without due process or cause. The newspaper staff wondered whether it would be legal to organize fundraising to help such families. Of course, not all Issei, Kibei, and Nisei were pro-American or without sentimental attachment to Japan in general and the militaristic and expansionist Imperial Japan in particular. Tanaka also writes of the sentiments some members of his staff felt for Imperial Japan by some Issei on this staff. One member on the newspaper's Japanese language news and editorial staff was "concerned about what he terms the 'pro-Japan' sympathies and attitudes of many Issei. He feels there is a great need for re-education of the resident Japanese so that they will better 'understand the undesirable nature of the present military government of Japan.' He is even doubtful of the 'American loyalty' of some of the other members of the Japanese section."[2] Similarly, some groups of German Americans and Italian Americans felt warmly toward the fascist governments that ruled their former homelands.

The stark injustice of the decision to forcibly remove Japanese Americans and their parents from their homes and into remote internment camps was matched by the hurriedness and severity which it was carried out. The army did not want responsibility for administering the internment policy for which it eventually advocated so a civil body, the War Relocation Authority (WRA), was hastily convened to register and resettle Japanese Americans. Initially, the army encouraged Japanese in coastal cities to relocate themselves. Francis Biddle, the US attorney general, remembers, "At first the evacuation was begun on a voluntary basis, the Japanese finding homes where they could. By February 24 it was estimated that about 15,000 persons had moved out of the prohibited zones along the West Coast."[3]

This voluntary movement of so many Issei and Nisei so quickly caused its own problems. Milton Eisenhower, the brother of General Dwight Eisenhower, was a well-respected federal government official who was against the internment program. Nevertheless, he was selected by Roosevelt to run the WRA. Looking back more than thirty years later, Milton Eisenhower recalls walking into the oval office on March 10 or 11, 1942, to be given this task, "I was startled by the change in the President . . . I had never seen him without his jaunty air . . . now . . . his lips were a tight grim line, and, as he looked up at me, I saw his eyes were bloodshot."[4] Roosevelt ordered Eisenhower "to set up a War Relocation Authority to move Japanese-Americans off the Pacific Coast" adding, "And Milton . . . the greatest possible speed is imperative." Agreeing to do the job because "President Roosevelt was the Commander-in-Chief and he had given me my war assignment," Eisenhower, "was determined to carry it out as effectively and humanely as possible." Eisenhower left the oval office to further discuss the order with Budget Director Harold Smith in his West Wing office.[5] Smith informed Eisenhower that forced relocation could apply to German and Italian aliens as well, but that those "nationals were not expected to constitute a problem." Eisenhower writes, "As I left the White House . . . it was clear to me that the question was not whether to evacuate the Japanese-Americans (since that was already under way) but rather how to carry out their relocation to the interior."[6]

Eisenhower, a former foreign service officer and official in the Department of Agriculture, knew little about Japanese Americans and next to nothing about the efforts toward their removal in western states. After getting his orders from Roosevelt, Eisenhower met with the main figures of Japanese American internment. These included Attorney General Biddle, a dove on the topic; Assistant Secretary of War John McCloy, a young former Wall Street lawyer who had distinguished himself in government service by working to secure congressional approval of Roosevelt's Lend-Lease Act to help Britain in the war before Pearl Harbor, who was somewhat hawkish on internment; and Karl Bendetsen, an attorney who had been an army reserve officer and was called up in 1940 to join the Judge Advocate General's office who was a definite hawk; and Western Defense Command head General John DeWitt, who as we have seen was a weather vane on the subject.

At this time, the army already had established over one hundred exclusion areas out of which Japanese Americans would be removed over the coming weeks to fifteen hastily constructed "assembly centers." Beyond that, it was up to Eisenhower to try to resettle Japanese Americans off of the West Coast, to try to find them employment, and to set up whatever type of "evacuation center" he deemed appropriate. At first, Eisenhower considered moving only military age men, leaving behind the women and children to maintain businesses and households. Internment hawks objected, thinking all Japanese American men, women, and children represented security threats. For his part, Eisenhower realized that breaking up families, even for the purpose of preserving some of their property and livelihoods, was even desirable from the point of view of the internees than sending away intact families.

Because almost all the people who would be affected by this executive order, the Issei and their Japanese American children, lived in the western states, Eisenhower chose to run the program from San Francisco. He located the nerve center of this slapped together federal program in a room in the Whitcomb Hotel on Market Street. Eisenhower soon learned that "a large number of agencies had their fingers in the pie, and without any great amount of over-all planning as to what was going to be done with the Japanese after they were evacuated."[7] Initially, the army promoted voluntary evacuation, and although this had been a mere "trickle" it was enough to upset the communities and labor markets in the areas to which these Issei and Nisei had relocated themselves.[8] Around 3,500 Issei and Nisei who migrated on their own to Colorado, Utah, Idaho, and other inter-mountain states before the forced internment found they were unwelcome there.[9] Eisenhower reports, "Despite the smallness of these movements, difficulties developed in a great many small communities and violence threatened. At Yerington, Nevada, for example, eight Japanese relocated voluntarily, only to be met by a local group which surrounded the evacuees and told them they would have to leave the community within a few hours; so the evacuees returned to California. Protest meetings [against incoming Issei and Nisei] developed in Colorado and elsewhere."[10]

Eisenhower got the army to stop voluntary evacuations by late March 1942 in favor of planned mass relocations. Japanese Americans and their parents had to wait until their numbers were called before they hurriedly sold their worldly possessions, usually for only pennies on the dollar, and reported for eventual relocation to internment camps that were just then being built in remote and desolate locations. Anticipating the financial hardships they would face when they were pulled from their homes and businesses, Eisenhower approached the Federal Reserve Bank in San Francisco which agreed to do all it could to protect the physical assets of evacuees. It failed miserably. "The bank undertook a definite policy of encouraging liquidation and by far the greatest number of evacuees sold their property at distress prices, gave it away, or stored it at their own expense and risk." The Federal Reserve made it clear that any property delivered to it would be "at the sole risk" of the owner. The form evacuees would have to sign to leave property with the Fed stated, "no liability or responsibility shall be assumed by the Federal Reserve Bank . . . for any act or omission in connection with [the property's] disposition. It is understood that no insurance will be provided on this property."[11]

The challenges the government faced with its hurried relocation policy were described in real time by the Japanese American Evacuation and Resettlement Study (JERS), an investigation of the assembly and resettlement of Japanese Americans during World War II under the direction of Berkeley sociologist Dorothy Swaine Thomas. The study was initiated in the same month President Roosevelt signed Executive Order 9066 and continued through December 1945 by the time the resettlement program nearly ended.[12] Thomas had come to Berkeley in 1940 as a full professor and already had a distinguished career. Her stature helped her win support for her study from UC President Robert G. Sproul and private funders including the Giannini and Rockefeller foundations. Thomas was an inspiring teacher who was noted for her support of her graduate students, encouraging them to write and publish.[13] A member of the JERS team, a graduate student in political science named Morton Grodzins, went on to write a seminal book about the project. Grodzins, who worked at Cal out of room 207 Giannini Hall (named in honor of benefactor A. P. Giannini, the son of Italian immigrants), soon discovered that then, as now, there was a severe shortage of housing in California. Even outside of coastal areas where most Issei and Nisei lived, there were few established communities that could accommodate ten thousand such families and none that were willing to. Attorney General Biddle notes, "The residents of eastern California did not want them to settle anywhere in the state; the officials of the Mountain States, such as Colorado, made it very clear that there would be trouble if they sought refuge further east. After the end of March [1942] mass evacuation was placed on a compulsory basis and applied to all Japanese in California."[14] To house the evacuees, internment camps would have to be built. These were located in areas away from population centers because officials in western states, and many of the citizens in those states, did not want Issei or their American born children coming to their communities.

Until the relocation camps were built, there were no places for the internees to go for the duration of the executive order, however long that might be, and no meaningful provisions for taking care of the property they were forced to leave behind. Eisenhower wrote a frank letter to the director of the Bureau of the Budget who cut the checks needed to pay for internment: "since permanent relocation centers cannot be located and constructed as rapidly as the military need of evacuation requires, it is necessary for the army to provide temporary assembly points where the people can be housed for a few weeks, perhaps for several months." In the rush to start internment, the WRA commandeered the only large, available parcels that were close to cities: unused fairgrounds and horse racetracks. These were never thought to be good locations for assembly centers, but they were the most expedient. Eisenhower writes, "Obviously the evacuees should not be held in such assembly points longer than is absolutely necessary. There is only enforced idleness at such points. This is terribly demoralizing to anyone."[15]

While they waited for the internment camps to be completed, some of the Issei and Nisei in San Francisco would live in the horse stables of Tanforan racetrack in San Bruno, thirteen miles south of the city. Those in

Los Angeles would live in the stables of the Santa Anita racetrack in Arcadia, California, under twenty miles northeast.[16] But what to do with the internees, torn from their homes, work, school, and communities, when they moved to the assembly centers? This too had not been thought out. When the official in charge of the Santa Anita Assembly Center reported that the internees would receive stipends of $54 to $94 per month, an amount more than American soldiers earned, there was an outcry from Congressman Leland Ford who represented Santa Monica, California. Ford had initially defended the loyalty of Japanese Americans but quicky changed his stance after receiving letters and telegrams from constituents and others expressing their hatred of Japanese and Japanese Americans.

Ford was the first congressman to pressure the government to remove Japanese Americans from the western states. Ford suggested to the Issei and Nisei that they look at internment as doing their bit for the war effort: "if an American born Japanese, who is a citizen, is really patriotic and wishes to make his contribution to the safety and welfare of this country, right here, is his opportunity to do so, namely by permitting himself to be placed in a concentration camp, he would be making his sacrifice and he should be willing to do it if he is patriotic and is working for us. As against his sacrifice, millions of other native-born citizens are willing to lay down their lives, which is a far greater sacrifice, of course, than being placed in a concentration camp."[17] Writing from the Whitcomb Hotel, Eisenhower explained to Congressman Ford that the source of the wage scale was the US Army which had used the subsistence wage scale of federal public works programs, "and in any event would charge against this wage the cost of subsistence, which would leave a net wage somewhat less in most cases than the army pay."[18] The WRA did not yet know how much internees would earn or what work they would be able to do, but they would pay for the privilege of their internment in stables and camps.

Eisenhower initially envisioned a benevolent program like the Civilian Conservation Corps (CCC), which had put millions of Americans to work managing forests and creating public parks during the Depression. Under this plan, CCC-like camps would "serve as staging areas for the evacuees as they were moved into private jobs as soon as possible and could resume something like a normal life away from the Western Defense Zone." This kind of more salubrious relocation quickly proved to be unfeasible. At a meeting on April 7 to discuss the plan, the governors of the states where these camps could be located "literally began shouting" at Eisenhower. He recalled, "[a] governor walked close to me, shook his fist in my face, and growled through clinched teeth: 'If you bring the Japanese into my state, I promise you they will be hanging from every tree!"[19] These officials would only accept Issei and Japanese Americans living in their states in concentration camps guarded by armed soldiers.

Milton Eisenhower was a smart and extremely effective administrator. Reading his letters to other federal authorities describing his plans for the WRA, the frustration he felt with this distasteful and hopeless job is palpable between the lines. The WRA wanted internees to have access to work, perhaps "useful public work to do . . . such as land subjugation" or growing produce for their own consumption or to sell, or bringing in light industry "which have always hired Japanese labor; for example, a knitting plant and a glove plant" that might wish to move out of the military area to one of the relocation camps. Eisenhower soon realized these schemes were hopeless. He was certainly aware of another irony he faced:

> Many of the same people who wished to have the Japanese evacuated in the first place are now asking that Japanese labor be kept available for various types of work. In the sugar beet and [other] crop areas of the west the demands for stoop labor are beginning to roll in. Politically this pressure is going to be hard to withstand, but if we break down the orderly program and begin to rush Japanese families here and there simply to meet demands for labor, we are once again going to raise fears in the West. Untoward incidents would not be unlikely. I am putting this statement in writing because I can assure you that I am going to become increasingly unpopular as the weeks go by and as I resist the demands from this area and that. I am going to meet the demands only if the Japanese can be fully protected.[20] This in turn means that group housing will have to be available for the Japanese families—housing to which all Japanese may return at night for protection.[21]

Eisenhower was right. Considerable pressure was applied to get Issei and Nisei labor to tend and harvest especially important crops such as sugar beets, which were used to make munitions. A few months later, Secretary of War Henry Stimson intervened directly with Lt. General DeWitt to have Japanese labor work the long staple cotton crop in Arizona. DeWitt, in a surprisingly forceful letter to Secretary Stimson acceded to the request but made it clear that he required the laborers genuinely volunteer for the work, that they be paid prevailing wage rates and provided adequate housing and protection, "employing federal troops for [their protection]."[22] At a time when the war was going badly for America, and the military was desperately short of troops in every theater of the global war it had recently entered, able-bodied soldiers were being used to protect farm workers, many of them American citizens, harvesting sugar beets and cotton, from threat posed by other Americans.

In April 1942, the plight of around 3,500 Nisei college students enrolled in institutions in the western states constituted a special problem. The college administrators Eisenhower contacted wanted no part in taking in Japanese American students. With the help of a prominent Quaker educator, he was able to form a group to help place these students at colleges in the Midwest and East. It was at this time that President Roosevelt received a letter from California governor Olson expressing his concern about the disrupted education of many loyal Japanese Americans. This is strange given the role Olson played in getting the internment bandwagon rolling. The letter moved Roosevelt. Eisenhower writes, "I felt the President had gained insight into the human problem that, had it come in February rather than May, might have promoted him to decide against mass evacuation."[23]

As Roosevelt's selected head of the WRA, it was up to Eisenhower to respond to whining congressmen and other federal officials. He also had to deal with reporters and columnists who fabricated statements they falsely attributed to him. One syndicated columnist wrote "Only about 20 percent of the approximately 75,000 American born Japanese in the three Pacific Coast states—California, Washington, and Oregon—are loyal to the United States, in the opinion of Milton S. Eisenhower, director of the war relocation authority." Eisenhower never said this in public or private and wrote the columnist to chide him for his "highly unethical" work.[24]

Eisenhower also had to face the few vocal critics of internment, including Ruth Benedict, chairman of the Legislative Committee for the Los Angeles branch of the Women's International League for Peace and Freedom. Benedict wrote to Eisenhower telling him that the Los Angeles branch of this group resolved at their recent meeting that "the detention of the Japanese and Americans of Japanese origin in reception centers is contrary to the fifth and fourteenth amendments of our Constitution." Benedict correctly termed internment "segregation . . . an act of racial discrimination engendered by pressure groups with ulterior motives." Benedict and her group called for due process and proper hearings to determine which specific Issei and Nisei persons "are dangerous to our country and those who are loyal and innocent."[25]

Eisenhower also heard from Edith Roberts of Cambridge, Massachusetts, who wrote to tell him: "The forced evacuation of the Japanese from the Pacific coast is one of the most distressing acts which the Government of the United States is carrying out in the prosecution of the war. The injustice of indiscriminate evacuation is absolutely contrary to the principles of democracy for which the war is supposedly being fought." Significantly, in her bill of particulars, Roberts writes, "It is highly significant that in Honolulu Chief of Police Gabrielson cabled on March 14 that there had been no acts of sabotage either on December 7 or thereafter. Why, then, should the entire body of Japanese in this country be under such suspicion?"[26]

She made an excellent point. Distressingly few Americans at that time shared the views of these two women. It was the incorrect but widespread belief that sabotage had been carried out by Issei and Nisei living in Hawaii leading up to and during the attack at Pearl Harbor that motivated much of the animus that propelled the drive for internment in California, Oregon, and Washington state. There were no provisions, however, for internment of Issei or Nisei on the Hawaiian Islands and there had been only very limited evacuation from Hawaii. Out of a total population of 160,000 persons of Japanese extraction living in the state of Hawaii, only 981 were interned or sent to relocation camps on the mainland in the first weeks of the war. Most of them were Issei or Kibei, that is Japanese Americans born in the United States but sent to Japan to be educated and reared. Ultimately, the army announced: "The shipping situation and the labor shortage make it a matter of military necessity to keep the people of Japanese blood on the island [Oahu]."[27]

When the time came to roll out internment on the West Coast, it was a mess. The family member responding to the summons registered the names of the members of his or her family and was told to report a few days later to be sent to an assembly center for an unknown period of time. They went into the WRA's system with names but quickly became numbers. A Japanese American woman recalled years later, "Henry went to the control station to register the family. . . He came home with 20 tags, all numbered 10710, tags to be attached to each piece of baggage, and one to hang from our coat lapels. From then on, we were known as Family No. 10710."[28]

Farmers had to abandon their lands and shopkeepers had to give up their stores, selling their property and inventory for pittances. The time allowed families to settle their affairs varied from place to place. One Japanese American reported, "We had about two weeks to do something. Either lease the property or sell everything." Another had less time: "the final notice for evacuation came with a four-day notice." All suffered from the emotional and monetary damage inflicted by internment. As one Japanese American testified,

> "It is difficult to describe the feeling of despair and humiliation experienced by all of us as we watched the Caucasians coming to look over our possessions and offering such nominal amounts, knowing we had no recourse but to accept whatever they were offering because we did not know what the future held for us." One woman sold a 37-room hotel for $300. A man who owned a pickup truck, and had just bought a set of new tires and a new battery for $125, asked only that amount of a prospective buyer. "The man 'bought' our pickup for $25." One homeowner, in despair, wanted to burn his house down. "I went to the storage shed to get the gasoline tank and pour the gasoline on my house, but my wife . . . said don't do it, maybe somebody can use this house; we are civilized people, not savages."[29]

When the time came to enter the assembly centers, internees were instructed to bring bedding and linens, toiletries, extra clothes, tableware and "essential personal effects." It was stressed to them that the amount of goods was "limited to that which can be carried by the individual or the family group." In practice, however, extra hand luggage beyond which a family could carry could be shipped to the assembly centers.[30]

Departures from San Francisco were fast and chaotic. By the first week of April, about half of the 5,280 Japanese and Japanese Americans in San Francisco were sent almost four hundred miles away to the assembly center at the Santa Anita horse racing track in Arcadia near Los Angeles. In the next weeks, most of the remaining Issei and Nisei in the Bay Area were sent to the assembly center at the Tanforan horse racing track in nearby San Bruno. By the third week of May the last group of 274 Issei and Nisei were gathered at the Raphael Weill public school in the middle of Japantown. They were escorted at rifle point onto six Greyhound buses that had been charted for the occasion and driven to Tanforan. The *San Francisco Chronicle* reported, "For the first time in 81 years, not a single Japanese is walking the streets of San Francisco."[31] Six Issei or Nisei remained in the city, for the time being, sick in San Francisco hospitals.

Most of the Issei and Nisei who lived in Northern California started their internment at the Tanforan race track. The place was famous among horse racing fans as the site of early victories of the legendary thoroughbred Seabiscuit. During the war, horse racing was postponed for the duration, so racetracks were abandoned. Thus, almost eight thousand men and women, boys and girls, elderly and infants were squeezed into Tanforan while they awaited relocation.[32] Most were housed in horse stalls that still smelled of the manure from the previous equine occupants. Rows of stalls were categorized as barracks. Several of the internees who were sent to Tanforan shared their experiences with JERS researcher Virginia Galbraith. In typed reports, postcards, and handwritten letters, they described life at Tanforan assembly center while they awaited relocation to a camp they knew not where, other than it would be far away from their homes. On May 2, 1942, when the Tanforan assembly center had been open for less than a week, Galbraith received a typed postcard from a member of the JERS team, Tom Shibutani, a twenty-two-year-old native of Stockton, California, and student at Berkeley. Shibutani set the typewriter on his cot and perched himself atop the machine's case and typed his first report, a brief card from Barrack 16, Apt, 49, Tanforan, San Bruno, California. Shibutani summarized the situation he and his wife Tomi faced in a single sentence, "We live in horse stalls with straw mattresses and what lousy food."[33] He promised to write more later.

Shibutani got a job as a barrack manager to have better access to the people and premises for his research with JERS. One of only twenty-five such managers at Tanforan, the position gave him and his JERS colleagues good insight into life at the assembly center. Two days later, he wrote a three-page typed letter to Galbraith giving her the details of his and his wife Tomi's experiences in their first days at Tanforan. He describes how the couple tried to make their assigned horse stall a home. Tomi nailed together pieces of scrap wood to make furniture for their "apartment." Shibutani's initial impressions centered around the physical structures of the assembly center such as the track, grandstands, and rows of horse stalls and the fence that separated them from freedom. The horse stall he and Tomi shared contained two bedframes, two straw mattresses (only invalids received cotton mattresses) and two electric bulbs. Shibutani wrote, "Some of the sections around here are just like slums. The houses are filthy with mud, and laundry is hung all over." The horse stalls did not keep out the persistent cold, as he and Tomi were lashed by winds that blew through the gaps between the roof and the wall. Mindful that he has been tasked with reporting on his environment, Shibutani adds, "These open rooms, incidentally, are useful for the purpose of our study. We can hear absolutely everything that's going on in the next couple of rooms, even if it's spoken in a whisper . . . It's hell though on the young married couples, because they have to restrain themselves more than they otherwise would."[34]

Theft was rife at Tanforan, which seems to have surprised Shibutani. He wrote, "Stealing is very uncommon among the Japanese. As one woman said to me in disgust, 'Before, whenever something was gone, we said that the Filipino or the Negro in the neighborhood did it. Now the Japanese are doing what the Filipino used to do!' Everything that isn't nailed down is taken."[35] Shibutani did not comment on the racism toward Black and Filipino Americans expressed in the woman's remarks.

After two weeks at Tanforan, Shibutani noticed tensions between the Issei, who were born in Japan and came to America as adult immigrants; Kibei, who were born in America and thus American citizens, but had been sent back to Japan for their education; and the Nisei who were born and grew up in America. He reports there was little division between the Nisei, Issei, and the Kibei living at Tanforan, except among the more progressive groups, "The 'liberals' claim that the Issei and the Kibei are 'fascists' at heart and in some ways try to avoid them." Shibutani notes there was some fascist sentiment among the Issei in a particular men's dormitory at Tanforan. One of the Nisei hung a large American flag in a conspicuous place in that dorm. "The Issei don't dare tear it down, but every time they go by they shout 'baka-tare'—equivalent to 'dope,' 'fool,' etc." He sensed unrest ahead, "This is a sad place." Shibutani picked up rumors of psychotic breaks in the camp and thought some of these men in this particular dorm were candidates for such trouble. "Elsewhere in the camp," Shibutani notes, "there doesn't seem to be any splits on the basis of place of birth or education (except among the 'liberals'). Shibutani notes that in most of the camp, the men seemed resigned, "the vast majority of the Issei and the Kibeis just don't give a damn what's going on just so long as they get their three squares [meals] a day."[36] He noticed that the American born and reared Nisei began speaking more Japanese in the camp while the usually far less Americanized Issei began to speak more English. The Kibeis, born in America but educated for a time in Japan, fit in easily with both groups, according to Shibutani.

In a letter to his boss, the program leader Dr. Dorothy Thomas, Shibutani lets down his guard a bit: "Living in this stall is no fun. Tomi and I try to make the best of things." He reports that he heard internees were expected to receive a stipend for personal expenses and salaries for those who work jobs at Tanforan, if any became available. Many outside the wire compared their lot with prisoners of war and thought the internees had it much better off by comparison. This attitude was too much for Shibutani who vented to Thomas, "What the hell. They take us out of our paths of life and put us in a rat-hole like this and expect us to be contented. Who do they think we are anyway?"[37]

Another JERS correspondent was Doris Shigeko Hayashi. A classmate of Tom Shibutani who recruited her to join the project, she graduated from Berkeley in 1942 with a degree in political science. The twenty-two-year-old native of Alameda, California, worked as a secretary in the assembly center employment office while interned at Tanforan.[38] Hayashi, like Shibutani, was among the first arrivals at the assembly center. At Tanforan she got a job interviewing internees about their work experience and recording that information to better match people with jobs, if any work became available. This gave her wide access to all the internees there. She also kept a diary which gives readers today insight into daily life at Tanforan. In May 1942 she wrote, "The whole atmosphere around the stables is rather dejecting because everyone has to sit in front of their homes since there's not enough room inside it seems almost like the slums . . . However, I think parts of this area aren't so bad."[39]

Like many of the internees, Hayashi seemed determined to make the best of her predicament. It was not easy. Some aspects of life at Tanforan had the feel of a very bad summer camp. Hayashi writes about some of the entertainment that was on offer, "Went to the talent show. It was lousy. The worst part was the man who sang a Japanese song. One could notice the antagonism of the Nisei to Japanese songs." Hayashi adds, "They make us sing *God Bless America* each time. It seems rather ironic . . . We all sing it, but it doesn't really seem quite appropriate. A more appropriate hymn would be the *Star Spangled Banner*."[40] But Tanforan was a prison and not a summer camp. Two days after that talent show, Hayashi writes, "The neighbor's father died in the county hospital and they had gone to the funeral . . . They had to get an okay from the top officials . . . Not very many people went . . . only five people including three in the family."[41]

From Hayashi we learn that Milton Eisenhower resolved the problem of wage rates for internees. Internees between the ages of sixteen and sixty were classified according to their skills and education. Hayashi and her team wrote these details on an index card for each person. If and when job opportunities were created at Tanforan or later on, internees with appropriate skills could be matched to those jobs. Not every internee had a background that could be easily classified on an index card. It was up to Hayashi and her colleagues to interview candidates to categorize their skills. The plan was to pay wages ranging from $8 per month for unskilled work, $12 per month for skilled labor, $12 per month for technical work, and $16 per month for professionals. Hayashi writes that wages were going to be paid in script to be spent at the camp, "Also part will be used for maintenance."[42] If and when jobs became available at the assembly center or at the permanent internment camps that were to become their homes indefinitely, internees would have to contribute to the cost of their incarceration.

Some Nisei leaders tried to buoy spirits by reframing the experience internees were living. Hayashi attended a talk about "How to Face Evacuation" given by a leader from the Young People's Fellowship, a group that formed at Tanforan. At first he portrayed Tanforan as something akin to a kibbutz rather than a temporary internment camp. The speaker, Hayashi writes said, "We have escaped to a great extent from the customary class and economic lines. We are on equal terms. Everything we value will be spiritual or internal, not material and external, since money will have little worth here, we will have to develop our internal ideas, beliefs, and talents to a great extent." But the façade that his audience were other than prisoners fell away with his advice to "attain a sense of achievement every time we accomplish any task, no matter how insignificant . . . [ours] is a situation which can't be prevented and for which we are not to blame. The main aim of each of us should be to do one task well and attain that sense of achievement."[43] It is not clear how many in the audience took the message to heart. Three days later Hayashi mentions in her diary, "The rumor is spreading that there is saltpeter in the coffee and tea, so quite a few of us are becoming more cautious about drinking it."[44] (There is a long and commonly held belief that potassium nitrate, also known as saltpeter, depresses male libido. Rumors of saltpeter added to food and coffee by authorities for this purpose were often rife in the military and in prisons.)[45]

The mixing of socioeconomic groups thrown together at Tanforan led to predictable frictions. Sophisticated urbanites and salt of the earth farmers did not always interact well. Hayashi says, "They are really crude in our eyes, though we may seem snobbish to them."[46] The way the Issei and Nisei got along with each other and with other mixed Japanese races at Tanforan was an issue both Tom Shibutani and Doris Hayashi discuss.

Hayashi writes, "It will be very interesting to watch how the question of intermarriage will be treated by the Japanese . . . I noticed that the lady next door was 'advising' her children not to play with the [half Filipino and half Nisei] children who live across the way." Hayashi goes on to write about a blond internee, the product of his Japanese and German parents, "I guess it's pretty difficult for [him]. He looks almost entirely Caucasian. It was interesting to note that the other day two blond boys came into the employment office to apply for work. Mr. Gunder [William Gunder, the personnel officer at Tanforan] was surprised to know they were Japanese. He thought they were Caucasian. He noted that they could probably escape without notice if everyone were not carefully searched on leaving the grounds."[47]

One Nisei woman who tried to avoid internment wound up in Tanforan. Hayashi writes, "A [Nisei] girl married to a Chinese and who also looks like a Chinese came in today from the San Francisco jail. She had been arrested for failure to register for evacuation. She had felt she would be able to go East for her husband is very wealthy, but some 'stooge' at the Chinese hotel at which she was staying must have reported her, so she was compelled to spend about ten days in jail with other women prisoners and lice and mice." This woman was likely to have an exceptionally difficult time in her internment. Hayashi writes, "I don't know how she will adjust herself to the Japanese since she has been away from them for a long time and she told the press that she 'Hated the Japanese.' Moreover, she is to live in the Hollywood Bowl [section of Tanforan] which is about the most condensed barrack, (circular and enclosed)."[48]

Confinement at Tanforan was similar to that at a minimum-security prison. Hayashi reports radios had to be turned off by 9:00 p.m., but there was no prescribed time for lights out.[49] The fact that their liberties had been taken way was made clear to all during the periodic sweeps of the camp. Camp security, bolstered by reinforcements from outside the camp, performed periodic searches of the barracks and stalls looking for contraband like "long knives, saws, bats, Japanese literature of any kind except hymnals and dictionaries and Bibles." The way the search was performed varied. In one part of Tanforan, Hayashi writes, "The [soldiers] dumped the beds upside down and searched every corner and crack [of the barracks] . . . In our barrack, a very friendly man . . . came and was . . . chatting with our family. We only had a [Japanese dictionary] had none of the other types of contraband so he didn't take anything from us. Thus our family didn't feel as bitter as some others might have."[50]

Although they were interned because the government felt it could not adequately assess their loyalty, Nisei men were not exempt from the military draft. The local draft board was keen to get their hands on the Nisei males of draft age. It was up to William Gunder, the personnel officer at

Tanforan, to register the men on a selected day. Registration was to begin at 8:00 a.m. on a given Monday. The local draft board wanted it started at 7:00 a.m. and to continue until midnight, but Gunder objected. Hayashi writes, "he was the only one [available to do the work] and would have no shifts."[51]

Nineteen-year-old Ben Iijima was a sophomore at Cal when he and his family were sent to Tanforan to await relocation. He became the youngest JERS fieldworker.[52] He arrived at the camp from his parents' home in Redwood City where he had been born and where his family had run a plant nursery. His drive in a truck to Tanforan was a melancholy ride. He writes, "When we began to pick up speed along Woodside Road and began to swing into stride along El Camino, I thought how for the last time I was looking at my home town. Redwood [City] wasn't a big city; but I thought it was big in the sense that people were liberal and not rabble-rousing here despite the feverish clamor of the papers—the residents had not a feeling of hatred toward me." The man driving the truck had graduated from Stanford, the cross-bay rival to Cal. The two men talked about Big Game parties, campus bon fires and hijinks, but Iijima writes, "we didn't talk a bit of evacuation or the war."[53]

Still new to Tanforan, Iijima takes in his surroundings. He runs into a young man, probably a high school student before he was interned. The two talk as they climbed the Tanforan racetrack grandstand bleachers to take in the view. Iijima writes, "From the highest row we could see the Bay in the distance and just beyond the barbed wire fences of Tanforan, the wooden homes of San Bruno, the white streak of Bayshore Highway, the smoke stacks of Bethlehem Steel. On the knoll above South San Francisco there is the imposing sign, 'South San Francisco The Industrial City.' How often I had seen that sign on my way to the University, and yet, from the grandstand seat, it seemed as though I were gazing on some strange landmark. 'Yes,' the fellow said rather quietly, 'it does seem funny, doesn't it?'"[54]

A similar sentiment was expressed to Dr. Thomas by Haruo Najima. After being at Tanforan for a few weeks Najima writes, "It is maddening to watch the neon lights of San Bruno go on at night, to see lights of some city across the bay, to see people working in the fields just outside, to see cars whizzing by on the highway just feet away or on Bayshore miles to the East. After being taught and educated that freedom of expression and movement is something worth while in the schools, it is extremely difficult to accept cooping up as if it were inevitable [that the] hand of fate had thrust us here, and that we should meekly accept that as such. The older folks [do], younger kids [do], and the rest of us will have to."[55]

To occupy his time, the young Cal sophomore Ben Iijima got a job on the assembly center's newspaper, the *Totalizer*. The work gave him scope to roam Tanforan and report findings to his JERS colleagues. He writes, "After the town hall meeting I went to a bull session up in the office of the *Totalizer*. We all seemed to agree that the attitude towards evacuation itself was not important, but its bearing to our later reinstatement after the war vital." Referring to the Japanese American Citizens League, the most well-known Japanese American organization that advocated cooperation with authorities regarding internment, Iijima continues, "One girl poised the question, 'Do the J.A.C.L. members feel differently about their former attitude of voluntary cooperation, now that we have come to camp and found conditions not as well as we had expected? Do you think we would have lost anything if we had fought vigorously before the military took a hand.' No one answered, but I think everyone was asking the same question individually. I came home in the dark, and I was impressed by the utter solitude and eeriness of the dark barracks around me. It's no pleasure walking alone in this camp after dark."[56]

All colleges and universities on West Coast were closed to Japanese Americans. One Sunday, Iijima runs into an old classmate who hopes to go to college in the Midwest or East Coast. He was hopeful that life would be better for him away from California and away from a big city. Iijima writes, "He told me the people were tolerant back east. When he does go, he intends to go to a rural town, where unlike the cities, the people will be more friendly." Later that afternoon, Iijima describes watching the two organized sports activities scheduled that Sunday: a sumo wrestling match and a softball game, bookends that capture some of the Nisei experience. Iijima writes, "In the afternoon I went to see a sumo contest ... The contestants were attired with only a heavy cloth wrapped around their waists. Some of the fellows wore their gym trunks, others, their briefs, but the rest were virtually naked ... The referee has a fan-like object in his hand which he uses to designate the winner. The older men shout out words of encouragement to their favorites and critically comment upon each man as the wrestlers come up in turn. After seeing several bouts I got unexplainably tired of it all, so I walked out to the track to watch the soft ball games. There were girls playing ball, too, throwing the ball with amazing speed and gusto."[57]

The next weekend Iijima observes the makeshift high school graduation for students who had attended Sequoia High School in nearby Redwood City. In a small room adjacent to the visitor's hall, seven teachers and the school principal came to present diplomas and awards to the graduating students. Iijima writes, "The principal spoke to the students telling them of the ceremonies they had [on campus]." It must have been wrenching to the students to think about the festivities they missed with their classmates. The next speaker was the school's history teacher, who was also a member of the American Legion, a group that advocated for Japanese American internment, to present the American Legion Medal in US history. Iijima writes,

I think [the history teacher] meant what he said when he said it was the proudest moment of his life. In awarding the medal he said [the winner] exemplified all that was the best of Americanism. Despite what I think of that organization [the American Legion], I think [he] is a truly fine person. He said he understood our position, but everyone is scared to speak in our behalf right now. Most of the seven women teachers were in tears. I don't know if they were all sincere or not but I guess it was a pathetic sight. The parents were there in their best clothes and they too were in tears . . . All the students were happy . . . as they clung to their school paper and diploma. One fellow that's always been complaining and look[ing] obviously unhappy, was smiling today and in good spirits.[58]

For Japanese Americans on the cusp of adulthood, internment was especially hard to understand. Some high school students at Tanforan wrote poignantly about the experience in a few class compositions that survive. In response to the theme "Relocation, its challenge to me" high school student Sachi Kawahara writes: "As an inhabitant of a relocation area I am invited to accept either one of two choices in determining my future. One of them is the attitude of defeatism and the other is that of continued self-improvement. I intend to follow the latter theory . . . The time will surely come when we can again trek back to our homes. If we keep the right attitude by being prepared, I know we will be welcomed back into the folds of American living."[59] Kawahara's teacher, Mr. Aki, gave her an A. Another essay on the theme "My Attitudes toward Evacuation" by high school student Rhoda Nishimura survives. She writes about her "melancholy" feelings when it came her family's turn to enter the camp. "[W]hen I feel like pouring out words of contempt towards the U.S. gov't." She remembers what a teacher told her before she departed for Tanforan, "To win this war everyone in the U.S. must make sacrifices. Your sacrifice is a much harder one than most of us have to bear. As a citizen always remember that this is your part in the war." Nishimura continues that she keeps this in mind even when she feels like a prisoner, "We aren't the only ones going through such trying days. The people in Greece are starving. In China there are famines each year . . . But do you not think in comparison to life in other suffering nations, our existence here in America though in camp is a much easier one? . . . Many men have given their lives for their country since Dec. 7. They gave their all for their native land. Let us drop our ill feelings and take on this life in camp as our duty in this war as loyal Americans."[60] No grade was indicated on the paper.

Ben Iijima sent the JERS team a few copies of the *Totalizer*, the camp newspaper. Among the notices for the dance band (the "Tanforan Tooters") and variety shows was this item about the American Legion group at the assembly center:

"Tatsu J. Ogawa, 46, who occupies Tanforan's [barrack] 15 [apartment] 50, carries on his forehead a scar of a wound received while fighting with the famous 91st 'Wild West' division in the Meuse-Argonne offensive of World War I." The item goes on to list his activities in the American Legion and Veterans of Foreign Wars, two groups that enthusiastically advocated for internment of Japanese Americans. The paper noted, almost as an aside, that Ogawa's wife and "four children are in Hawaii, unable to return here after going to the islands to visit her ailing father, just before Dec.7."[61]

When the ten relocation camps that had been constructed in remote and desolate areas including Manzanar, California; Tule Lake in Newell, California; Topaz (Central Utah) in Delta, Utah; and Gila River in Rivers, Arizona were ready, the internees took busses and trains from the assembly centers to their new homes far away. Early in the summer of 1942, Tom and Tomi Shibutani left Tanforan for their relocation camp at Tule Lake, 370 miles northeast from San Francisco near the Oregon border. For Shibutani, the hastily built relocation camp was preferable to the horse stall he and his wife shared at the assembly center. He writes: "Compared to Tanforan it's paradise . . . Physical facilities wonderful; so is administration. Men in office personally conducted us to our quarters, which are among the best in the camp—all completed.[62]

By June 1942, Milton Eisenhower had had enough. He describes his time running the WRA as a "nightmare."[63] Eisenhower, who began his career in government service under President Calvin Coolidge and ended it working on special projects for President Nixon had a long view into how organizational decisions are made, especially in government. About the disastrous decision to intern Issei and Japanese Americans, he writes, "Many forces were at work—military, political, economic, emotional and racial. The principal actors in the drama frequently acted independently of each other. Often they were unaware of what the others were doing or thinking or how their decisions or actions related to other decisions or actions. I doubt that anyone saw the over-all pattern that was emerging or how his actions contributed to that pattern." Eisenhower surmised, "Misunderstanding, rumor, fear, misinformation, prejudice, and ignorance were dark winds that blew across the land. An incident here, a rumor there, a political move, a military decision, an official memorandum—all fell like pieces into a mosaic that no single individual could perceive or had created." Eisenhower sadly observed, "And as the days passed and the pressures mounted, the ultimate decision began to take shape . . . the reality is that in such major movements, the decision is not *made*, it happens."[64]

NOTES

1. Issei refers to a person born in Japan who immigrated to the United States or Canada. These people were prohibited from becoming US citizens by the Exclusion Act of 1924. They lived and worked in the United States. Their American or Canadian born children are referred to as Nisei. These people were birthright citizens of the United States or Canada. Kibei designates a Nisei, i.e., a person of Issei parents who is born in the United States, but educated largely in Japan. Sansei refers to a person born in the United States or Canada whose grandparents were immigrants from Japan.
2. Togo W. Tanaka, "Journal." bk0014b1h3g-FID1.pdf. Japanese Americans—Evacuation and relocation, 1942–1945, Japanese American Evacuation and Resettlement Study, University of California, Berkeley Bancroft Library.
3. Biddle, *In Brief Authority*, 220.
4. Milton Eisenhower did not keep a diary and this visit is not recorded in the president's calendar on either of those days. Eisenhower reports that Harold Smith, the budget director, was present in the Oval Office when Eisenhower received this order. Milton S. Eisenhower, *The President is Calling* (New York: Doubleday and Co., 1974), 95.
5. Eisenhower, *The President is Calling*, 98.
6. Eisenhower, *The President is Calling*, 97.
7. Letter from Milton Eisenhower to E. H. Wiecking on March 26, 1942, University of California, Berkeley Bancroft Library. WRA bk0013c8x6r-FID1.pdf.
8. Letter from Milton Eisenhower to E. H. Wiecking on March 26, 1942, University of California, Berkeley Bancroft Library. WRA bk0013c8x6r-FID1.pdf.
9. "By February 16, 1942, the Justice Department had detained 2,192 Japanese; 1,393 Germans, and 264 Italians. Close to 250 German and Italian individuals were interned for up to two years in camps in Montana, Oklahoma, Tennessee, and Texas. Source: Inada, *Only What We Could Carry*, 191.
10. Milton S. Eisenhower letter to Harold D. Smith, Director, Bureau of the Budget, April 5, 1942, University of California, Berkeley Bancroft Library. bk0013c8x6r-FID1.
11. Dorothy Swaine Thomas and Richard S. Nishimoto with Rosalie A. Hankey, James M. Sakoda, Morton Grodzins, Frank Miyamoto, *The Spoilage* (Berkeley: University of California Press, 1946), 15. Thomas and Nishimoto cite the Federal Reserve form as Personal Property Form, Wartime Civil Control Administration, Form FRB-2.
12. Thomas and Nishimoto with Hankey, Sakoda, Grodzins, Miyamoto, *The Spoilage*, xiv.
13. "Dorothy Swaine Thomas October 24, 1899–May 1, 1977," American Sociological Association. Asanet.org.
14. Biddle, *In Brief Authority*, 220.
15. Milton S. Eisenhower letter to Harold D. Smith, Director, Bureau of the Budget, April 5, 1942, University of California, Berkeley Bancroft Library. bk0013c8x6r-FID1.
16. Milton S. Eisenhower letter to Harold D. Smith, Director, Bureau of the Budget, April 5, 1942, University of California, Berkeley Bancroft Library. bk0013c8x6r-FID1.

17. Morton Grodzins, *Americans Betrayed, Politics and the Japanese Evacuation* (Chicago: University of Chicago Press, 1949), 65.

18. Letter from Milton Eisenhower to E. H. Wiecking, March 26, 1942, University of California, Berkeley Bancroft Library. bk0013c8x6r-FID1.

19. Eisenhower, *The President is Calling*, 118.

20. In a letter from Milton Eisenhower to Dave Davidson dated April 28, 1942 (on WRA Stationary from the California Office in the Whitcomb Hotel Building), Eisenhower estimates that he did not have enough federal troops to protect groups of fewer than 5,000 internees. This constraint meant that almost all work projects would have to be done at the assembly centers. There were few work projects that could be usefully performed at a racetrack or fairground on short notice. University of California, Berkeley Bancroft Library. bk0013c8x6r-FID1.pdf.

21. Milton S. Eisenhower letter to Harold D. Smith, Director, Bureau of the Budget, April 5, 1942, University of California, Berkeley Bancroft Library. bk0013c8x6r-FID1.

22. J. L. DeWitt, "Letter to Henry Stimson, September 12, 1942," University of California, Berkeley Bancroft Library, Japanese American Evacuation and Resettlement Records 1930–1974, BANC MSS 67/14 c, folder D2.046.

23. Eisenhower, *The President is Calling*, 121.

24. Letter from Milton Eisenhower to Cole E. Morgan, King Features Syndicate, April 30, 1942, University of California, Berkeley Bancroft Library. bk0013c8x6r-FID1.

25. Letter from Ruth Benedict to Milton Eisenhower on June 11, 1942, University of California, Berkeley Bancroft Library. bk0013c8x6r-FID1.

26. Letter from Edith Roberts to Milton Eisenhower dated May 9, 1942, University of California, Berkeley Bancroft Library. bk0013c8x6r-FID1.

27. Mathew M. Briones, *Jim and Jap Crow: A Cultural History of 1940s Interracial America* (Princeton: Princeton University Press, 2012), 458.

28. John Hersey, "Behind Barbed Wire," *The New York Times Magazine*, September 11, 1988, 56. Complete testimonies are available at Commission on Wartime Relocation and Internment of Civilians, National Archives. Archives.gov.

29. Hersey, "Behind Barbed Wire," 56.

30. Thomas and Nishimoto with Hankey, Sakoda, Grodzins, Miyamoto, *The Spoilage*, 14.

31. "S.F. Clear of All But 6 Sick Japs," *San Francisco Chronicle*, Thursday, May 21, 1942, 1.

32. "Tanforan (detention facility)," Densho Encyclopedia. Densho.org.

33. Tom Shibutani to Virginia Galbraith, Japanese Americans—Evacuation and relocation, 1942–1945, Japanese American Evacuation and Resettlement Study, University of California, Berkeley Bancroft Library, bk0013c8x2j-FID1.pdf.

34. Tamotsu Shibutani to Virginia Galbraith, Japanese Americans—Evacuation and relocation, 1942–1945, Japanese American Evacuation and Resettlement Study, University of California, Berkeley Bancroft Library, bk0013c8x2j-FID1.pdf, Letter dated May 4, 1942, 1.

35. Tamotsu Shibutani to Virginia Galbraith, Japanese Americans—Evacuation and relocation, 1942–1945, Japanese American Evacuation and Resettlement Study, University of California, Berkeley Bancroft Library, bk0013c8x2j-FID1.pdf, Letter dated May 4, 1942, 3.

36. Tamotsu Shibutani to Virginia Galbraith, Japanese Americans—Evacuation and relocation, 1942–1945, Japanese American Evacuation and Resettlement Study, University of California, Berkeley Bancroft Library, bk0013c8x2j-FID1.pdf, Letter dated May 11, 1942, 2–3.

37. Tamotsu Shibutani to Virginia Galbraith, Japanese Americans—Evacuation and relocation, 1942–1945, Japanese American Evacuation and Resettlement Study, University of California, Berkeley Bancroft Library, bk0013c8x2j-FID1.pdf, Letter dated May 11, 1942, 2–3.

38. https://encyclopedia.densho.org/Doris_Hayashi/.

39. Doris Hayashi, "Diary, May 5, 1942," Vol. 1, Japanese Americans—Evacuation and relocation, 1942–1945, Japanese American Evacuation and Resettlement Study, University of California, Berkeley Bancroft Library, bk0013c5j52-FID1.pdf.

40. Doris Hayashi, "Diary, May 14, 1942," Vol. 1, Japanese Americans—Evacuation and relocation, 1942–1945, Japanese American Evacuation and Resettlement Study, University of California, Berkeley Bancroft Library, bk0013c5j52-FID1.pdf.

41. Doris Hayashi, "Diary, May 16, 1942," Vol. 1, Japanese Americans—Evacuation and relocation, 1942–1945, Japanese American Evacuation and Resettlement Study, University of California, Berkeley Bancroft Library, bk0013c5j52-FID1.pdf.

42. Doris Hayashi, "Diary, May 15, 1942," Vol. 1, Japanese Americans—Evacuation and relocation, 1942–1945, Japanese American Evacuation and Resettlement Study, University of California, Berkeley Bancroft Library, bk0013c5j52-FID1.pdf.

43. Doris Hayashi, "Diary, May 31, 1942," Vol. 1, Japanese Americans—Evacuation and relocation, 1942–1945, Japanese American Evacuation and Resettlement Study, University of California, Berkeley Bancroft Library, bk0013c5j52-FID1.pdf.

44. Doris Hayashi, "Diary, June 3, 1942," Vol. 1, Japanese Americans—Evacuation and relocation, 1942–1945, Japanese American Evacuation and Resettlement Study, University of California, Berkeley Bancroft Library, bk0013c5j52-FID1.pdf.

45. https://www.militarytimes.com/off-duty/military-culture/2021/09/22/saltpeter-for-sex-drives-and-the-urban-legend-of-the-militarys-libido-manipulation/.

46. Doris Hayashi, "Diary, June 26, 1942," Vol. 2, Japanese Americans—Evacuation and relocation, 1942–1945, Japanese American Evacuation and Resettlement Study, University of California, Berkeley Bancroft Library, bk0013c5j6m-FID1.pdf.

47. Doris Hayashi, "Diary, June 4, 1942," Vol. 1, Japanese Americans—Evacuation and relocation, 1942–1945, Japanese American Evacuation and Resettlement Study, University of California, Berkeley Bancroft Library, bk0013c5j52-FID1.pdf.

48. Doris Hayashi, "Diary, June 23, 1942," Vol. 2, Japanese Americans—Evacuation and relocation, 1942–1945, Japanese American Evacuation and Resettlement Study, University of California, Berkeley Bancroft Library, bk0013c5j6m-FID1.pdf.

49. Doris Hayashi, "Diary, June 6, 1942," Vol. 1, Japanese Americans—Evacuation and relocation, 1942–1945, Japanese American Evacuation and Resettlement Study, University of California, Berkeley Bancroft Library, bk0013c5j52-FID1.pdf.

50. Doris Hayashi, "Diary, June 23, 1942," Vol. 2, Japanese Americans—Evacuation and relocation, 1942–1945, Japanese American Evacuation and Resettlement Study, University of California, Berkeley Bancroft Library, bk0013c5j6m-FID1.pdf.

51. Doris Hayashi, "Diary, June 27, 1942," Vol. 2, Japanese Americans—Evacuation and relocation, 1942–1945, Japanese American Evacuation and Resettlement Study, University of California, Berkeley Bancroft Library, bk0013c5j6m-FID1.pdf

52. https://encyclopedia.densho.org/Ben%20Iijima.

53. Ben Iijima, "Diary," pages 4–5, Japanese Americans—Evacuation and relocation, 1942–1945, Japanese American Evacuation and Resettlement Study, University of California, Berkeley Bancroft Library, bk0013c8w7s-FID1.pdf. This diary entry was undated.

54. Ben Iijima, "Diary, May 22, 1942," page 2, Japanese Americans—Evacuation and relocation, 1942–1945, Japanese American Evacuation and Resettlement Study, University of California, Berkeley Bancroft Library, bk0013c8w8b-FID1.pdf.

55. Letter from Haruo Najima to "Jean and George" of the JERS Project dated May 9, 1942. bk0013c5k64-FID1 https://oac.cdlib.org/ark:/28722/bk0013c5k64/?brand=oac4.

56. Ben Iijima, Diary, June 3, 1942," page 14, Japanese Americans—Evacuation and relocation, 1942–1945, Japanese American Evacuation and Resettlement Study, University of California, Berkeley Bancroft Library, bk0013c8w8b-FID1.pdf.

57. Ben Iijima, "Diary, June 7, 1942," page 21, Japanese Americans—Evacuation and relocation, 1942–1945 Japanese American Evacuation and Resettlement Study, University of California, Berkeley Bancroft Library, bk0013c8w8b-FID1.pdf.

58. Ben Iijima, "Diary, June 13, 1942," page 26, Japanese Americans—Evacuation and relocation, 1942–1945, Japanese American Evacuation and Resettlement Study, University of California, Berkeley Bancroft Library, bk0013c8w8b-FID1.pdf.

59. Japanese Americans—Evacuation and relocation, 1942–1945, Japanese American Evacuation and Resettlement Study, University of California, Berkeley Bancroft Library, bk0013c5m0b-FID1.pdf.

60. Japanese Americans—Evacuation and relocation, 1942–1945, Japanese American Evacuation and Resettlement Study, University of California, Berkeley Bancroft Library, bk0013c5m0b-FID1.pdf.

61. The *Totalizer*, June 20, 1942, 6. Ben Iijima, "Diary, June 13, 1942," page 26, Japanese Americans—Evacuation and relocation, 1942–1945, Japanese American Evacuation and Resettlement Study, University of California, Bancroft Library, bk0013c8w8b-FID1.pdf.

62. Ben Iijima, "Diary, June 13, 1942," page 26, Japanese Americans—Evacuation and relocation, 1942–1945, Japanese American Evacuation and Resettlement Study, University of California, Berkeley Bancroft Library, bk0013c8w8b-FID1.pdf.

63. Eisenhower, *The President is Calling*, 114.

64. Eisenhower, *The President is Calling*, 126.

12

✠

Nearer to Free
Black Migration to San Francisco

Marguerite Johnson, the three-year-old Black girl in Oakland who ran home to her grandmother with the news of Pearl Harbor, soon moved with her mother and brother to the Western Addition, also known as the Fillmore, in San Francisco. A mostly Japanese neighborhood, the Fillmore was one of the few areas in San Francisco where the small population of Black San Franciscans in the city could rent or buy property. For years Black Americans, Filipino Americans, Japanese Americans, and other races lived side by side in that neighborhood. It was the place where the teenager Marguerite Johnson grew up to become the woman, Maya Angelou. In her beautiful memoir, *I know Why the Caged Bird Sings*, Angelou writes about the changes that the internment of Japanese Americans had on her street, block, and neighborhood,

> In the early months of World War II, San Francisco's Fillmore district, or the Western Addition, experienced a visible revolution. On the surface it appeared to be totally peaceful and almost a refutation of the term "revolution." The Yakamoto Sea Food Market quietly became Sammy's Shoe Shine Parlor and Smoke Shop. Yashigira's Hardware metamorphosed into La Salon de Beauté owned by Miss Clorinda Jackson. That Japanese shops which sold products to Nisei customers were taken over by enterprising Negro businessmen, and in less than a year became permanent homes away from home for the newly arrived Southern Blacks. Where the odors of tempura, raw fish and cha had dominated, the aroma of chitins, greens and ham hocks now prevailed . . . as the Japanese disappeared, soundlessly and without protest, the Negroes entered with their loud jukeboxes, their just-released

animosities and the relief of escape from Southern bonds. The Japanese area became San Francisco's Harlem in a matter of months.¹

Those months would have been March, April, and May of 1942 when most Issei and Japanese Americans were pushed into assembly centers like the Tanforan racetrack to await indefinite internment in relocation camps.

The "negroes" who Angelou says "escaped from Southern bonds" were Black Americans who left near peonage in the South for good employment in Bay Area shipyards that were operating twenty-four hours a day to build ships for America's war effort. This was a continuation of the "Great Migration" of Black Americans from the South to the North, Midwest and West that had been ongoing since before World War I. In the Great Migration's initial phase, Black southerners left the South for jobs in the North and Midwest. When World War I started in 1914, immigration from Europe declined and bans on immigration of non-White people from other parts of the world created opportunities for Black Americans in a variety of industries, especially when America entered that war in 1917. In the years between World War I until World War II, an estimated two million Black people left the South for other parts of the country.² In the 1920s and 1930s, industries in the Pacific Coast states developed.

When America entered World War II, burgeoning demand for war work again created employment opportunities. In this second phase of the Great Migration, Black Americans moved West to Los Angeles, Oakland, and San Francisco in California and Portland, Oregon, and Seattle, Washington.³ During World War II, the West Coast "suddenly became the nation's new racial frontier." As late as 1940, Black Americans constituted only 1.5 percent of the total population of the three West Coast states. Only in Los Angeles was there a Black community of any considerable size in the West. In the advent of World War II, however, Black people made up 10 percent of the two million migrants who came to the West Coast.⁴ The emigration of Americans brought about by World War II was unprecedented. "Probably never before in the history of the United States has there been internal population movement of such magnitude" as occurred during World War II.⁵ In San Francisco, the city's Black population increased more than 600 percent during the war as Black migrants from the South came to the Bay Area seeking and finding good jobs and leaving behind the poor schools and racial violence that they had lived with.⁶

When World War II started, the singer and actor Joseph James and his wife Alberta were living in San Francisco. In addition to their work as entertainers, the Jameses were active in Black civic life. James describes the San Francisco that greeted the Black migrants that arrived in large numbers seeking war work. Citing statistics from the 1940 census, he writes, "There was a total population of 634,536 [in San Francisco]. Of this, only 4,846 were Negroes. Moreover, Negroes were so widely scattered that the visitor to San Francisco at that time would have easily received the impression that there were almost no Negroes in the city. There was only one point of relatively high concentration of Negro residence—the well-known Fillmore District; but even this was in no sense a Negro area. Here, White people were most numerous, with the Japanese ancestry group second with upwards of five thousand. There were, also, small numbers of Filipinos and Chinese. Negroes did not number more than one thousand."[7] When he came to San Francisco, James would have encountered the city's chapter of the National Association for the Advancement of Colored People (NAACP). Founded in New York, 1909, the NAACP was the largest and most influential advocacy group for Black people in the country. Its initial focus was on promoting legal equality for Black Americans. Over time, its mission expanded to promote economic equity and voting rights.

San Francisco's Black population remained relatively small between 1900 and 1940. Black workers in the city were excluded from organized labor and the industrial jobs in the area.[8] Although Black emigrants and Chinese immigrants began coming to San Francisco "at roughly the same time, lived in proximity to one another and shared similar aspirations to better their economic and social position, and occasionally even shared the same recreations facilities," while Chinese residents were largely confined to Chinatown in San Francisco, there were no Black ghettos in San Francisco before World War II.[9]

By the start of World War II, the San Francisco Bay Area was one of the biggest shipbuilding centers in America. This work also created demand for many other industries in the region. In addition to war work, the Bay Area was home to important military installations including US Navy air stations at Treasure Island, Alameda, and Moffett Field near Palo Alto. There were also vast navy yards at Hunter's Point, Mare Island, and Port Chicago, all along different parts of bays near San Francisco. The US Army had numerous bases in the region, including the majestic Presidio and Fort Mason in San Francisco, Hamilton Field in Marin County, and Fort McDowell on Angel Island. "Few metropolitan areas in the West were as fully girded for a full-scale war as the Bay Region."[10] When America entered the war, however, Bay Area cities were unprepared to receive the more than half-million people who came from all over the country seeking good paying industrial jobs. There was little available housing and overcrowded schools and hospitals. Historian Gerald D. Nash writes, "San Francisco buckled under the influx of more than 125,000 new residents, most of whom worked in Bay Area defense establishments. In addition, the city was host to tens of thousands of 'war tourists,' relatives or friends of servicemen departing to or arriving from Pacific battle areas. At the same time it continued to provide the traditional function as an entertainment capital in the West for thousands of servicemen and women."[11] Housing in California in general, and San Francisco in particular, has always been in short supply. Wartime demand meant there was a housing crunch in most cities in America. For Black people facing informal and formal restrictions on where they could live, finding housing was especially challenging. War work attracted approximately fifteen thousand new Black migrants to San Francisco. Most sought homes in the Fillmore in properties recently vacated by the interned Issei and Nisei. The number of Black people seeking homes greatly exceeded the available houses, flats, and apartments available to them. Black emigrants made homes in subdivided apartments and even stores, rear porches and "practically any space available in the Fillmore."[12]

The sizeable Black migration to San Francisco attracted the attention of noted sociologist Dr. Charles S. Johnson, then a professor at Fisk University and codirector of race relations for the Julius Rosenwald Fund, a philanthropy with a special interest in Black education and uplift. Johnson came to San Francisco to study conditions on the ground for Black migrants. He found that in San Francisco, as in most other cities in the country, restrictive covenants determined which neighborhoods non-Whites could live. Johnson's team interviewed civic improvement clubs, real estate firms, insurance companies, loan companies, merchant associations, and the real estate board. Johnson was not surprised to learn, "All groups admitted unquestionably to the presence and operation of restrictive agreements against Negroes." Perhaps sheepishly, "only about half of them admitted," to the Black interviewer, "that the areas covered by their organizations were involved."[13]

The areas in San Francisco where restrictive covenants were most prevalent included tony neighborhoods like: the Marina, Pacific Heights, Nob Hill, and Russian Hill; the suburb-like Mira Loma Park district and the working-class Bayview. Johnson found that all building contractors putting up three or more houses used restrictive clauses. This helped reinforce the practice, Johnson notes, because "racial restrictions covering the land can go in only with the original subdivision. Thereafter, restrictions must be managed through contracts of all property owners not to sell or rent to minority groups. These restrictive contracts are registered with the Recorders Office and become legally binding."[14] Before the war, few Black San Franciscans could afford to live in the small single-family homes typical of the Bayview district; and fewer still could afford the more expensive neighborhoods. When Black people found good paying defense industry jobs, Johnson noted, "There has been agitation for restrictive contracts in the Pacific Heights district where a Negro family bought a home on Pacific and Laguna [an intersection in affluent Pacific Heights]. In the working class Bayview district near Hunter's Point six months ago hand bills were distributed from door to door threatening to burn down the house of anyone selling property to Negroes."[15] As late as 1940, when the navy purchased the shipyard at Hunter's Point, there were only seven Black people living among the fourteen thousand residents of the Bayview.[16]

During the war, San Francisco's population boomed, growing by over 30 percent. From its small base,[17] the city's Black population increased well over 600 percent.[18] Restrictive covenants forced the new Black migrants, like the Issei and Nisei who came decades before them, into the few neighborhoods where they could live. Chief among them was the Fillmore. For Maya Angelou, then a Black high school girl living there, it was a vibrant neighborhood. She writes, "On Post Street, where our house was, the hill skidded slowly down to Fillmore, the market heart of our district. In the two short blocks before it reached its destination, the street housed two day-and-night restaurants, two pool halls, four Chinese restaurants, two gambling houses, plus diners, shoeshine shops, beauty salons, barber shops and at least four churches. To fully grasp the never-ending activity in San Francisco's Negro neighborhood during the war, one need only know that the two blocks described were side streets that were duplicated many times over in the eight-to-ten square block area."[19]

This was the neighborhood studied by sociologist Charles S. Johnson. He managed a team of workers who interviewed 278 Black families in San Francisco. Joseph James's wife Alberta was part of this team.[20] Johnson was careful to interview Black people who had lived in the city for years or even decades as well as new arrivals.[21] He learned that family heads who were already established in San Francisco, "look with considerable disfavor upon the new Negro population." He speculated, "this reflects the fear of the older Negro residents that the Negro migrants will augment racial difficulties in the city."[22] Indeed, San Francisco had been spared much of the worst racial violence that plagued other cities. Historian Albert S. Broussard writes, "Most whites were civil in their contacts with blacks, irrespective of their personal prejudices, and displayed what one historian has called 'polite racism.'"[23]

Maya Angelou concurred, "San Franciscans would have sworn on the Golden Gate Bridge that racism was missing from the heart of their air-conditioned city," she writes, "But they would have been sadly mistaken."[24] There also was some simple snobbery of established Black families toward the newcomers. Angelou remembers, "Native San Franciscans, possessive of the city, had to cope with an influx, not of awed respectful tourists but of raucous unsophisticated provincials."[25] Another description of the established Black community in the Bay Area comes from the nurse, self-taught historian, and writer Delilah L. Beasley. Born two years after the Civil War, she came to Oakland, California, around 1910. She wrote a weekly column titled "Activities among Negroes" in the

Oakland Tribune, and published a book, *The Negro Trail Blazers of California* about black pioneers "dating back to early Spanish exploration of the region."[26] Beasley writes, "The colored people now living in the northern part of the State and around San Francisco remind one much of persons living around Boston and New England towns; they are so fond of their own little corner of the world; they are so self-satisfied."[27]

Indeed, Black Americans were able to make better lives for themselves in the Bay Area than was possible in most other parts of the country. Still, they were constrained in both their opportunities for work and within the community. Black women usually held jobs as domestics. Very few worked in established companies where wages were better. Black men often were employed by the railroad, usually as red cap porters, or as longshoremen or teamsters. The small number of Black entrepreneurs in the area operated grocery stores, shoeshine stands, or barber shops.[28] The three Black churches in San Francisco, the Bethel AME, the Third Baptist Church, and the Zion Church, each boasting congregations of five to six hundred members played a large role in Black social life.[29] As historian Douglas Henry Daniels writes in his excellent book *Pioneer Urbanites: A Social and Cultural History of Black San Francisco,* "While they did not leave race discrimination, or even segregation behind them, San Francisco-bound southerners managed to escape Jim Crow laws and humiliation."[30]

Daniels captures the voice of former Texan Martel Meneweather, who came to San Francisco in 1919 when she was twenty-nine years old. She was a college graduate and the daughter of college graduates at a time when only around 2 percent of Americans had a college degree. Even as a young girl, Meneweather had been acutely aware of the constraints binding her in the Jim Crow South. She said, "I never liked the south. I didn't like the tradition and to me, south was like slavery . . . I wanted to find a place where I would be free to bring my children and my children would be reared as free citizens . . . To me [San Francisco] was heaven. It was like coming from hell to heaven. That's how I feel about it."[31]

Where the Great Migration brought rural Southern Black Americans to cities there was usually some mild frictions within the expanding Black community. W.E.B. DuBois, the pioneering sociologist, intellectual, and cofounder of the NAACP, saw this phenomenon play out time and again, "Yet it has everywhere been manifest in the long run that while a part of the negroes were native-born and trained in the culture of the city, the others were immigrants largely ignorant and unused to city life . . . Thus the history of the negro in Northern cities is the history of the rise of a small group growing by accretions from without, but at the same time periodically overwhelmed by them and compelled to start over again when once the new material had been assimilated."[32]

One native San Franciscan saw the new Black migrants from his viewpoint as a well-established Black man in the city. Aurelious P. Alberga was in his late fifties when defense work brought Black people in large numbers to the Bay Area. Alberga had been a boxer and one of the few Black officers in the US Army during World War I. He fought in the trench warfare in the Vosges mountains in France rising to the rank of 1st lieutenant.[33] He recalls being the only Black San Franciscan to be commissioned in the army.[34] Earlier in his career, at the time of the 1906 earthquake, Alberga worked for a prominent and wealthy blind businessman in San Francisco, helping him manage his various properties and serving as an aide. Alberga was active in the Republican party, at a time when most Black Americans were loyal to what had been "the party of Lincoln." Later, Alberga owned an eight-chair bootblack stand in the Ferry Building, the result of Republican political patronage from California's governor Friend Richardson, whom Alberga helped elect. Later still, he owned businesses in commercial real estate, insurance, and bail bonds. He also helped organize the Northern California chapter of the NAACP and its local chapter in San Francisco.

Interestingly, Alberga had been attracted to Marcus Garvey's Universal Negro Improvement Association and even toyed with joining the charismatic Black leader's Back-to-Africa movement in the 1920s when Garvey came to San Francisco. Speaking of the Black people who came to San Francisco during World War II, Alberga saw, "quite a bit of difference [in the newer Black migrants]." In particular, they showed "a great deal of timidity," characterized by the new southern migrants. "They [had no] confidence in themselves . . . [or] in anything that they done . . . Their English was very, very bad. And they took—quite a bit of repeating, almost, on all—nearly all occasions, to understand what they were endeavoring to try to impress you with . . . Their demeanor in their way of walking down the street here . . . They walked with that attitude, as though something was behind them . . . You could pick them out from among all the others, just like that (snaps his fingers), and they needed seven, eight, or nine years before they seemed to get Americanized."[35]

Among the newly arrived Black emigrants to San Francisco was Dr. Daniel Collins, who was a dentist who arrived in San Francisco in 1942 to teach at the University of California Dental School. He was one of the few Black professionals to move to San Francisco in the early 1940s. Collins came to California aboard the Union Pacific Railroad's steam locomotive, the Challenger. He was one of many Black men on that train seeking a new and better life in California. Collins recalled, "They were people looking for a job, who could take a one-way ticket to California, with no destination in mind except to California. You knew there were war jobs out here, knowing you could get a job. And on the Challenger, on that train, there was not a single seat, every seat was taken. And, in fact, the men's room, there were two or three seats around the men's room, they were filled. There was a guy sitting on the can so if you had to go, he had to get up. That's how crowded that train was."[36]

The overcrowding presented entrepreneurial opportunities for people, Black or White, who had a foothold on property in the Fillmore. Sociologist Charles S. Johnson's report cites two examples: "Mrs H. rents rooms to 17 couples and two single men in a house next door for which she pays 75 dollars a month and takes in 60 to 100 dollars weekly depending upon if they pay their rent." And there was this, "The room the Z's live in is a front bedroom. They rent the entire half of the house originally intended for two families, sub-let the other bedrooms with two other couples. The three families apparently live completely to themselves. The other couples each pay $17.00 a week for room and kitchen sharing privileges." The living conditions that many of San Francisco's newest residents encountered in the Golden State must have been something of a disappointment, even if they had experienced worse in their old hometowns. Johnson's study offers revealing details. "The family of three lives in one room. It has a double bed, a dresser, two chairs, a two-burner gas stove, a small work table and an orange box nailed to the one window for a cooler. There is a small clothes closet, and for this accommodation the family pays $8 a week."[37] Among the study sample, only a little more than half the people interviewed had accommodations with access to a bathroom.

Dr. Collins described the overcrowding he found when he arrived in San Francisco, "In fact, you know, we laugh about it now but I knew one guy who was a very small old man named Merle Gadles. He was a wise, wise old-timer. Merle Gadles rented some guy a big chifforobe. The guy stayed in a big chifforobe. That was just a big enough drawer for a guy to sleep in. Well that was the circumstances on the ground level."[38] Hard as it was, it must have been worth it. As a high school student, Maya Angelou watched Black migrants move into the Fillmore. Many, like her, came from the South and found for the first time in their lives new economic and social opportunities. Angelou writes of the Black Americans who came to San Francisco, "For the first time he could think of himself as a Boss, a Spender . . . The shipyards and ammunition plants brought to booming life by the war let him know that he was needed and even appreciated. A completely alien yet pleasant position for him to experience." As for any sympathy Black San Franciscans might feel for the Issei and Nisei who used to live in the Fillmore, Angelou surmised: "Who could expect this man to share his new and dizzying importance with concern for a race that he had never known to exist."[39]

Across the country, over one million Black Americans entered civilian employment during the period between 1940 to 1944. The number of Black workers employed in skilled jobs doubled as did the number of single-skilled and semiskilled Black workers. The number of Black women employed as domestics fell sharply as black women found much better paying jobs and careers in industries from which they had been excluded by race and gender in the past. Economist Robert C. Weaver said of the phenomenon of good jobs becoming available to Black people during the war, "These changes in a period of four years, represented more industrial and occupational diversification for Negroes than had occurred in the seventy-five preceding years."[40] Most of the Black newcomers of World War II migrated to the West Coast from the western region of the South—Texas, Louisiana, and Arkansas—to meet the needs of the expanding war economy in California. It was said that Henry J. Kaiser, the famous industrialist who built ships fast using assembly line methods during the war, "brought Blacks here from all over the south—every state—and he brought them in train loads. He brought one to three train loads every day for six months."[41]

In the Bay Area, it was in shipyards that most Black migrants found the best economic opportunities of their lives up to that time. Job opportunities abounded in Bay Area shipbuilding. Johnson writes, "The sharecropper from Louisiana is now a welder in a shipyard, the bootblack has become an electrician at Bethlehem Steel, the longshoremen from Texas and Louisiana are employed in their usual occupation as longshoremen, and the musician from Oklahoma is now a musician in San Francisco. On the other hand, the editor from Virginia, a graduate of college, is now a rigger on a marine ship working on the swing shift; the owner of a filling station from Houston, Texas, is now a welder in Oakland, California; but his son a college graduate who was a draftsman in Texas is a draftsman in San Francisco."[42] Left unsaid in his report was that all these men and women breathed a little easier in the Bay Area and the jobs paid far better than any opportunities they had back home. Urgent wartime demand for their labor trumped Jim Crow institutional racism that excluded them from good paying industrial jobs in the past. Johnson found, however, that other industries remained unwelcoming to Black workers, even in the face of increased wartime need. His interviewer was told, "The shipyards get the better type of Negro worker and since they are few, only the inferior type remains to be used. Insomuch as the company maintains the highest standards for its workers, it does not hire those Negroes who are available now."[43] This executive added, "To employ Negroes more fully and use them in higher job categories would invite union trouble and reaction from white workers, thus the company is forced to follow a policy of expediency."[44]

Up to this time, across the country non-Whites had been excluded from most industrial unions. That was also the case in the shipyards near San Francisco, whose laborers were represented by the American Federation of Labor's Boilermakers Union Local 6. Black laborers who wished to work in the closed shop shipyards were compelled to join the union, but because they were Black, they were prohibited from joining the regular union and instead had to enter the segregated auxiliary union. Charles S. Johnson writes, "The major problem of labor unions and Negro workers in the Bay areas is the burning issue of segregated union auxiliaries for Negroes within the Boilermakers' set-up. This is by no means the only important labor union problem involving Negro workers, but it is the principal one. Since the majority of Negro workers are in the shipyards and bargaining agreement represented under the 'maser contract' are maintained by the Boilermakers Union to which the auxiliaries are attached, the bulk of the Bay area Negro workers are directly involved."[45] Dissatisfaction with this situation showed up in interviews with Johnson's survey sample. He notes in his report, "A high proportion of Negro head of household union members were dissatisfied with the AFL, particularly the Negro auxiliary of the Boilermakers Union."[46]

Black job seekers faced routine discrimination and even violence as they moved to urban areas in the north and the west to find jobs in defense plants that were building up prior to America entering the war. One of the most prominent Black labor leaders of that time, A. Philip Randolph, president of the Brotherhood of Sleeping Car Porters, threatened to organize protests, bringing "ten, twenty, fifty thousand Negroes on the White House lawn" if President Roosevelt did not issue an executive order stopping discrimination in the defense industry, where the federal government was the main buyer and had direct sway. Roosevelt, and especially his wife Eleanor, were sympathetic to labor and the struggle Black Americans faced with racism in America. The president, who believed Randolph's threat, was also keen to avoid the social unrest of a massive demonstration of Black Americans at a time when the country was girding for a war that was obviously on the horizon but for which America was still woefully unprepared. On June 25, 1941, Roosevelt signed Executive Order 8802 "banning discriminatory employment practices by federal agencies and all unions and companies engaged in war-related work. The order also established the Fair Employment Practices Commission (FEPC) to enforce the new policy."[47] It was the first presidential directive on race since Reconstruction. With the executive order in hand, Randolph called off the march. Randolph would be a driving force of the March on Washington twenty-two years later where two hundred thousand demonstrators heard Martin Luther King deliver his celebrated "I Have a Dream" speech from the steps of the Lincoln Memorial.

The shipyard known as Marinship in beautiful Marin County offers a good microcosm of the economic, social, and strategic impact of defense work in the Bay Area during the war. Within three months of breaking ground on its site along the tidal marshes of Richardson Bay, near the

San Francisco Bay and the Golden Gate to the Pacific Ocean, the keel to the first ship built was laid. The shipyard specialized not in building warships like aircraft carriers or destroyers, but constructed the vital cargo carriers known as "Liberty Ships" and fuel tankers. If America was the Arsenal of Democracy, Marinship and shipyards like it in the Bay Area and elsewhere built the means to deliver that arsenal across the Atlantic and Pacific Oceans to the war.

The need was great. Before America entered the war, almost all of its commercial maritime fleet was old and nearing obsolescence.[48] Commissioning, building, and operating Marinship illustrates the cooperation between government and business that was refined during World War II and still exists today. In early March 1942, San Francisco's Bechtel Corporation received a request for a proposal to build and operate a West Coast shipyard. The Federal government retained ownership of the shipyard. "Bechtel responded within 24 hours with a tentative plan for a plant on the Sausalito waterfront, one of the few vacant industrial sites left along San Francisco Bay with good rail and highway access . . . ten days later Bechtel signed a Commission contract to build and operate the proposed facility and deliver 34 ships by the end of 1943."[49] This was an audacious plan. It was met. As historian Charles Wollenberg writes, "During its three-and-a-half year career, Marinship delivered 93 vessels: 15 Liberty Ships and 78 T-2 tankers . . . the yard also outfitted and repaired an additional 23 vessels and began building barges for the invasion of Japan, a project that was abruptly ended when Japan surrendered . . . Marinship [was] a military-industrial comet, briefly lighting up the Bay Area economic skyline."[50]

German U-boat commander Peter Cremer was a man with a unique point of view on the importance of the hastily constructed cargo and tanker ships that came out of shipyards like Marinship. He writes, "The capacity of American shipyards . . . and their new method of building Henry Kaiser's Liberty and Victory ships in sections, threw out all our calculations. Although in 1942 we were still confident of destroying seven hundred thousand tons (of shipping) a month and outstripping new additions, we had in fact already lost the race between sinkings and new construction—the cardinal factor of the U-boat war." Creamer pointed to the central fact of Marinship and other shipyards, "They built faster than we could sink. And as for the durability of these 'off-the-peg' ships, built in a few months on the conveyor-belt system . . . they were still to be found decades later on every sea, under every possible flag. Against such [numbers of ships] we could do nothing with our few U-boats."[51]

Many of the new ships that crossed the oceans carrying vital food, fuel, and ammunition to the fighting were built near San Francisco. Federal contracts for defense work seemed to rain down upon California and the Bay Area in particular. This bonanza "changed Bay Area society more than any other event since the California Gold Rush."[52] Almost 17 percent of all wartime ship construction workers in the United States were employed in Bay Area facilities.[53] To meet this demand, when so many of the able-bodied White men who usually filled these positions had enlisted or been drafted into the military, necessitated the hiring and training of thousands of men and women of all colors who previously knew nothing about ships or shipbuilding. More than 90 percent of Marinship employees had never worked in a shipyard before and had never worked in the craft that they used, such as welding, electrical, clerical, or myriad others, before working there.[54] Together, they got the job done. Marinship alone built ninety-three Liberty ships and tankers and employed nearly twenty thousand workers.[55]

NOTES

1. Angelou, *I Know Why the Caged Bird Sings*, 209.
2. "The Great Migration (1910–1970)," African American Heritage, National Archives. Archives.gov.
3. Within twenty years of World War II, a further three million Black people migrated throughout the United States. "The Great Migration (1910–1970)," African American Heritage, National Archives. Archives.gov.
4. Carey McWilliams, *Brothers under the Skin* (Boston: Little, Brown & Co., 1964), 7.
5. Marilynn S. Johnson, *The Second Gold Rush: Oakland and the East Bay in World War II* (Berkeley: University of California Press, 1993), 2, citing US Bureau of the Census, Current Population Reports, Populations Characteristics, ser. P-20, no. 14, Internal Migration in the United States: April 1940 to April 1947 (Washington, DC, Bureau of the Census), 1.
6. Broussard, *Black San Francisco: The Struggle for Racial Equality in the West, 1900–1954*, 4.
7. Joseph James, "Race Relations on the Pacific Coast," *The Journal of Educational Sociology* 19, no. 3 (November 1945): 166.
8. Broussard, *Black San Francisco: The Struggle for Racial Equality in the West, 1900–1954*, 3.
9. Broussard, *Black San Francisco: The Struggle for Racial Equality in the West, 1900–1954*, 5.
10. Gerald D. Nash, *The American West Transformed: The Impact of the Second World War*, 66–67.
11. Nash, *The American West Transformed: The Impact of the Second World War*, 66–67.
12. Nash, *The American West Transformed: The Impact of the Second World War*, 97. Nash quotes San Francisco Public Health director J. C. Geiger.
13. Charles S. Johnson, Grace Jones, Herman Long, "The Negro War Worker in San Francisco: A Local Self-Survey," May 1944. Project financed by a San Francisco citizen, administered by the YWCA, and carried out in connection with the Race Relations Program of the American Missionary Association, Dr. Charles S. Johnson, Director, and the Julius Rosenwald Fund.

14. Johnson, Jones, Long, "The Negro War Worker in San Francisco: A Local Self-Survey," 30.

15. Johnson, Jones, Long, "The Negro War Worker in San Francisco: A Local Self-Survey," 31.

16. By the end of the war, that number had grown to nine thousand or 20 percent of the population of the neighborhood. Katherine Petrin and Matthew Davis, "South San Francisco Opera House," National Register of Historic Places Registration Form, Bayview Opera House. Bvoh.org.

17. Charles S. Johnson: "The 1940 census reports 634,536 inhabitants for San Francisco. Of this number, 4,846 were Negroes, constituting .8 percent of the population of the city . . . There were 17,782 Chinese and 5,280 Japanese residents." (Page 2) "The civilian population of California was increased by more than a million persons during the three and a half years following the 1940 Census, according to estimates of the Federal Census Bureau. This growth took place despite the evacuation of almost 100,000 Japanese inhabitants, inductions into the armed forces and a sizeable out migration . . . Proportionally, the San Francisco area has experienced the larger growth with a population increase of 26 percent over 1940 compared with 13 percent increase in the Los Angeles area. These figures relate only to the civilian population. The number of military personnel stationed in or in transit through California, is not a matter of public information." (Page 1) More than 13 percent of California's inhabitants were foreign born compared with 8.8 percent for the nation as a whole in 1940. Johnson, Jones, Long, "The Negro War Worker in San Francisco: A Local Self-Survey," 1.

18. Broussard, *Black San Francisco: The Struggle for Racial Equality in the West, 1900–1954*, 135.

19. Angelou, *I Know Why the Caged Bird Sings*, 179.

20. She was credited in the report as Mrs. Joseph James. Her first name, Alberta, was not given.

21. This sample covers 1,316 individuals, in 272 households. One hundred forty-nine migrant households (54.8 percent) and 123 non-migrant households (45.2 percent) are in the sample. Johnson, Jones, Long, "The Negro War Worker in San Francisco: A Local Self-Survey," 9.

22. Charles S. Johnson, Grace Jones, Herman Long, "The Negro War Worker in San Francisco A Local Self-Survey," May 1944, 18.

23. Broussard, *Black San Francisco: The Struggle for Racial Equality in the West, 1900–1954*, 7.

24. Angelou, *I Know Why the Caged Bird Sings*, 213.

25. Angelou, *I Know Why the Caged Bird Sings*, 212.

26. "Delilah L. Beasley and the Trail She Blazed," California State University, Northridge University Library. Library.csun.edu.

27. Douglas Henry Daniels, *Pioneer Urbanites: A Social and Cultural History of Black San Francisco* (Berkeley: University of California Press, 1990), 162.

28. Albert S. Broussard, "Interview with Aurelious P. Alberga Conducted on December 7, 1976," *Afro-Americans in San Francisco Prior to World War II*, San Francisco Public Library Oral History Project, 15–16.

29. Broussard, "Interview with Aurelious P. Alberga Conducted on December 7, 1976," 18.

30. Daniels, *Pioneer Urbanites: A Social and Cultural History of Black San Francisco,* 163.

31. Daniels, *Pioneer Urbanites: A Social and Cultural History of Black San Francisco,* 180.

32. Daniels, *Pioneer Urbanites: A Social and Cultural History of Black San Francisco,* 162.

33. Broussard, "Interview with Aurelious P. Alberga Conducted on December 7, 1976," 8.

34. Broussard, "Interview with Aurelious P. Alberga Conducted on December 7, 1976," 21.

35. Daniels, *Pioneer Urbanites: A Social and Cultural History of Black San Francisco,* 171.

36. Paul T. Miller, *The Postwar Struggle for Civil Rights: African Americans in San Francisco 1945–1957* (New York: Routledge, 2010), 6–7.

37. Johnson, Jones, Long, "The Negro War Worker in San Francisco: A Local Self-Survey," 25.

38. Miller, *The Postwar Struggle for Civil Rights: African Americans in San Francisco 1945–1957*, 11–12.

39. Angelou, *I Know Why the Caged Bird Sings*, 210.

40. Carey McWilliams, *Brothers under the Skin* (Boston: Little, Brown & Co., 1964), 9.

41. Daniels, "Pioneer Urbanites: A Social and Cultural History of Black San Francisco," 165.

42. Johnson, Jones, Long, "The Negro War Worker in San Francisco: A Local Self-Survey," 82–83.

43. Johnson, Jones, Long, "The Negro War Worker in San Francisco: A Local Self-Survey," 67.

44. Johnson, Jones, Long, "The Negro War Worker in San Francisco: A Local Self-Survey," 68.

45. Johnson, Jones, Long, "The Negro War Worker in San Francisco: A Local Self-Survey," 69.

46. Johnson, Jones, Long, "The Negro War Worker in San Francisco: A Local Self-Survey," 18.

47. "Executive Order 8802: Prohibition of Discrimination in the Defense Industry (1941)," Milestone Documents, National Archives, Archives.gov. To investigate "complaints of discrimination in violation of the provisions of this order" Executive Order 8802 established the "Committee on Fair Employment Practice." More commonly known as the Fair Employment Practice Committee (FEPC), it has been disregarded by most historians as a powerless and ineffectual agency, especially in the South. After World War II, the FEPC almost became a permanent agency, but a strong voting bloc in Congress prevented it. Shortly after the dismantling of the FEPC, President Truman issued Executive Order 9981 banning segregation in the military.

48. Charles Wollenberg, *Marinship at War: Shipbuilding and Social Change in Wartime Sausalito* (Berkeley: Western Heritage Press, 1990), 17.

49. Wollenberg, *Marinship at War: Shipbuilding and Social Change in Wartime Sausalito*, 3.

50. Wollenberg, *Marinship at War: Shipbuilding and Social Change in Wartime Sausalito*, 5

51. Peter Cremer with Fritz Brustat-Naval, *U-Boat Commander*, trans. Lawrence Wilson (Annapolis: Naval Institute Press, 1984), 81.

52. Wollenberg, *Marinship at War: Shipbuilding and Social Change in Wartime Sausalito*, 2.

53. Wollenberg, *Marinship at War: Shipbuilding and Social Change in Wartime Sausalito*, 3.

54. Wollenberg, *Marinship at War: Shipbuilding and Social Change in Wartime Sausalito*, 6.

55. Jack Tracy in forward to Wollenberg, *Marinship at War: Shipbuilding and Social Change in Wartime Sausalito*, viii.

13

The Baritone Who Broke the Jim Crow Union

When Japan attacked Pearl Harbor, Joseph James was in Hollywood rehearsing the song "Good News" for the movie, *Tales of Manhattan*. Participating in this movie, featuring big White movie stars including Charles Boyer, Rita Hayworth, Henry Fonda, and popular Black stars Paul Robeson, Ethel Waters, and Eddie "Rochester" Anderson was bread and butter work for James.[1] The Hall Johnson Choir sang the choral numbers and their leader directed the vocal arrangement for the film. At the beginning of the war, singing and acting jobs became harder for James to find so he returned home to San Francisco. Unable to find much work in show business in San Francisco, James took a welding course at the Samuel Gompers Trade School, a public high school in the Mission District, to train for the plentiful jobs in the shipyards. The work paid well; dayshift Journeymen welders earned about $270 per month, those on the nightshift earned even more.[2] Before the war, the median income for a man in the United States was about $80 per month.[3]

In the summer of 1942, James was hired as a welder at Marinship.[4] With his interest in mechanics and his good training, James had been successful at the shipyard. He was quickly promoted to Journeyman welder and earned a position on the "Flying Squadron" of expert welders sent to wherever trouble spots arose in ship production.[5] His experience, education, and personality made him a leader and organizer. James also continued performing concerts at Marinship, setting aside his welder's helmet and torch from time to time to sing in shipyard programs and ship launches, including at the launch of the Liberty SS *William A. Richardson*, the first ship constructed there, where James sang for a crowd of twenty thousand people who came to witness its launch. The exposure reinforced his popularity at the shipyard. After only a year on the job, James emerged as the leading Black figure at Marinship and this helped him become a highly effective labor organizer there. It was from this position that he undertook to overthrow the Jim Crow auxiliary unions that Black workers were forced to join at shipyards on the West Coast.

The International Brotherhood of Boilermakers, a union within the American Federation of Labor had traditionally excluded Black members. To maintain segregation while at the same time taking on Black workers in closed shops, in which all eligible workers were required to join the union, in 1937 the Boilermakers started creating all-Black auxiliary union locals. These segregated union lodges charged the same amount of dues as the regular Boilermakers union but were unequal in various ways, including paying only about half the insurance benefits as the White lodges. Further, auxiliary lodges had to rely on White governing lodges to approve job promotions and represent auxiliary members in grievances. Finally, auxiliary members or the auxiliary lodge itself could be thrown out of the union at the discretion of the international president of the governing lodge. By contrast, members of the White governing lodge or a local lodge could only be thrown out of the union by the international president acting in conjunction with the union's executive counsel and only after having been proved guilty of violation of the union's constitution and by-laws.[6]

Near the time America entered the war, the union negotiated closed-shop agreements with West Coast shipbuilders. This agreement forced over thirty thousand Black workers in shipyards in Los Angeles, Oakland, Portland, Oregon, and Marinship in Sausalito, where Joseph James worked, to accept this unequal union representation. As James explained later,

> The boilermakers' union, which has jurisdiction in all of the crafts in which most Negroes work, has provided an auxiliary into which Negroes are obliged to go. Other labor groups, like the machinists, do not accept Negroes as members, but allow them to work in the craft on a permit basis. The unions of the stage riggers, shipwrights, pile drivers, electricians, and street railway men (in San Francisco) accept Negroes into full membership. These are all A.F. of L. unions. The C.I.O. [the Congress of Industrial Organization at that time was a rival governing union], in accordance with its well-known policy of non-discrimination, not only accepts Negroes as members but has paid officials who are Negroes. The C.I.O. in this area is represented by the International Longshoremen's and Warehousemen's Union, the ship-scalers, United Office and Professional Workers, United Federal Workers, and, most recently, the Transport Workers' Union.[7]

For a time, Bay Area Black workers received clearances to work in local shipyards without having to join the auxiliary union or pay union dues. By February 1943, as more Black workers were hired, the Boilermakers union set up auxiliary unions at East Bay shipyards and forced Black workers to join those, and pay the same dues as the members of the governing White unions. Black shipyard workers there did not like the order, but complied. As the NAACP wrote in its magazine, *Crisis*, Black workers "knew jim crow, segregation and second-class citizenship when [they] saw it," but they paid their dues anyway, "much in the same manner as [Black people] took a rear seat on a bus in Memphis . . . [they] regarded the payments as a necessary bribe for the privilege of working at a job that paid more than [they] ever dreamed."[8] Black workers and White workers in these shipyards earned the same handsome pay.

Joseph James objected to this separate and unequal union representation forced upon Black ship workers. Unable to interest the San Francisco chapter of the NAACP to help him fight the Jim Crow auxiliary, James organized the San Francisco Committee Against Segregation and Discrimination to rally Black ship workers to fight auxiliary unions.[9] When the same order for Black workers to join the auxiliary union came down at Marinship in August 1943, many Black workers looked to him for guidance. So did management at Marinship, which that August devoted a special issue of its employee magazine, *Marin-er,* to the topic of race relations at the shipyard. The lead article was written by James in his role as a respected Journeyman welder and head of Marinship's Negro Advisory Board. He writes, "Here we are, workers from many far-flung sections of the country and the world, representing nearly every conceivable shade of political and social philosophy, working together for the realization of a common goal! Here, therefore, we have a complete refutation of the oft-heard assertion that 'Negroes (or Chinese, Mexicans or Filipinos) and whites just won't work together. There's a natural antagonism that keeps them fighting one another.'" James writes that at Marinship, working together in racial harmony was the "rule, not the exception!"[10]

Over the next three months, around half of the approximately 1,100 Black workers at Marinship refused to join the auxiliary union. "On November 24, the union ordered management to fire 430 Black workers unless they paid their auxiliary dues in 24 hours and warned an additional 150 workers that they faced similar treatment."[11] That evening in San Francisco James's Committee Against Segregation and Discrimination held a meeting that attracted a few hundred people to discuss what to do. James told the attendees that he did not want to destroy the Boilermakers union but rather make it stronger with all members given full and equal rights. The participants agreed to continue the boycott of the auxiliary union. The vote was unanimous.[12] Two days later, on Friday, November 26, dozens of Black workers who had not joined the auxiliary were denied access to the shipyard and informed that they no longer had permission to work there. Very quickly, two hundred workers were dismissed at

Marinship, including Joseph James.[13] This at a time when the Bay Area faced a severe labor shortage and any able-bodied man or woman, White or Black, could get a job at a shipyard.[14]

On that Saturday hundreds of Black men and women gathered at a Marinship gate to protest the firings. The local paper called it "Marin's greatest labor demonstration and most critical situation to arise since the San Francisco General strike in the summer of 1934."[15] Despite this breathless claim, it was an orderly protest. That Sunday, about a thousand people attended a meeting of James's Committee in the Fillmore in San Francisco. Some committee leaders advocated a boycott of jobs that demanded Jim Crow unions. James and other leaders insisted they wanted to end segregated unions while continuing to work in the shipyards. The meeting voted to pursue James's course supported by legal action against the auxiliary union. That Monday, the committee's attorneys, San Francisco lawyers George Andersen and Herbert Resner, filed suit in Federal District Court on behalf of James and a group of other Black workers at Marinship seeking to be reinstated. The judge issued a temporary restraining order preventing the firings pending a hearing. Marinship officials said they would halt further dismissals but refused to reinstate the dismissed workers until they received union approval. Another court ordered this action and after some foot-dragging by the union, dismissed workers were allowed to return to Marinship. To get the word out, James's committee hired trucks with loudspeakers to drive around the Fillmore in San Francisco and Marin City, the neighborhood where most of the Black ship workers lived, urging them to return to work.[16] Still the Boilermakers union refused to back down and allow Black workers into the regular union.

When Joseph James formed the committee, there were few civic or political organizations for Black people at that time in San Francisco. He noted that before the war, the small Black community in San Francisco "was extremely conservative. There were five small churches ministering to the spiritual needs of the Negro community. None of these exhibited any appreciable social consciousness."[17] The city's branch of the NAACP had only 585 members, and this was at the end of a membership drive in 1943, during the height of the action against the auxiliary union. Disagreement remained among Black workers about whether they should submit to the auxiliary union system. Some wanted to strike, others were content to leave well enough alone—the jobs and pay provided were good—even if the union conditions were blatantly unequal. The resigned submission of the latter group troubled Thurgood Marshall, legal counsel for the national body of the NAACP in New York. Marshall told his boss, the group's president Walter White, "a large group of Negroes in the Bay Area . . . are in favor of auxiliaries in the Boilermakers union."[18] Marshall was making a case to his boss to dedicate scarce NAACP headquarters resources to support James's action in San Francisco.

James wanted Black workers to boycott the auxiliary unions without stopping their vital wartime work. The NAACP supported this position. This left Joseph James navigating a middle course between his fellow Black workers content with the auxiliaries on one side, and his colleagues willing to strike a defense plant during wartime on the other. When a strike of Black workers at Marinship was held on November 27, 1943, James showed up at the shipyard gates to urge workers with union authorizations to return to work. Other committee members urged strikers to continue their stoppage. With the help of the NAACP, James filed his lawsuit against Marinship, protesting the firing of the Black shipbuilders. Joseph James and Thurgood Marshall wrote each other frequently about the situation at Marinship. In early 1944, James had become president of the San Francisco chapter of the NAACP and the San Francisco Committee Against Segregation and Discrimination dissolved. Most of the committee members followed James to the NAACP, enlarging its ranks.[19] James needed Marshall's legal help, in turn, Marshall and the national NAACP benefitted from the revitalization of the once sleepy San Francisco chapter of the organization and its work toward the NAACP's mission to advance employment opportunities for Black Americans.

During World War II, the leaders of the NAACP considered employment discrimination and voting rights as the two most important problems facing Black people in America.[20] This represented a shift for the organization. Before the war, the NAACP had focused its resources on cases that benefited and helped expand the Black middle class, and on pressing social justice issues like lynching and involuntary servitude, "whose shock value garnered support from liberal whites," who along with Black middle class members had been the group's main sources of the group's funding.[21] By the 1940s, the NAACP sought and litigated cases for working class Black Americans, like shipbuilders, in state and federal courts. The court cases advanced the group's mission and brought notoriety which, the group hoped, would increase its dues paying membership among the broader Black community and increase its ties to organized labor. During the war, the national office of the NAACP dedicated one staff attorney out of its team of only five lawyers to specialize in employment discrimination cases.[22]

Thus it was that the special counsel to the NAACP, Thurgood Marshall, an attorney still only in his mid-30s, took an expensive cross country flight from the group's national headquarters in New York City to San Francisco to help Joseph James in his court fight. In some Black circles, especially on the East Coast, Marshall was already a kind of celebrity. Legal scholar Mark Tushnet, who clerked for Marshall after he had been elevated to the Supreme Court writes, "[Marshall's] effusive personality made him a speaker sought out by nearly all the NAACP's local branches around the country, and his talks and travels provided moral support to the local lawyers and their clients, who had to face the assaults of the Jim Crow systems daily."[23] Asked on a local San Francisco radio show to discuss the Joseph James case, Marshall told listeners why he came so far to join a local fight. He explained that "as a negro and an attorney" he believed "the right of the negro to nondiscriminatory employment" and the right to vote as the two most pressing long-term problems Black Americans in the United States faced. He added, "When those problems are solved other questions will settle themselves."[24] Marshall preferred the term "negro" throughout his life, long after it fell from currency.[25]

As early as 1940 Marshall had determined that the NAACP should fight against discrimination in the already burgeoning defense industries.[26] President Roosevelt's Executive Order 8802, signed in July 1941, established the Fair Employment Practices Commission (FEPC) and banned discriminatory employment practices by federal agencies and all unions and companies engaged in war-related work. The FEPC turned out to be a toothless organization, but the ban described in the executive order gave Joseph James and the NAACP more ammunition to fight workplace discrimination.

Marshall began his career at the NAACP as the head of its Legal Defense Fund. In this role, he coordinated the work of other lawyers rather than working on many of the briefs himself.[27] In 1938 Marshall became the NAACP's chief lawyer. He became famous for his courtroom oral advocacy. Legal scholar Mark Tushnet describes Marshall's courtroom manner, "He was a master at striking the right tone: sometimes engaged in what seemed to be a simple conversation with the justices about how they all should handle a difficult legal problem, sometimes the eloquent orator whose words went to the heart of the moral case for his clients."[28] "Marshall thought of himself primarily as a trial lawyer," Tushnet writes, "adept not so much at the cutting cross-examination (a tactic unlikely to help his clients in the South) but rather at carefully compiling a record that would maximize the chance that some appeals court would reverse the adverse trial court decisions that were to be expected. As an oral advocate, Marshall was a master as well."[29]

Marshall had been well trained. This son of Baltimore, Maryland, was a graduate of the Black college Lincoln University in Pennsylvania. He received his law degree from Howard University Law School in 1933. At that time, Howard University School of Law trained three-quarters of the Black lawyers in the United States. There were not many. The year Marshall graduated, he had only ten classmates at Howard.[30] The school's growing prominence reflected the hard work of its dean, professor Charles Hamilton Houston, a Black Harvard Law School educated attorney. Legal scholar Randall Kennedy described how Houston shaped Howard's law school, "[Houston]was charged with helping the institution gain accreditation, and used strong methods to achieve it: [he] expelled underachieving students, fired weak faculty, and phased out Howard's night school, even though his own father had earned his law degree there."[31] Also, Houston ran one of the few law schools with an integrated faculty, five of the twelve law professors were White.[32] Thurgood Marshall stood out at Howard and was noticed by Houston who used the law student to work on real legal cases. Marshall often recounted how he learned "to be a trial lawyer by riding in the back seat of Houston's car, balancing a typewriter on his knees while pounding out a motion to exclude evidence."[33]

When Marshall graduated from Howard, he opened a law office in Baltimore. In one of his important early cases in private practice in 1935, on behalf of a local NAACP chapter he successfully challenged University of Maryland Law School over its segregation policy. This victory in court was especially pleasing for Marshall who had wanted to attend that school but knew it did not accept Black students. Years later Marshall admitted that he dreamed about "getting even with Maryland for not letting me go to its law school." Shortly before his death in 1993 Marshall admitted to an interviewer that he was "still angry" at the school. Marshall used a strategy adopted by the NAACP to challenge segregation by proving in court how its practice violated equal protection rights enshrined in the Constitution. Under the "separate but equal" doctrine deemed lawful by the Supreme Court since 1896, segregation would be unlawful unless schools for Black students and schools for White students were equal in every way. NAACP strategists knew this was not achievable in practice. States and localities could not afford to maintain segregation under these terms. "The South would go broke," Marshall recalled years later, "paying for truly equal, dual systems."[34] This was a sharp chisel Marshall used to carve away at segregation beginning in the 1930s. He wielded it again and again in cases around the country, with its greatest effect in the landmark US Supreme Court decision in *Brown v. Board of Education* in 1954, in which Earl Warren who rose to become chief justice played a vital role in finding that separate but equal educational facilities for racial minorities to be inherently unequal.

After three years of private practice, when he failed to get hired to teach at Howard Law School, Marshall joined the NAACP as chief legal counsel. To that time, the NAACP had focused on Black education. Marshall persuaded its board to also fight segregation. In 1940, Marshall founded the NAACP's Legal Defense Fund. In was in this role that he joined the Joseph James case.[35] There was a great need all over the country for the NAACP's legal representation. In a speech in 1944, Marshall pointed out that it wasn't until 1939 that the US Department of Justice established its Civil Rights Section to enforce civil rights statues already on the books. Prior to that time, Marshall said, "Negroes were unable to persuade the U.S. Department of Justice to enforce any of the civil rights statues where Negroes were the complaining parties."[36] Worse, it wasn't until Francis

Biddle became attorney general in 1941, that members of lynch mobs were prosecuted, Marshall said, "for the first time in the history of the United States Department of Justice."[37]

Thurgood Marshall had much important legal work to do around the country, but very few resources at his disposal. During the time of the Marinship case, the entire NAACP Legal Defense Fund was staffed by only three attorneys, Marshall and two colleagues. Based in New York City, Marshall was far away from the courts hearing James's case. Joseph James was lucky to find two San Francisco attorneys, George R. Andersen and Herbert Resner, who also were willing to work his case. Andersen had labored as an ironworker as a teenager in San Francisco during World War I, and in a nice coincidence was a member of the Boilermakers Union Local 6, the same union and local involved in the Marinship case. After graduating from night law school in San Francisco, Andersen became active in labor law cases, often representing unions and their workers. Resner was a graduate of the more prestigious law school at UC Berkeley. Neither Andersen nor Resner had been civil rights attorneys before they joined forces with Joseph James. Both San Francisco attorneys made names for themselves fighting in courts for labor cases and noted for their left wing clients and causes. Andersen represented the Communist Party of California, which might have given some pause to the more conservative Marshall and the NAACP.[38]

When James's legal team returned to federal court on December 12, 1943, historian and writer Charles Wollenberg writes, "the courtroom was crowded with Black spectators."[39] Andersen argued that if Black Americans could be forced into separate auxiliary unions, so could Irish Americans such as the judge or Armenian Americans such as the union's attorney. On January 6, 1944, James's team was handed a defeat. The court dismissed James's case on the grounds that no diversity of citizenship was involved (that is to say all concerned parties were residents of California so the case did not cross state lines) nor was there sufficient federal question to warrant such action in the federal courts. The NAACP, Andersen, and Resner got a secondary temporary injunction, this time from the local courts.[40] Historian Wollenberg writes, "The order was served just fifteen minutes before a work shift was to change at Marinship. The company already had removed Black worker's time cards from the rack, but clerks hurriedly replaced the cards, and the shift changed without incident."[41] So *James v. Marinship* lived on to fight again.

When not all of the Black workers who were benefitting from the NAACP's legal support joined and paid NAACP dues, Marshall leaned on James to urge his colleagues to join and pay up. Marshall wrote to James, "To be perfectly frank, it seems to me that the men working in the Marinship yard who are not paying any labor union dues are getting something for nothing." What they are getting, Marshall pointed out "is full protection by the courts as a result of this case. If they are not willing to pay for the expenses of this case, I do not see how they can expect anyone to have too much sympathy for them." Marshall then hammered home his point, asking James to explain to fellow Black workers, "that if they do not pay for the case it might be necessary to use the funds sent to the Association by soldiers." Those are Black military members, Marshall added, who "earn about one-tenth of the money [Black ship workers] earn, who are constantly up against the proposition of being killed and who are, nevertheless, sufficiently interested in the advancement of their people to send money from India, China, France, Italy, Africa, and other theaters of war."[42]

While the Marinship case was in the courts, Joseph James continued his direct activism. In March 1944, he led a group of several dozen workers to the Boilermakers Local 6's union hall, where they again tried to join the union. In a letter sent to the media and the union, James wrote: "It is ironical that a group of people who believe in and adhere to the principle of trade unionism as sincerely as we do should be placed in the position of fighting the leadership of a union in order to obtain full membership in that union."[43] James was taking pains to demonstrate that he wanted workers to join the union in good faith and dispel the union's contention that Black workers did not want to join the union and that the demonstrators were just a bunch of troublemakers and agitators. James reported that his group was met by "the head of the plain clothes [police] detail [who] suggest that we 'move on'; and since our point had been made, there was no use staying."[44]

On February 17, 1944, a Marin County Superior Court judge, Edward Butler, ruled that the Boilermakers' policy of "discriminatin against and segregating Negroes into auxiliaries is contrary to public policy of the state of California." Butler prohibited the union from requiring Black workers to join auxiliaries as a condition of employment and also barred Marinship from laying off workers who refused to pay auxiliary dues. Butler found that if the Boilermakers wished to maintain a closed shop, they must "admit Negroes as members on the same terms and conditions as white persons." Despite this defeat, the Boilermakers still refused to accept Black workers as full members. The union and Marinship management appealed the case to the California Supreme Court. The union, however, could not require Black workers to join the auxiliary union as a condition of employment at Marinship. Judge Butler's decision applied only to Marinship, but, during 1944, cases similar to James's suit were brought into various Bay Area courts. During this time, the toothless FEPC tried to cajole the union in accepting Black workers as full members, but failed, so the issue awaited the decision of the California Supreme Court.

Writing about the case in the May 1944 issue of the NAACP's magazine, *Crisis*, Marshall called *James v. Marinship* "epoch making," adding at that time, "at least fifteen unions exclude Negroes from membership by provisions in either their constitution or ritual [practice]. Nine international unions bar Negroes from admission to their regular unions and locals, admitting them only to 'Jim Crow' auxiliary bodies."[45] Marshall continued, "While the Boilermakers permitted the Negroes to work, they did not intend for them to have full membership in the union. So in order to protect their closed-ship agreements, they began to inaugurate the policy of setting up 'Jim Crow' auxiliary unions. On the West Coast many Negroes, while paying their dues, including initiation fees to the regular locals of the Boilermakers, at the same time refused to be relegated to the status of members in auxiliary locals. This situation prevailed for some time."[46]

While the California Supreme Court considered *James v. Marinship*, Thurgood Marshall returned to the Bay Area at the behest of Joseph James to help with another case, this one stemming from an acute tragedy. On the night of July 17, 1944, a giant explosion rocked the East Bay and lit the night sky with a massive fireball. There had been an accident at a Bay Area ammunition depot. While loading ordnance onto two Liberty ships at the Port Chicago Naval Magazine, thirty-five miles northeast of San Francisco, five thousand tons of munitions ignited. The explosion completely destroyed the two ships and their docks and damaged most of the buildings on the base and many in the neighboring town of Port Chicago. In this disaster 320 men, including the 202 Black sailors who were loading the munitions, were instantly killed in the explosion. An additional 400 people were injured. It was the worst disaster on the homefront since America entered the war.[47] The Black sailors were working in segregated units "subjected to disparate treatment from their white counterparts because of their race, and had not received any training for the dangerous work of loading ammunition onto ships."[48]

A few weeks after the explosion, 328 surviving members of the groups of Black sailors in the ordnance battalion were ordered to resume work several miles away at the Mare Island Navy Shipyard. Of this group, 258 refused their orders to resume loading munitions. The 258 men were confined for three days on a barge docked there.[49] The men ultimately agreed to return to work but were tried and convicted in summary court-martial proceedings. These men were sentenced to bad conduct charges and fined three months' pay. The navy singled out fifty of the men as ringleaders and charged them with mutiny. This is when Joseph James called on Thurgood Marshall to help. James was "well aware of the pattern of discrimination practiced in the Navy and very much concerned about this trial."[50] In a press release the NAACP said: "Following an urgent telephone call from Joseph James, president of the local NAACP Branch, asking that National Office assistance be given to the defendants immediately, Mr. Marshall flew to San Francisco where he has been reviewing testimony and interviewing the men."[51]

After Marshall arrived at the court-martial in August and reviewed the testimony and interviewed the charged men, he thought the sailors were being railroaded into a mutiny charge. Noting that many of the accused men had been injured at the Port Chicago explosion, Marshall said when they refused to load ammunition, "Their officers including the Admiral talked to them. Then their officer asked them the following: 'All of you are willing to obey all lawful orders stand fast. All who are not fall out and give your names to the officers.' Some stood fast and other fell out. Those who fell out were arrested. There were 257 altogether but it ends up that only 50 are charged with mutiny." The men, Marshall explained, had not considered that to be an order—to load the ammunition—and that "what they meant by their actions was that they did not want to load ammunition. They did not intend to disobey an order." Marshall then cited the example of a seventeen-year-old sailor who had one week of experience loading ammunition and was assigned as a hatch tender directing the winch operator as to how to lower the ammunition into the ship's hold. "No wonder they were all afraid to load ammunition." Marshall concluded, "There is no sufficient evidence of mutiny or conspiracy. There is no evidence of refusal to obey a direct order. These men are being tried for mutiny solely because of their race or color."[52] The court-martial disagreed. All fifty men were convicted of mutiny and sentenced to fifteen years in prison and a dishonorable discharge.[53]

This outcome must have weighed on the minds of James and Marshall as they awaited the verdict of *James v. Marinship*. On the second to the last day of the year, the state supreme court ruled unanimously, however, in favor of James. In an opinion written by Chief Justice Phil S. Gibson, the court cited all the ways in which auxiliary lodges were inferior to the regular union writing, "in our opinion, an arbitrarily closed or partially closed union is incompatible with a closed shop."[54] The court ruled that the Boilermakers union could not retain both its discriminatory membership practices and a closed shop. Although the decision did not prohibit unions from racial discrimination (it only disallowed racial discrimination combined with the "monopoly" power of the closed shop) still, in early 1945, the NAACP called the James case "a splendid victory."[55] As early as 1942, the Black newspaper *The Pittsburg Courier*, urged its readers to strive for twin victories—the "Double V" campaign—to defeat fascism overseas and obtain freedom from Jim Crow constraints at home. James, Marshall, and the Black workers at Marinship did their parts.[56]

As legal scholar Reuel Schiller notes, even after the *Marinship* decision, many Black ship workers were reluctant to "abandon the auxiliaries even after the court declared them to be illegal. Marshall, in particular, did not seem to understand, the way James did, the complexity of the African-American feelings about the auxiliaries [Marshall wrote to James] 'it seems to me that at this stage [the San Francisco Branch of the NAACP] has a real job in educating Negro Boilermakers.'"[57] Black workers had gained much in the Bay Area, many of them were reluctant to risk losing those gains. It was there that they found good and important work and a home. In a 1944 press conference, San Francisco Mayor Roger Lapham asked Tom Fleming, a well-known journalist and founding editor of San Francisco's only Black newspaper, *The Reporter,* his thoughts about when the Black migrants would want to return home to the south. Lapham asked, "Mr. Fleming, how long do you think these colored people are going to be here?" Fleming responded: "Mr. Mayor, you know how permanent the Golden Gate is? Well, Blacks are just as permanent as the Golden Gate."[58]

NOTES

1. Joseph James is uncredited in this film. The Hall Johnson Choir is credited as "Themselves."
2. Wollenberg, *Marinship at War: Shipbuilding and Social Change in Wartime Sausalito,* 52.
3. Linton Weeks, "The 1940 Census: 72-Year-Old Secrets Revealed," National Public Radio. Npr.org.
4. Dana Whitson and Larry Clinton, "Joseph James, Entertainer," February 13, 2019, Sausalito Historical Society. Sausalitohistoricalsociety.com.
5. Joseph James, "Marinship Negroes Speak to Fellow Workmen," *The Mariner,* August 21, 1943.
6. J. Clay Smith, Jr., editor, *Supreme Justice: Speeches and Writings; Thurgood Marshall* (Philadelphia: University of Pennsylvania Press, 2003), 18.
7. Joseph James, "Profiles: San Francisco," *The Journal of Educational Sociology* 19, no. 3 (November 1945): 169.
8. Charles Wollenberg, "James vs. Marinship: Trouble on the New Black Frontier," *California History* 60, no. 3 (Fall 1981): 267.
9. Reuel Schiller, *Forging Rivals: Race, Class, Law, and the Collapse of Postwar Liberalism* (New York: Cambridge University Press, 2015), 54.
10. James, "Marinship Negroes Speak to Fellow Workmen."
11. Wollenberg, "James vs. Marinship: Trouble on the New Black Frontier," *California History,* 269.
12. Wollenberg, "James vs. Marinship: Trouble on the New Black Frontier," *California History,* 269.
13. Quintard Taylor, "African American Men in the American West," *The Annals of the American Academy of Political and Social Science* 569 (May 2000): 112.
14. Wollenberg, "James vs. Marinship: Trouble on the New Black Frontier," 266.
15. Wollenberg, "James vs. Marinship: Trouble on the New Black Frontier," *California History,* 270.
16. Wollenberg, "James vs. Marinship: Trouble on the New Black Frontier," *California History,* 271.

17. Joseph James, "Profiles: San Francisco," *The Journal of Educational Sociology* 19, no. 3 (November 1945): 167.

18. Schiller, *Forging Rivals: Race, Class, Law, and the Collapse of Postwar Liberalism*, 54.

19. Schiller, *Forging Rivals:: Race, Class, Law, and the Collapse of Postwar Liberalism*, 56.

20. Risa Lauren Goluboff, "Let Economic Equality Take Care of Itself: The NAACP, Labor Litigation, and the Making of Civil Rights in the 1940s," *UCLA Law Review* 52 (2005): 1393.

21. Goluboff, "Let Economic Equality Take Care of Itself: The NAACP, Labor Litigation, and the Making of Civil Rights in the 1940s," 1423.

22. Goluboff, "Let Economic Equality Take Care of Itself: The NAACP, Labor Litigation, and the Making of Civil Rights in the 1940s," 1395.

23. Mark V. Tushnet, ed, *Thurgood Marshall: His Speeches, Writings, Arguments, Opinions, and Reminiscences* (Chicago: Lawrence Hill Books, 2001), xx.

24. Goluboff, "Let Economic Equality Take Care of Itself: The NAACP, Labor Litigation, and the Making of Civil Rights in the 1940s," 1394–1395.

25. Stephen L. Carter, "What Thurgood Marshall Taught Me," *The New York Times Magazine*, July 18, 2021.

26. Goluboff, "Let Economic Equality Take Care of Itself: The NAACP, Labor Litigation, and the Making of Civil Rights in the 1940s," 1395.

27. Tushnet, *Thurgood Marshall: His Speeches, Writings, Arguments, Opinions, and Reminiscences*, 1.

28. Tushnet, *Thurgood Marshall: His Speeches, Writings, Arguments, Opinions, and Reminiscences*, 2.

29. Tushnet, *Thurgood Marshall: His Speeches, Writings, Arguments, Opinions, and Reminiscences*, xx.

30. J. Clay Smith Jr., "Thurgood Marshall: An Heir of Charles Hamilton Houston," *Hastings Constitutional Law Quarterly* 20, no. 3 (Spring 1993): 507.

31. Brett Milano, "The Man Who Killed Jim Crow: The Legacy of Charles Hamilton Houston," Harvard Law Today, September 5, 2019. Today.law.harvard.edu.

32. Smith Jr., "Thurgood Marshall: An Heir of Charles Hamilton Houston," 508.

33. Tushnet, editor, *Thurgood Marshall: His Speeches, Writings, Arguments, Opinions, and Reminiscences*, 1.

34. Juan Williams, "The Courts: Poetic Justice," *New York Times*, January 18, 2004, 4.

35. After founding the NAACP Legal Defense Fund in 1940, Marshall became the key strategist in the effort to end racial segregation, in particular regularly challenging *Plessy v. Ferguson*, the Supreme Court–sanctioned legal doctrine that called for "separate but equal" structures for White and Black people. Marshall won a series of court decisions that gradually struck down that doctrine, ultimately leading to Brown v. Board of Education, which he argued before the Supreme Court in 1952 and 1953, finally overturning "separate but equal" and acknowledging that segregation greatly diminished students' self-esteem. Asked by Justice Felix Frankfurter during the argument what he meant by "equal," Mr. Marshall replied, "Equal means getting the same thing, at the same time, and in the same place." See "Thurgood Marshall," NAACP Legal Defense Fund. Naacpldf.org.

36. Tushnet, *Thurgood Marshall: His Speeches, Writings, Arguments, Opinions, and Reminiscences*, 93.

37. Tushnet, *Thurgood Marshall: His Speeches, Writings, Arguments, Opinions, and Reminiscences*, 93.

38. More biographical information is available in the obituaries of the two men in the *San Francisco Chronicle*. "George R. Andersen Dies at 65, *San Francisco Chronicle*, December 30, 1965, 28 and "Herbert Resner," *San Francisco Chronicle*, October 17, 1995, 18.

39. Wollenberg, "James vs. Marinship: Trouble on the New Black Frontier," 271.

40. Smith, Jr., editor, *Supreme Justice: Speeches and Writings; Thurgood Marshall*, 19–20.

41. Wollenberg, "James vs. Marinship: Trouble on the New Black Frontier," 274.

42. Goluboff, "Let Economic Equality Take Care of Itself: The NAACP, Labor Litigation, and the Making of Civil Rights in the 1940s," 1426–1427.

43. Schiller, *Forging Rivals: Race, Class, Law, and the Collapse of Postwar Liberalism*, 66.

44. Schiller, *Forging Rivals: Race, Class, Law, and the Collapse of Postwar Liberalism*, 66–67.

45. Smith, Jr., *Supreme Justice: Speeches and Writings; Thurgood Marshall*, 17.

46. Smith, Jr., *Supreme Justice: Speeches and Writings; Thurgood Marshall*, 19.

47. "320 Americans Killed in WWII Naval Magazine Accident," Port Chicago Naval Magazine National Memorial, National Park Service. Nps.gov.

48. "320 Americans Killed in WWII Naval Magazine Accident," Port Chicago Naval Magazine National Memorial, National Park Service. Nps.gov.

49. "320 Americans Killed in WWII Naval Magazine Accident," Port Chicago Naval Magazine National Memorial, National Park Service. Nps.gov.

50. Charles Wollenberg, "The Mare Island 'Mutiny,'" July 22, 1979, *San Francisco Chronicle*, 34.

51. "Race Not Mutiny Is Issue in Trial of 50 Negro Seamen," October 13, 1944, NAACP Press Release, Library of Congress.

52. "Race Not Mutiny Is Issue in Trial of 50 Negro Seamen," October 13, 1944, NAACP Press Release, Library of Congress.

53. At the end of the war the fifty men were released from prison, granted clemency, and finished the remaining months of their enlistment in the Pacific.

54. SCOCAL, James v. Marinship Corp., 25 Cal.2d 721.

55. Goluboff, "Let Economic Equality Take Care of Itself: The NAACP, Labor Litigation, and the Making of Civil Rights in the 1940s," 1434.

56. "The Courier's Double 'V' For a Double Victory Campaign Gets Country-Wide Support," *Pittsburgh Courier*, February 14, 1942, 1.

57. Schiller, *Forging Rivals: Race, Class, Law, and the Collapse of Postwar Liberalism*, 74.

58. Miller, *The Postwar Struggle for Civil Rights African Americans in San Francisco 1945–1957*, 13.

14

Out of LeConte and into Los Alamos

Ernest Lawrence enjoyed a status and esteem among government, military, and corporate leaders that few scientists achieve. By contrast, the FBI and many US Army security officials continued to have suspicions about Robert Oppenheimer's loyalty to the American government, or more precisely, what they perceived to be his sympathy with communism and the Soviet Union. Lawrence trusted Oppenheimer and believed the government needed his talents. In January 1943, Lawrence wrote a carte blanche reference for Oppenheimer, characterizing him as "a close personal friend" and "a man of great intellectual caliber" while also praising his character and integrity.[1]

General Groves did not need Lawrence's vote of confidence in Oppenheimer. The general made his own decisions about people. He decided that he liked Oppenheimer, that he trusted him and, most importantly, needed him. He would not be swayed by the concerns of the FBI or his own army security personnel. In June 1942, General Groves selected Oppenheimer to be the scientific director of the weapons development lab for the Manhattan Project. Even before making the selection, Groves asked Oppenheimer to weigh in on the decision where to locate the top secret research laboratory that would create the design of the fission weapon. Now with Oppenheimer on board, the two men set out to find a suitable location for a top secret laboratory that could host a growing number of scientists and technicians and their families. Groves specified that the site needed good transportation options from Washington DC, as well as Chicago and San Francisco, the latter two cities locations of much of the scientific leadership in nuclear research at that time. Also important, Groves wanted it to be somewhat remote so any disasters would not be detected, "If we had any experiments that [exploded] ... in the vicinity of Los Angeles, [the public would] know it in a hurry."[2]

Oppenheimer identified two possibilities: the Albuquerque area in New Mexico; and a remote location in eastern California, about eight hours from Los Angeles. Transportation difficulties quickly ruled out the remote California site, so Groves and Oppenheimer traveled to Albuquerque. Traversing the region, Oppenheimer suggested they look at Las Alamos. Oppenheimer knew that area well because his family had a ranch in the nearby Sangre de Cristo Mountains. The site Oppenheimer had in mind was a private boarding school for boys. Its owner wanted to sell because he thought it would be too difficult to run during the war. The site met Groves's requirements so he bought it and set about acquiring national forest land that surrounded the school.

By the summer of 1942 America's bomb effort was making up for lost time. Enrico Fermi and his team were on their way to creating a self-sustained nuclear reaction. They accomplished this in December, creating a makeshift nuclear reactor in a squash court under the stands of the stadium at the University of Chicago. Such was the growing sense of urgency felt by the government that even before Fermi's feat the Dupont corporation was tasked with building a production reactor before such a device had been shown to work in prototype. Plans were made to produce useful quantities of fissile plutonium (an element that Seaborg and his team had created only a year and a half earlier) and fissile uranium. Two methods to enrich uranium were selected. The separation of uranium-235 by the electromagnetic method, though extremely expensive, seemed very likely to succeed; the separation by gaseous diffusion was less certain. The committee in charge of the uranium project also began a serious study of the assembly of a weapon. Lawrence thought this step could wait. Groves disagreed and dedicated scarce scientific resources upfront to designing the atomic bomb. He proved prescient. In 1945, the preparations for the assembly of the weapon were finished just about the same time that the necessary amounts of fissile material first became available.

In the autumn of 1942, Oppenheimer set out to build a large research complex at Los Alamos and fill it with experimental and theoretical physicists to work on the problem of how to design a fission bomb. Oppenheimer got most of the physicists from his summer session at LeConte Hall in Berkeley to come to Los Alamos. He next traveled to campuses where work on some aspect of fission research was going on, including Cornell, the University of Minnesota, Princeton, and Stanford, to recruit scientists to come to this secret location to work on a secret project. It is a sign of the high regard fellow scientists held for Oppenheimer that so many would abandon their campuses and turn down other important research to come to the desert to work with Oppenheimer on a project so secret that he could not describe it to them until they agreed to join. He got most of the scientists he pursued. In mid-March 1943, Oppenheimer, Kitty, and their son moved to the site. The scientists he was recruiting would begin arriving a few months later. Oppenheimer made certain the site had good views, telling an interviewer more than twenty years later, "my feeling was that if you are going to ask people to be essentially confined, you must not put them in the bottom of a canyon. You have to put them on the top of a mesa. I think that was even more important than the technical details." He also made sure that the houses the scientists and their family occupied each had a fireplace and balcony. Oppenheimer joked, "that was my big contribution."[3] The population of scientists, technicians and their families at Los Alamos doubled every four months.

Oppenheimer and his staff at Los Alamos were wrestling with how to design a fission bomb and what method to use to explode the bomb. Fissile uranium could be exploded with a "gun-type" mechanism in which a quantity of uranium-235 was fired into another quantity of uranium-235, creating a "supercritical mass," that is, an amount of fissile uranium more than sufficient to sustain a nuclear reaction. This straightforward method was thought to be so reliable as to be what Oppenheimer reaching back to his student days at Göttingen in Germany called a *"stumpfsinnig"* or a dull method. The other source of fissile material, plutonium, that Seaborg and his team first created at Gilman Hall at Berkeley, required a different method to explode. This was an implosion method in which a subcritical sphere of fissile plutonium is surrounded by explosives. When detonated, the explosives compress the plutonium sphere creating a supercritical mass. This was novel work and fraught with theoretical and technical challenges. Oppenheimer said, "we knew we had to do this and did not know whether we could."[4]

So the Manhattan Project set out to develop two types of bombs, one using uranium and the other plutonium. Oppenheimer was officially in charge of leading the team at Los Alamos to design the bombs. Uranium production, or enrichment, to use the term or art, was done at a huge facility at Oak Ridge, Tennessee. Uranium had never before been enriched on an industrial scale. Several methods were proposed at the S-1 conference Lawrence led at Bohemian Grove, but General Groves, hedging his bet, selected two. One method, suggested by Ernest Lawrence, used electromagnetic separation to accomplish the task. This method was based "on the principle that charged particles of the lighter isotope would be deflected more when passing through a magnetic field."[5] Lawrence and his team converted a cyclotron and its magnet into a device to separate isotopes electromagnetically. They named their new machine the "Calutron" after Cal. It separated scarce fissionable isotope uranium-235 from the more abundant uranium-238. The other method, gaseous diffusion, had been proposed by physicist George Kistiakowsky. This method was "based on the principle that molecules of the lighter isotope, uranium-235, would pass more readily through a porous barrier."[6] Two huge plants were built at Oak Ridge, Tennessee, to enrich uranium using the respective methods.

While uranium enrichment was taking place at Oak Ridge, Tennessee, plutonium enrichment was going on across the country at Hanford, Washington. The plutonium they would use had to be manufactured. To produce plutonium on an industrial scale, nuclear reactors were built at Hanford. Natural (i.e., not enriched uranium) was used as the fuel for these reactors. Three reactors were built at Hanford. Work started in mid-1943 and the first reactor was operational in late September 1944. By early February 1945, Oppenheimer and his team at Los Alamos were receiving the first shipments of enriched plutonium from Hanford.[7]

While Oppenheimer was scientific director and in charge of the work being done at Los Alamos, Ernest Lawrence was first among equals in the project to develop fissile uranium-235. During the war Lawrence officially remained at Cal, but crisscrossed the country constantly, especially as the Manhattan Project was getting started. His secretary remembered, "He was out of town almost more than he was in town during that war period . . . [H]e would come in from Oak Ridge and have these meetings with the different ones and find out what was wrong. Then he would fly off again to meet with other groups across the country." Lawrence's well-mannered upbringing remained with him, however, even during this hectic time. "He was the kind of person who would take a trip and the one thing he would do the very next day, or even that same day if he had time, was to have a little list of all the people he saw and did things for him. Everyone got a thank-you letter. It made no difference what they did. It went right down the line. . . . Each one was separately dictated . . . and a personal note in it."[8]

With his Nobel Prize, fame, and his easy familiarity with leaders in academia, philanthropy, business, and now government, Lawrence had long worn the mantle of leadership easily. Oppenheimer's starring role in the Manhattan Project was much more surprising. For much of the 1930s, he was a fey academic, almost as interested in the arts as he was the sciences. Socially awkward as a young man, in his thirties Oppenheimer gained savoir faire and stature. He had matured from being ungainly to a man that women noticed and were attracted to. For his part, Oppenheimer began to reciprocate. A woman in his social circle since the 1930s said Oppenheimer's "precocity and brilliance already legend . . . a Jewish Pan with his blue eyes and his wild Einstein hair."[9] He dated a number of women casually, often bringing them to social functions with his students.

In 1936, Robert Oppenheimer met Jean Tatlock, the daughter of a distinguished Berkeley English professor. She was in medical school at Stanford at the time, already set on becoming a psychiatrist. Jean was young, ten years younger than Oppenheimer, very smart (medical school "seemed easy for her"), beautiful, but troubled by depression, and "very private about her despair."[10] Oppenheimer recalls, "and in the autumn [of 1936], I began to court her, and we grew close to each other. We were at least twice close enough to marriage to think of ourselves as engaged."[11] A friend who knew both Tatlock and Oppenheimer and traveled in their left wing political circles remembers, "All of us were a bit envious [of Tatlock] . . . When we came to know [Oppenheimer] at the parties for Loyalist Spain, we knew how those eyes would hold one's own, how he would listen as few others listen and punctuate his attentiveness with 'Yes! Yes! Yes!' and how when he was deep in thought he would pace so that all the young physicist-apostles who surrounded him [emulated his] jerky, pronated walk and punctuated their listening with 'Yes! Yes! Yes!'"[12]

Until the mid-1930s, Oppenheimer did not display much interest in politics. His family's wealth spared him from any personal experience with the privations of the Great Depression. In so far as he had any political orientation, it was gently left wing, out of sympathy for people who suffered economic hardships that he had not. As the Depression wore on and fascism grew in Germany, many people in America looked toward communism to solve the problems that America's traditional center-right politics, prior to Franklin Roosevelt, could not. Kai Bird and Martin J. Sherwin, authors of the definitive biography of Oppenheimer, *American Prometheus*, write, "It was Tatlock who 'opened the door' for Robert into this world of politics."[13] The politics were mostly communist and Spanish Loyalist. At the time, Spain was riven by a civil war that pitted a fascist military and its right wing supporters against Spain's democratically elected republican government, whose supporters tended to be left wing or communist. Nazi Germany supported the Spanish fascists and left wing sympathizers in America and Britain supported the Spanish Loyalists. So did communists in those countries after the Soviet Union sided against Spanish fascists. Atrocities committed by Spanish fascists galvanized left wing attention in America and elsewhere. Tatlock's political activism pushed Oppenheimer out of his ivory tower and into political activism. It was a journey he was ready to make. Oppenheimer said, "I should not give the impression that it was wholly because of Jean Tatlock that I made left wing friends, or felt sympathy for causes which hitherto would have seemed so remote from me, like the loyalist cause in Spain, and the organization of migratory workers . . . I liked the new sense of companionship, and at the time felt that I was coming to be part of the life of my time and country."[14]

Tatlock was not just another girlfriend for Oppenheimer. Where he used to introduce his girlfriends to his students, Tatlock he kept separate. She was trim, shapely, and tall with "dark curly hair, hazel-blue eyes with heavy black lashes."[15] She was both attractive and socially adept. The two socialized mostly with her friends who were communists or fellow travelers. Tatlock also grew close to Oppenheimer's younger brother, the physicist Frank Oppenheimer and Frank's wife Jacquenette (Jackie). The three joined the Communist Party USA.[16] Robert, despite his sympathy for many its espoused causes, did not join the party. (Some scholars think he did join the party in secret.)[17]

Oppenheimer described his political activism: "This was the era of what the communists then called the 'united front,' in which they joined with many non-communist groups in support of humanitarian objectives. Many of these objectives engaged my interest." Oppenheimer contributed to the longshoremen's union leader Harry Bridges strike fund during the San Francisco Waterfront general strike in 1934 and as he elaborated, "I subscribed to the [communist newspaper] *People's World*; I contributed to the various committees and organizations which were intended to help the Spanish loyalist cause. I was invited to help establish the Teacher's Union, which included faculty and teaching assistants at the University, and school teachers of the East Bay. I was elected recording secretary. My connection with the Teacher's Union continued until sometime in 1941, when we disbanded our chapter."[18] Ernest Lawrence did not share Oppenheimer's interest in political action. Lawrence's biographer relates this anecdote: "One Sunday Oppie entered the [Rad Lab] and wrote on the blackboard . . . 'Cocktail Party Benefit for Spanish Loyalists at Brode's, everybody at Lab invited.' Half an hour later . . . Lawrence came in and noticed Oppie's message. He stood for perhaps half a minute, clenching and unclenching his jaws. Then he walked slowly to the board and erased Oppie's message, without a word." Later Lawrence approached Oppenheimer and told him "You're too good a physicist to get mixed up in politics and causes."[19]

Oppenheimer and Tatlock had a stormy romance. Oppenheimer's former student, close friend and colleague Robert Serber said, "Jean was Robert's truest love. He loved her the most. He was devoted to her."[20] Tatlock twice declined Oppenheimer's marriage proposals. At times, Tatlock "disappeared for weeks, months sometimes" and taunted Oppenheimer mercilessly "about whom she had been with and what they had been doing. She seemed determined to hurt him, perhaps because she knew Robert loved her so much."[21] Further tying the couple, Tatlock was a close friend of Oppenheimer's friend and landlady Mary Ellen Washburn who with her husband John lived above him in the upper flat of their duplex home on Shasta Road. After Tatlock graduated Stanford Medical School she began residency training in psychiatry at Mt Zion hospital in San Francisco. The couple had broken up but from time to time whenever Tatlock phoned him in a low mood Oppenheimer went to her and talked her out of her depression. They remained close friends, and occasional lovers.

After his relationship with Tatlock ended, Oppenheimer again was playing the field, dating a string of attractive, young women.[22] Then he dated Estelle Caen, the attractive sister of San Francisco columnist Herb Caen. Oppenheimer and a young post doc physicist attended a New Year's Eve party at Estelle Caen's apartment. "Oppenheimer could not recall the address, but he knew her apartment was on Clay Street and that the address was divisible by seven." So the two physicists "tooled up Clay Street peering at houses on the way until [they] found Estelle's apartment at 3528."[23] It would have been a fun party. Her brother Herb writes, "She was one of those remarkable cooks who could keep four pots and five conversations going at the same time—she soon assembled a salon. Harry Bridges was there, and Frank and J. Robert Oppenheimer . . . The young Bill Saroyan would drop in out of the blue and pull up a chair in the big kitchen on Russian Hill. Dong Kingman, Doris and Pierre Monteux, Artie Shaw, Benny Goodman, Albert Elkus: the mix was heady, the dialogue crisp, the politics left."[24] Herb Caen recalled "that Oppenheimer hated swing music." One night he played a Goodman quartet for the physicist and said, "Not much different from a Mozart quartet, really." Oppenheimer said: "How would you know?"[25]

While on one of his regular visits to Caltech, Oppenheimer met, fell in love with, and married Katherine ("Kitty") Harrison, the wife of a physician doing research at the university. Like Jean Tatlock, Kitty was smart, attractive, and a communist. She had been married three times before meeting Oppenheimer. Her second husband was well-known American communist Joe Dallet, who had been killed fighting in the Abraham Lincoln Brigade for the Loyalists in the Spanish Civil War. Kitty's interest in the party waned after she married Oppenheimer. Her focus switched to her family as she and Robert began having children. Oppenheimer's former student and colleague Robert Serber commented, "[Kitty Oppenheimer's] career was advancing Robert's career, which was the overwhelming, controlling influence on her from then on."[26]

After his marriage to Kitty, from time-to-time Jean Tatlock called Robert when she was in the despair of depression. Robert Serber, who knew Jean, Kitty, and Robert says, "Kitty told me that she knew all about it. [Oppenheimer] would tell her that Jean was in trouble, and he was going to try and see what he can do." Oppenheimer was always concerned that Tatlock might commit suicide while in a depression.[27] He stayed in contact with Tatlock after he married Kitty. Oppenheimer and Tatlock spent New Year's Eve of 1941 together at the Top of the Mark. She socialized with Oppenheimer and his wife in their home in Berkeley, which was around the corner from her father's house. It seems there were some trysts between Oppenheimer and Tatlock during this time before he joined the Manhattan Project. Oppenheimer later said, "There was still deep feeling when we saw each other."[28] Kitty's third husband (Oppenheimer was her fourth) later told the FBI that he, Kitty, and Oppenheimer "had modern views concerning sex."[29]

One encounter Oppenheimer had with Tatlock after he became the scientific director of the program to build the bomb was noted by the FBI. After Oppenheimer got involved with the Manhattan Project, he knowingly came under surveillance. On June 14, 1943, after Oppenheimer and his family had left for Los Alamos, he returned to Berkeley for business. Tatlock had asked to see him. Oppenheimer agreed because as he later testified, "She was undergoing psychiatric treatment. She was extremely unhappy." Oppenheimer made plans to meet Tatlock at her home on Telegraph Hill in San Francisco. Asked why Tatlock wanted to see Oppenheimer, he responded, "Because she was still in love with me."[30] It seems likely Oppenheimer was still in love with her too.

An FBI agent trailed Oppenheimer on his date with Tatlock. The agent spiced up his official written report with a little colorful editorializing. It reads: "Oppenheimer arrived at 9:45 PWT. He rushed to meet a young lady, whom he kissed and they walked away arm in arm. They entered a 1935 green Plymouth coupe and the young lady drove. The car is registered to Jean Tatlock. She is five foot seven, 128 [pounds], long dark hair, slim, attractive."[31]

Ten years later, Oppenheimer had to discuss this meeting under oath. Asked point blank,

"You spent the night with her, didn't you?"

Oppenheimer responded, "Yes."

"That is when you were working on a secret war project?"

"Yes."

"Did you think that consistent with good security?"

"It was as a matter of fact. Not a word— it was not good practice."

"Didn't you think that put you in a rather difficult position [because Tatlock was a] Communist?"

"Oh, but she wasn't."

"How did you know?"

"I knew her."[32]

Oppenheimer says Tatlock had drifted away from the Communist Party, that it "never seemed to provide for her what she was seeking."[33] Oppenheimer, who at the time of this tryst was married, the father of a child, and the head of the most secret project of the war, was not in a position to provide what she might be seeking.

The next morning Tatlock drove Oppenheimer to the airport. "I never saw her again," Oppenheimer said. On January 3 or 4, 1944, Tatlock committed suicide at her home.[34]

Her body was discovered by her father. The door of her Telegraph Hill apartment was bolted so it must have been with a sense of dread at what he might find that J. S. P. Tatlock, the sixty-eight-year-old emeritus professor of medieval literature and specialist in Chaucer, climbed through a window to look for her. He found his daughter lying dead in her bathtub. She had taken an overdose of sleeping pills. Her father found the note she left, it read: "All love and courage."[35]

General Groves knew of Oppenheimer's relationship with Jean Tatlock, but he did not understand it. He thought their relationship was "purely sex."[36]

It was not his affair with Tatlock that caused Oppenheimer the most trouble later. Instead he came to be haunted by an approach from another friend, Haakon Chevalier, a professor of French literature at Berkeley. Oppenheimer and Chevalier were very close. They shared a love of languages, literature, and left wing politics. They both attended communist and leftist meetings. Chevalier and Oppenheimer remined close after he married Kitty; so close that after a troublesome pregnancy, Kitty and Robert left their firstborn with Chevalier and his wife for nearly two months as the Oppenheimers left to set up housekeeping at Los Alamos. In the spring of 1943, the Chevaliers hosted the Oppenheimers to dinner in their home. With their wives in the living room and the two friends in the kitchen, Chevalier told Oppenheimer that he knew a way to pass information to the Soviets. Oppenheimer declined the offer, but waited eight months before reporting this approach and even then invented an incriminating subterfuge, what he later called "a cock and bull story" instead of naming his friend Chevalier as the source.

This was ten years in the future. During the war, the FBI snooped on Oppenheimer for its own purposes. For all of their wiretaps, informants and shadowing, the FBI did not find any legitimate evidence that he was disloyal to his country. Certainly, they found nothing that would have made General Groves distrust his favorite physicist. As work at Los Alamos got underway, Groves did worry about Oppenheimer's physical security. He would have known Oppenheimer was a notoriously bad driver. But Groves also worried about other threats too. During the war he authorized an American plan to capture or kill the famous German physicist Werner Heisenberg, the Nobel laureate thought to be heading the Nazi atomic bomb project, when that scientist was visiting neutral Switzerland. Groves worried about German assassins targeting Oppenheimer in addition to more routine dangers.[37] A little over a month after Oppenheimer's evening with Tatlock, Groves sent him this letter:

July 29, 1943.
　Dr. J. R. Oppenheimer P. O. BOX 1663
　Santa Fe. New Mexico
　Dear Dr. Oppenheimer:
　. . . It is requested that:
　Day-to-day operations
　(a) YOU refrain from flying in airplanes of any description; the time saved is not worth the risk.
　(b) You refrain from driving an automobile for any appreciable distance (above a few miles) and from being without suitable protection on any lonely road, such as the road from Los Alamos to Santa Fe. . . .
　(c) . . . In driving about town a guard of some kind should be used, particularly during hours of darkness. The cost of such guard is a proper charge against the United States.
　I realized that these precautions may be personally burdensome . . .[38]

The precautions had nothing to do with Oppenheimer's affair with Jean Tatlock. As Groves recognized, Oppenheimer was becoming too important to the Manhattan Project and the country to drive himself or travel without an armed guard.

NOTES

1. Letter of recommendation for J. Robert Oppenheimer from Ernest O. Lawrence, 1943 January 15, Ernest O. Lawrence Papers, ca. 1920–1968, University of California, Berkeley Bancroft Library, BANC MSS 72/117 c, brk00007741_24a_k.jpg

2. Groueff, "Interview with General Leslie Groves Conducted on January 5, 1965, Part 11."

3. Groueff, "Interview with J. Robert Oppenheimer, 1965."

4. Groueff, "Interview with J. Robert Oppenheimer, 1965."

5. "Electromagnetic Separation," The Manhattan Project Interactive History, US Department of Energy. Otsi.gov.

6. "Electromagnetic Separation," The Manhattan Project Interactive History, US Department of Energy. Otsi.gov.

7. "The Plutonium Path to the Bomb," The Manhattan Project Interactive History, US Department of Energy. Otsi.gov.

8. Groueff, "Interview of Eleanor Irvine Davisson Conducted on February 8, 1965, at Berkeley, CA."

9. Edith A. Jenkins, *Against a Field Sinister* (San Francisco: City Lights Books, 1991), 22.

10. Jenkins, *Against a Field Sinister*, 21–2 2.

11. Oppenheimer, "Testimony to the Atomic Energy Commission," vol. 1, 20–22.

12. Jenkins, *Against a Field Sinister*, 22.

13. Bird and Sherwin, *American Prometheus: The Triumph and Tragedy of J. Robert Oppenheimer*, 115.

14. Oppenheimer, "Testimony to the Atomic Energy Commission," vol. 1, 20–22.

15. Bird and Sherwin, *American Prometheus: The Triumph and Tragedy of J. Robert Oppenheimer*, 111.

16. Shirley Streshinsky and Patricia Klaus, *An Atomic Love Story* (Nashville: Turner Publishing, 2013), 103.

17. Gregg Herken website for his book "Brotherhood of the Bomb." Brotherhoodofthebomb.com.

18. Oppenheimer, "Testimony to the Atomic Energy Commission," vol. 1, 20–22.

19. Childs, *An American Genius: The Life of Ernest Orlando Lawrence*, 266–267. "Brode's" might have referred to Berkeley physicist Robert B. Brode.

20. Bird and Sherwin, *American Prometheus: The Triumph and Tragedy of J. Robert Oppenheimer*, 111.

21. Goodchild, *J. Robert Oppenheimer: Shatterer of Worlds*, 35.

22. Martin J. Sherwin, "Haakon Chevalier's Interview, Part 2, Conducted on June 29, 1982." Voices of the Manhattan Project, Atomic Heritage Foundation. Manhattanprojectvoices.org.

23. Walter Gratzer, *Eurekas and Euphorias: The Oxford Book of Scientific Anecdotes* (Oxford: Oxford University Press, 2002), 111.

24. Herb Caen, "Days of Our Years," *San Francisco Chronicle*, May 16, 1995.

25. Jack Smith, "Raising Caen to the Level of an L.A. Idol," *Los Angeles Times*, August 17, 1988.

26. Bird and Sherwin, *American Prometheus: The Triumph and Tragedy of J. Robert Oppenheimer*, 164.

27. Martin J. Sherwin, "Robert Serber's Interview Conducted on January 9, 1982." Voices of the Manhattan Project, Atomic Heritage Foundation, Manhattanprojectvoices.org.

28. Oppenheimer, "Testimony to the Atomic Energy Commission," vol. 3, 502–505.

29. Bird and Sherwin, *American Prometheus: The Triumph and Tragedy of J. Robert Oppenheimer*, 162.

30. Oppenheimer, "Testimony to the Atomic Energy Commission," vol. 3, 502–505.

31. Streshinsky and Klaus, *Atomic Love Story*, xxiv. NB: the time designation "PWT" in the FBI report refers to "Pacific War Time" as daylight savings time was re-branded during WWII.

32. Oppenheimer, "Testimony to the Atomic Energy Commission," vol. 3, 502–505.

33. Oppenheimer, "Testimony to the Atomic Energy Commission," vol. 3, 502–505.
34. This was located at 1405 Montgomery Street, San Francisco.
35. Jenkins, *Against a Field Sinister*, 24.
36. Groueff, "Interview with General Leslie Groves Conducted on January 5, 1965, Part 6."
37. Thomas Powers, *Heisenberg's War* (Boston: DeCapo Press, 2000), 250.
38. Judith M. Lathrop, ed., "Los Alamos Science," Winter/Spring 1983, 13.

15

The World Comes to San Francisco

During the lean times of the Great Depression, social life in San Francisco, high, low, and in-between, from the louche dancehalls along its Barbary Coast to the dignified and ornate mansions atop Pacific Heights, quieted a bit. When America entered World War II, the muted days of the Depression were over. The war that laid to waste so many cities in Asia and Europe reinvigorated San Francisco. Situated midway between Asia and Europe, the two largest theaters of the war, San Francisco once again felt a gold rush giddiness. The entertainment industry's leading trade paper *Variety* in Manhattan could see it from 2,500 miles away. Early in the war the paper ran a page-one story using the city's nickname that locals hate: "Frisco is again a boom town, a pleasure-seeking town, and, yes, in some respects, a hell-raising town."[1] The journalist and bon vivant, Lucius Beebe, whose expansive beat encompassed disreputable dens and the shiniest cotillions in the city agreed. "The town is in the chips," he writes, "the fleet is always in; the plush cord is up in the hot spots and you can't fight your way to the bar at cocktail time at the Top of the Mark, the Fairmont . . . or the St. Francis."[2] More than 1.65 million soldiers and sailors shipped out from San Francisco during the war. It is safe to say most of them had been intent on having a good time before they sailed out of the Golden Gate, maybe never to return.[3]

San Francisco is a little city of seven hills. The top of one of those hills, Nob Hill, named for the "Big Four" robber baron nabobs who once had their mansions there, became famous for the luxurious hospitality of the three hotels that surmount it. What Beebe calls "the show place of Nob Hill" was the Top of the Mark, a cocktail lounge that takes the entire nineteenth floor of the Mark Hopkins Hotel, which stands tall at the apex of the storied hill. What had been a penthouse suite was transformed in 1939 into a glass walled showplace meant to shake off the Depression for good. It became an instant classic with locals and tourists alike. Two elevators were required to service the bar's traffic, "while a single lift is sufficient for the other requirements of the house." When war came, the Top of the Mark did its duty, its oval "bar is jammed three deep with the armed services after sundown, while older officers and their ladies prefer window tables overlooking" the Golden Gate or the Bay and Berkeley and Oakland in the near distance.[4] On Saturday nights lines of two hundred thirsty soldiers, sailors, Marines, and civilians queued up for hours in the hotel lobby to wait their turn to whisk up to the bar.[5]

The hotel claimed that the Top of the Mark served thirty thousand service men each month.[6] This impressive statistic understates the impact the bar had on the many service members who visited on their leaves. As the journalist Richard W. Johnson writes, the Top of the Mark, "has become a sort of symbol of the kind of delights any serviceman could enjoy before the war and hopes to return to." Whether shooting the breeze on troop carriers, standing in chow lines or in the middle of a firefight, when officers and enlisted men alike reminisced about shipping out from or their last leave in San Francisco, a common refrain was "how would you like to be at the Top of the Mark tonight?" The worse the circumstance, the more sweetly the memory soothed. At the bloody atoll of Tarawa, where the fighting was so intense and the terrain so difficult that eighty years later the remains of more than one hundred American soldiers and Marines still await identification, Johnson recalled, "a Marine officer from Kansas sagged down beside me in my foxhole. We listened to the snipers' bullets singing overhead and after a while he said: 'Know where I'd like to be tonight?' . . . 'Sure,' I said, 'at the Top of the Mark.' He looked at me in the gathering dusk. 'Yeah,' he said slowly."[7]

A poignant tradition was started at the Top of the Mark during World War II. Servicemen with money in their pockets before shipping out to the war could buy a bottle of liquor and leave it in the care of the bartender. The next patron to come from that soldier's, sailor's or airman's squadron could drink from it for free, on the condition that the man who finished the bottle bought a replacement. During World War II, navy aviator Aaron Seidler was shipping out. But his orders and pay were delayed so he found himself broke on his leave in San Francisco. Still, he was in luck. There was a bottle of scotch earmarked for his navy fighter squadron in the cabinet. He and his buddies, aviators Joseph Mooney and Robert Johnson Sr. finished the bottle of Cutty Sark left by a predecessor. Per the new custom, it was up to the three skint fliers to replace it. Tradition was upheld when a civilian at the bar drinking next to them treated the aviators to two bottles, one which they finished that night and the other trusted to the barman to replace the empty squadron bottle.[8] Sailor Floyd Beaver went to the Top of the Mark in 1943 and returned with his wife in 2012 to celebrate their sixty-fifth wedding anniversary. For those who did not make it to the bar on leave, the longing grew over the years. Dave Whitmore, a former navy ensign, since retired to Wisconsin, did not make it to the Top of the Mark during the war. Seventy years later, he and his wife Alice were seated at one of the coveted tables overlooking the west view. "I have been wanting to get to the Top of the Mark since early in WWII," he said, "I finally made it!"[9]

Over time, nobody remembers when, the tradition died. Bottles were drunk but not replaced. Service men and women who had heard about the tradition went to the Mark and were disappointed to discover there were no bottles for any squadrons. That changed in 2009 when a young navy lieutenant named Mike Hall from Pacifica, a town just south of the city, was home on leave and like so many servicemen before him, visited the Top of the Mark. Before he left, he purchased a bottle of Wild Turkey bourbon and left it in the care of the bartender to provide a shot to any other servicemembers who made their way to the bar. Hall also left a logbook for the soldiers and sailors to write messages to those that came after. In doing so, the squadron bottle tradition was reestablished and attracted old veterans and young active-duty personnel on leave. Former sailor Roger Benner, a veteran of World War II, reliving his time on leave in San Francisco seven decades earlier came to dedicate a bottle to his shipmates from the USS *Bullhead* that were lost on patrol in the South Pacific on August 8, 1945. Another sailor, a young woman born more than sixty years after him, navy Lieutenant Lupei Chou, fighting in a newer and longer war, came to the Top of the Mark in 2011. Like so many sailors before her, she shared a familiar refrain: "While sitting in a tent at Camp Marmal, Afghanistan, eating MRE, I frequently dream of the wonderful fare at the Top of the Mark."[10]

Of course, as Jimmy Stewart's character says in Alfred Hitchcock's classic movie *Vertigo*, there were plenty of street-level bars and restaurants in the town. The Palace Hotel (locals referred to it simply as the Palace) boasted both a spacious and airy Palm Court and a more intimate paneled cocktail lounge overseen by a large painting of the Pied Piper by Maxfield Parrish running the length of the bar. It was a local landmark even then and the head barman there attracted a following of patrons like the piper depicted in the painting, "Nick . . . can charge $2.50 for a couple of mixed drinks without batting an eye, but he has been known to be generous with enlisted men and is one of the town's highly esteemed citizens," Beebe notes. If drinks in the better bars and lounges were pricy, food was more affordable, "even in the poshest places and dinner at Omar Khayyam's, the Mark or Maiden Lane Solari's comes to no more than similar establishments elsewhere in the world."[11] The feeling of bonanza seemed to grip many of the men and women who found themselves in San Francisco during the war, whether they were on a twenty-four-hour pass and visiting the city for the first time in their lives before shipping out, or a multigeneration native to San Francisco.

It was called "seeing the elephant," doing the rounds in the city that boasted attractions for all kinds of people. Some people liked the posher establishments in hotels like the Cirque Room at the Fairmont Hotel, the Redwood Bar at the Clift Hotel or Persian Room at the Sir Francis Drake. Others made their way downtown to new clubs that opened including Slapsy Maxie's on O'Farrell Street, Richelieu Casino on Geary, and the Troc on Geary Blvd that featured dining and dancing. The floor shows at these clubs were slow to change because talent was so hard to find, but few patrons noticed or cared. Some took in shows at the established jazz clubs in the city, the scene of a "Great Revival" of the Golden Age of Jazz, at places like Dawn Club, a basement joint and former speakeasy located on Annie Street between the kitchen and the service entrance to the Palace, and the CIO Hall on Golden Gate Avenue.[12] Then there was the Fillmore, only ten blocks away from Nob Hill but a world apart.

One cornerstone club in the Fillmore was Joe Tenner's Café Society—Uptown at 1733 Fillmore Street. It was a dark and smoky basement club at the end of a long flight of stairs from the street. There was no special access for celebrities then, dustmen and duchesses alike had to walk down those stairs to enjoy the shows. There was not even a stage door for the performers.[13] Jazz was intimate there, great artists stood by your table, practically sat in your lap while they performed. The club billed itself as "an intimate supper club with top-flight entertainment. Admission was $1.50 and dinner started at $3. Open from 8 p.m. until 2 a.m., two shows nightly."[14] Also in the Fillmore were Jack's Tavern on Sutter Street and Club Alabam on Post Street. These were joined by clubs springing up fast including the New Orleans Swing Club, the Long Bar, the California Theater, Elsie's Breakfast Nook, and the Texas Playhouse, all within a few blocks of each other.

Lively entertainment was also available at the so-called International Settlement, boasting a concentration of attractions including the Arabian Nights cocktail lounge, Gay 'N Frisky club, Hippodrome club, the Bella Pacific, and Moulin Rouge.[15] Nobody, least of all those shipping out, knew what tomorrow held so seeing the elephant meant taking in as much as possible as fast as possible. Inevitably revelers grow tired. Accommodations, however, were "at a fabulous premium" and hard to find even if one's pockets were full. San Francisco was largely tolerant of servicemen heading out to war, those who failed to find a bed often "slept unmolested in the lobbies of the smartest" hotels.[16]

As the tide of war in Europe turned conclusively against the Axis, the "Big Three" leaders of the Allied powers, President Franklin Roosevelt, British Prime Minister Winston Churchill, and Soviet Premier Joseph Stalin, met at the Yalta Conference in 1945 to strategize about the end of the war in Europe, the continued fighting against Japan in the Pacific, and the beginning of the postwar world. At Yalta, the Big Three outlined the creation of a United Nations body. Roosevelt wanted the organizing conference of the UN to take place in San Francisco. The continental United States was unscarred by the war. The United States paid the most treasure, if not blood although its service members lost lots of that as well, to fight the war. It also would pay most of the costs of establishing the United Nations, so the president got his way. Roosevelt wanted the UN's organizing conference held in San Francisco and its permanent body hosted in the United States. Those locations, if not the idea of the UN itself, suited Churchill and Stalin. Roosevelt wanted to have the conference in America to provide "a New World setting and atmosphere for the discussions . . . The choice of San Francisco was made with the idea of emphasizing America's world-wide interests by directing attention to the Pacific battlefield."[17]

Anne O'Hare McCormick, a reporter who interviewed the president about his plans for the UN elaborates, "New enterprises flourish [in San Francisco], unblurred by too much bother about ways and means, are as tall as indigenous redwoods, the oversize rhododendrons, the roller-coaster terrain."[18] It would be a monumental undertaking. As the military historian John Keegan notes, "Four times in the modern age men have sat down to reorder the world—at the Peace of Westphalia in 1648 after the Thirty Years War, at the Congress of Vienna in 1815 after the Napoleonic Wars, in Paris in 1919 after World War I and in San Francisco in 1945 after World War II. Sometimes the new orders held, and sometimes they didn't. Keegan adds, "The consequences of the settlement of 1648 persist, since it established the principle that states are sovereign. The settlement of 1815, which re-established the power of kings, did not last. The settlement of 1919 . . . is with us yet. The borders it drew for the 'successor' states of the German, Austrian, Russian and Ottoman empires remain, with trifling exceptions, and so does the principle of 'self-determination' by which the statesmen worked."[19] What would happen in San Francisco? Roosevelt did not live to see it. He died thirteen days before the conference was launched.

The conference went on as planned. Thus it was that 282 delegates from forty-six nations descended upon the city in the four days of April 22–25, 1945.[20] It took America's military to pull it off. The army and navy provided 215 cars, 25 jeeps, 50 buses and 48 limousines to transport delegates and other officials around the city. For those without access to this motor pool, conference organizers arranged for eight hundred taxi cabs to be available and hired shuttle busses to run every ten minutes between the conference sites and hotels.[21] One cab company, eager for business touted it had drivers who spoke Czech, French, Norwegian, Portuguese, Russian, Yugoslav, Spanish, Turkish, Greek, Syrian, and Farsi. Diplomatic immunity was passed out like beads at Mardi Gras and San Francisco police officers were told that delegates and other officials had freedom from arrests or imprisonment.[22]

The conference took place in two grand buildings, the American Renaissance style Opera House and the French Renaissance style Veterans Building—separate but linked by a formal court. The complex, along with San Francisco City Hall, was the pride of the civic center. The Opera House, with well over three thousand seats was used for the plenary sessions. The stage there had been designed by Broadway set and lighting designer Jo Mielziner, who created four golden, velour columns representative of FDR's "Four Freedoms" placed in front of a blue backdrop, the semicircle of forty-six United Nations flags all illuminated with floodlighting. "The effect," wrote *Time*, "was just about right—not dull, not gaudy." A band was placed backstage to entertain the galleries while the delegates arrived. Early comers expecting to hear more august music might have been surprised by the choices including showtunes and popular numbers like "Lover, Come Back to Me," "Stout-Hearted Men," and "Wanting You."[23]

The morning of the plenary session, April 25, had been warm and bright. By mid-afternoon clouds moved in and it began to rain. The flags, flown at half-staff to honor the late Franklin Roosevelt, looked mournful as the delegates streamed into the Opera House to occupy the plush red seats of the orchestra section. The many men and few women who would make up the nascent bodies of the United Nations: the General Assembly, Security Council, Court of International Justice, trusteeships, multilateral and unilateral, collective security, for the most part just as Roosevelt had hoped and planned arrived and took their seats. At 4:30 p.m. the US Secretary of State Edward R. Stettinius Jr. stood at the podium, struck his gavel three times and declared: "The first plenary session of the United Nations Conference on World Organization is hereby convened."[24]

The city, long a tourist destination, had discouraged unnecessary visits during the conference. Still, hotel rooms were hard to find. About five thousand people were expected for the conference. Supplies were expected to be tight, for example, in that smokey age, hotel patrons had to show their room key to buy cigarettes from the cigar stand in their lobby.[25] Even the secretive and exclusive Bohemian Club agreed to house some delegates. Roosevelt had been slated to stay in the James Flood penthouse of the Fairmont Hotel. A collector of rare books, the president would have liked to browse the two-story circular library in the suite, but would have been frustrated not being able to navigate his wheelchair to the second level.[26] Because most of the Allies were being bled dry, financially and otherwise, by the war, Washington, as host, paid all of the costs of the conferences including transportation to and from San Francisco. Only the personal expenses of the delegates were not covered by Uncle Sam. Initially expected to run for four weeks, the conference lasted nine weeks and cost the government $2 million in direct expenses (over $33 million today). Not included in that figure were the considerable funds spent by the army and navy, FBI and other federal agencies and departments.[27]

Among the first delegations to arrive were the Russians. Fifty of their officials flew in on three airplanes. Other Russians arrived on the 2,153-ton ship, *Smolny*, rumored to be loaded with caviar and vodka and had capacity for 138 passengers, including twenty-eight first class accommodations.[28] The ship was linked by a secure telephone line to a soundproof room in the Russian suite at the St. Francis hotel on Union Square. The ship then relayed messages via radio to Moscow. If the Soviets had done any electronic eavesdropping, such as bugging rooms or intercepting cables, this party ship could get the intelligence back to Stalin instantly.[29]

The Russians indeed might have been up to espionage in San Francisco. The Americans certainly were. American signal intelligence personnel worked twenty-four hours a day during the UN conference intercepting coded messages and breaking them down. The army officer in charge of the American signals operations at the conference felt "the success of the conference may owe a great deal to [his branch's work]." The information received was unsurprising: the French worried about the dents in their image as a major world power, the Spanish in Franco's right-wing regime disliked the communist Russians, and Czechoslovakian delegates, whose country had been dismembered by treaty and subsequently invaded by Germany, opposed the inclusion of Argentina, whose leaders had been openly sympathetic to Hitler and very, very late to declare war against Germany.[30]

Delegations hosted receptions, teas, and cocktail parties all over the city. To prevent the city's grande dames from competing with quasi-official festivities, the US State Department forbid "a hostess from entertaining more than 28 guests at one time."[31] Still, the *San Francisco Chronicle* called it the "greatest entertainment opportunity in history ... The social events seemed endless ... the town and Peninsula clear down to Palo Alto were peppered with parties."[32] That may have been so, but the names, ranks and hometown addresses of the numerous causalities, dead and wounded, from Northern California that the ongoing fighting in Europe and Asia produced still appeared on page two of the *Chronicle* as they had since the beginning of the war and would continue until the war was over.

On May 8, 1945, known as Victory in Europe or V-E day, when Germany surrendered unconditionally, the British Foreign Minister Anthony

Eden, Deputy Prime Minister Clement Attlee and more than one hundred members of the British delegation clustered around a radio at the Top of the Mark, which had closed for the day, to listen to an address from King George VI broadcast from London. His stammer mostly under control except for a few halts, the King's speech echoed over the oval bar and against picture windows. "The atmosphere of the room, which usually sparkles with cocktail hour gossip was church-like as the King reported one foe had been vanquished and 'we did not falter. Now we have yet to deal with the Japanese, a determined and cruel foe.'"[33]

NOTES

1. Sherman Miller, "Barbary Coast Is Recalled by Frisco Boom," *Variety*, November 4, 1942, 1.

2. Lucius Beebe, "San Francisco: Boom Town De Luxe," *American Mercury*, January 1942, 66.

3. https://www.nps.gov/articles/000/the-u-s-army-s-san-francisco-port-of-embarkation-in-world-war-ii.htm.

4. Beebe, "San Francisco: Boom Town De Luxe," 71. Source of thirty thousand service men a month is an advertisement for the Mark Hopkins Hotel appearing in the *San Francisco Chronicle*, June 17, 1944, 5.

5. "*Life* Visits the Top of the Mark," *Life*, July 31, 1944, 75.

6. Advertisement for the Mark Hopkins Hotel in *San Francisco Chronicle*, June 17, 1944, 5.

7. Richard W. Johnson, "Mention San Francisco's Top of the Mark to Service Men—That Brings on Nostalgia," United Press International, February 22, 1944. Source regarding remains of American servicemen at Tarawa: Dave Philipps, "New Tools to Find Soldiers Also Reveal Old Mistakes," *New York Times*, June 12, 2022, 16.

8. Aaron Seider Recollection, Top of the Mark Squadron Bottle log book.

9. Dave Whitmore Recollection, Top of the Mark Squadron Bottle log book.

10. Lupei Chou Recollection, Top of the Mark Squadron Bottle log book.

11. Beebe, "San Francisco: Boom Town De Luxe," 70–71.

12. "The Great Jazz Revival," The San Francisco Traditional Jazz Foundation Collection, Stanford Libraries. Exhibits.stanfprd.edu.

13. John Wesley Noble, *Never Plead Guilty: The Story of Jake Erlich* (New York: Farrar, Straus and Cudahy, 1955), 237.

14. "Fortnight," *The Newsmagazine of California* 6, no. 4 (February 18, 1949): 28. https://www.google.com/books/edition/Fortnight/IT87AQAAIAAJ?hl=en&gbpv=1.

15. This stretch of Pacific Avenue between Kearney and Montgomery Streets use to be called the Barbary Coast.

16. Beebe, "San Francisco: Boom Town De Luxe," 73.

17. Anne O'Hare McCormick, "His 'Unfinished Business'—And Ours," The *New York Times Magazine*, April 22, 1945, 43.

18. Anne O'Hare McCormick, "San Francisco: Battlefield for Peace," The *New York Times Magazine*, May 6, 1945, 9.

19. John Keegan, "Peace in Their Time," *Washington Post*, December 15, 2002.

20. Townsend Hoopes and Douglas Brinkley, *FDR and the Creation of the U.N.* (New Haven: Yale University Press, 1997), 184.

21. Stephen C. Schlesinger, *Act of Creation: The Founding of the United Nations* (Cambridge: Westview, 2004), 115.

22. "San Francisco: Beautiful City of the Golden Gate Plays Host at Security Conference," *Life*, April 30, 1945, 26.

23. "The Conference: The Second Beginning," *Time*, May 07, 1945. The designer pronounced his surname as "mellzeener."

24. "The Conference: The Second Beginning," *Time*.

25. "Party Ship Is Sent to Parley by Soviet," *New York Times*, March 21, 1945, 6.

26. "The San Francisco Conference Will Go On as Planned," *Life*, April 23, 1945, 38.

27. Schlesinger, *Act of Creation: The Founding of the United Nations*, 111.

28. "Party Ship Is Sent to Parley by Soviet," *New York Times*, March 21, 1945, 6.

29. Schlesinger, *Act of Creation: The Founding of the United Nations*, 102–103.

30. James Bamford, *Body of Secrets* (New York: Anchor, 2002), 22–23.

31. "Press at San Francisco," *Life*, May 14, 1945, 43.

32. "To Meet the Delegate from . . . Visitors Continue to Hold Spotlight," *San Francisco Chronicle*, May 9, 1945, 8.

33. "One Foe Is Vanquished," *San Francisco Chronicle*, May 9, 1945, 6.

16

✣

Jack Kennedy Present at the Creation

At a time when most people got the news from newspapers, radio, and newsreels that played before movies, around 1,200 people were accredited as journalists to cover the United Nations Conference on International Organization—six for every delegate. These included newspaper and wire service reporters, newspaper columnists and less conventional correspondents such as movie stars Rita Hayworth, Lana Turner, and Orson Wells. Those three did not stay long.[1] The journalists were joined by six hundred radio technicians and twenty-seven newsreel cameras.[2] Most of the big-name reporters stayed at the Palace Hotel.[3] Soon they were going to be joined there by a new, if temporary, member of the fifth estate.

While San Francisco prepared to host the world, a skinny twenty-seven-year-old recently discharged navy lieutenant checked into the Beverly Hills Hotel almost four hundred miles south. John F. Kennedy, Jack to his family and friends, was the second son and second-born child of Rose Kennedy and her husband Joseph P. Kennedy, the former US ambassador to Great Britain and formidably wealthy businessman who was the equivalent of a billionaire today. John and his older brother Joseph "Joe Jr." and their younger sister Kathleen "Kick" were familiar with the glamorous parts of California the way they were familiar with the best spots in London or the French Riviera. They were regular visitors to these places when they weren't at their family's estates on Cape Cod, in their home state of Massachusetts, or Palm Beach in Florida. Their good looks, senses of humor, savoir faire, and their father's money made them welcome everywhere they ventured. When America entered the war, each found a call to duty. Joe Jr. became a naval aviator flying search and destroy missions at dangerously low altitudes in a four-engine B-24 Liberator bomber from England against German U-boats, submarines that for a time imperiled the allies more than anything else that enemy possessed. Jack captained a PT (patrol, torpedo) boat, a small, swift vessel armed with torpedoes, mortars, machine guns and cannons that struck at the ships of the Japanese Imperial Navy in the South Pacific. Kick joined the American Red Cross in London and faced bombs and V-1 rockets and V-2 missiles that killed so many civilians throughout the war. Each did their duty, but one became a national hero.

In the summer of 1944, the *New Yorker* ran a story about John F. Kennedy's exploits in the navy when a Japanese destroyer sliced apart his PT boat in action near the Solomon Islands in the South Pacific. In the early morning dark of August 2, 1943, Kennedy's boat was rammed by a Japanese destroyer. The craft wrecked and aflame, Kennedy ordered his crew to abandon ship. Two crew members had disappeared, probably killed in the impact. That left Kennedy and the ten surviving crew members swimming amid the debris of their wrecked boat. Some of the crew were good swimmers, others weren't. Some were injured in one way or another. With no good options left to them, Kennedy ordered the crew to swim to an islet two and a half miles away; part of a chain of small islands, some of which were occupied by the Japanese. Two crew members who could not swim at all were tied to floating planks of ship debris and pushed and pulled the distance by other crewmates. Kennedy, perhaps the best swimmer of the crew, swam for five hours towing an injured crewman by clinching in his teeth a strap from the man's life vest.[4]

The surviving crew spent the next several days swimming from one island to another in search of food and drinkable water. As before, Kennedy again towing the injured crewmember the entire distance while the other crew members brought along the two non-swimmers lashed to the wreckage flotsam. All battled thirst and hunger while at the same time looking out for and evading the Japanese soldiers and sailors. After close calls with the enemy and long nighttime swimming treks by Kennedy and another officer looking for passing Allied vessels to rescue them, two indigenous coast watchers working with the Allies, Eroni Kumana and Biuku Gasa, finally found Kennedy and asked him to carve a message into a coconut husk. Kennedy scratched:

NAURO ISL
COMMANDER ... NATIVE KNOWS
POS'IT ... HE CAN PILOT ... 11 ALIVE
NEED SMALL BOAT ... KENNEDY[5]

Kumana and Gasa passed his message on to Lt. Arthur R. Evans, an Australian coast watcher hidden on a nearby island. Evans radioed Kennedy's message to his commander and asked the two men to bring Kennedy to him. Evans and Kennedy, communicating with their superiors over the radio, planned the rescue mission where Kennedy would rendezvous with two PT boats and guide them through reefs and shallows that he learned so well over the past few days. Under the cover of late night on August 7 in enemy waters, the surviving eleven crew members of PT 109 were rescued. For his actions after the sinking, Kennedy was awarded the Navy and Marine Corps Medal. He and his crew also received the Purple Heart in recognition of their injuries sustained in the collision.

Whatever the circumstances of how his boat was sunk, John F. Kennedy certainly was a hero in the aftermath, leading his men who survived on an arduous trek to their eventual rescue. Fearful that not everybody in the country read about the exploits of his second son in the *New Yorker*, Jack's father arranged to have the article appear in the much more widely circulating *Reader's Digest*. Joseph Kennedy Sr., who was a master at promoting himself and his children, noted that the coverage, "would be a great boost for the Kennedy clan."[6] Word of Jack's exploits reached far and wide. Joe Jr. from his airbase in England wrote to his parents that one of the crewmates on his B-24, "told me the other day he couldn't swim far and [if their plane ended up crashing in the ocean] he expected me to tow him as brother Jack did."[7] Already Jack was becoming a demi-celebrity. His father worked to keep Joe Jr., who carried his father's political aspirations, and Jack, whose trajectory was less certain, in the limelight.

Before America entered the war, John F. Kennedy had published a book, *Why England Slept*, about British appeasement of Nazi Germany. Kennedy reworked his senior thesis at Harvard University into a book that in many ways repudiated the position his father was taking at that time as ambassador. Still, Joseph Kennedy used his influence to provide Jack with materials not available at the vast Harvard library and people to interview, such as the British ambassador to the United States, that a typical college senior could not access. If Joseph Kennedy's influence provided a sharp machete to cut through a thicket, Jack had his own trail map. That Jack's ideology was shifting from his father's did not bother the senior Kennedy. As historian Fredrik Logevall writes, "[Joe Kennedy] could be domineering and overbearing in any number of ways, but not [with ideology] . . . he urged [his children] to come to their own judgements on things. It was and would remain one of his most appealing personal qualities."[8] With his father's help, Jack found a publisher. The book was well received, and Joseph Kennedy used his resources and contacts to promote the book, including, according to one writer, secretly buying thirty thousand copies, turning it into a best seller that year.[9]

It was as a graduate of Harvard and the author of a new and successful book that Jack came west to spend the fall quarter of 1940 auditing classes at Stanford University. It was a notable enough event to be featured in story with a photograph of Jack in the *The Stanford Daily*. Kennedy cut a wide swath as he tooled around quiet Palo Alto in his brand-new cactus-green 1941 Buick convertible. The car cost his father over $1,300 dollars, almost twice the cost of the average new car that year. The invoice for it, like the other large charges made by Joseph Kennedy's nine children, was paid by his office. Even apart from his access to wealth, Jack was not an ordinary recent graduate. At a party with students and faculty, an undergraduate remembered the "deference and respect shown Kennedy by the faculty members . . . and by Kennedy's earnestness, facile mind and powers of persuasion." A week later, the same student noticed Kennedy in his convertible parked illegally in front of the campus bookstore. Kennedy was talking with a "strikingly beautiful co-ed . . . She stood on the curb next to the car. . . laughing delightedly at something Jack Kennedy had said . . . Kennedy sat beaming up at her expansively, thoroughly enjoying the moment, one arm hooked over the top of the car door, the other stretched along the tip of the green leather seat."[10] Jack had joked in a letter to a friend from his recently passed Harvard days that at coeducational Stanford he spends his nights reading, "with occasional breaks to hawk autographed copies of *Why England Slept* around the local sororities at a reduced price."[11]

The West Coast agreed with John F. Kennedy. He caught the eye of *San Francisco Chronicle* columnist Herb Caen who noticed that, "Jack Kennedy, son of Ambass. Joseph Kennedy, is taking but one graduate course at the Stanford Bus. and Govt. School—a course known to all the students as a 'pipe' [easy class]; young Kennedy spends so little time at the school that recently it took the Dean a week to locate him!"[12] A week earlier a Boston newspaper noted that Jack was in Hollywood visiting a movie studio and meeting actresses as the guest of actor Robert Stack. Joseph Kennedy Sr.'s office clipped both articles for his files. It was while he was auditing classes and thoroughly enjoying himself in Palo Alto that Jack, who in his few weeks on campus, was already one of "Stanford's leading figures" according to the school's paper, registered for the first peacetime draft lottery in the county's history, an event captured in a photograph of the front page of the school paper. Seventeen million men between the ages of 21 and 35 put down their names for the draft and each was assigned a unique draft number. The 800,000 men selected in this draft would be obligated to serve one year in the military where they would get "a gun, clothing, food, shelter, training and $21 a month."[13]

Twelve days later in a ceremony in Washington, DC, led by President Roosevelt, Secretary of War Henry Stimson, blindfolded with a strip of linen, reached his hand into a ten-gallon fishbowl filled with nine thousand blue capsules, each containing the draft number of a man who had registered. One by one, Stimson handed the capsules to the president who, speaking before newsreel cameras and radio microphones, opened them and read the numbers drawn. This continued for the first fifteen draws before Roosevelt departed. Stimson carried on and the eighteenth number drawn belonged to Jack, an honor that again got his picture on the front page of the campus paper and was noted around the country. A friend from prep school sent Jack a telegram with congratulations to the "president's 18th choice."[14]

During the war, the large, close-knit Kennedy family dispersed. Joe Jr. and Kick both were in England, he at various air bases and she in London working with the American Red Cross. At his insistence and using his father's political pull, Jack was sent into combat in the South Pacific. The younger members of the family were in various prep schools and colleges. The family stayed in touch with each other though long, chatty, and funny letters, many between Joseph Sr. and his children. The letters show the social nous and fun that characterized the three eldest Kennedy children. Kick's letters are full of stories of evenings out with royalty including the Queen, aristocrats such as members of the Mitford and Cavendish families, generals, admirals, diplomats and celebrities in Blitz-ravaged London or grand country estates like Cliveden and of course the stately Chatsworth House, which her future husband, the eldest son of the 10th Duke of Devonshire, stood to inherit. Her letters discussed parties and the many people she met in wartime England. Jack, reading her letters while stationed in the hot, humid, and remote Solomon Islands teased her that she "is getting to sound like a character out of Louisa May Alcott."[15] Joe Jr.'s letters are also interesting, showing more humor than he is sometimes depicted as having. But Jack's letters are the most thoughtful and sensitive. There are fewer of them available, which makes those that remain all the more poignant.

In a letter to his parents dated May 14, 1943, Kennedy talks about beautiful nights on patrol in his PT boat cutting through "water that is amazingly phosphorescent—flying fishes which shine like lights" and racing porpoises "who lodge right under the bow and no matter how fast the boat goes keep just about six inches ahead"[16] Kennedy goes on to discuss the stateside popularity of Army General Douglas MacArthur. Kennedy contrasts that with the lack of esteem the general enjoyed among Marines and sailors he is serving with in the Pacific. "Here," Kennedy writes, "[General MacArthur is] . . . very, very unpopular. His nick-name is 'Dug-out-Doug' which seems to date back to the first invasion of Guadalcanal. The Army was supposed to come in and relieve the Marines after the beach-head had been established. In ninety-three days no Army. Rightly or wrongly (probably wrongly) MacArthur is blamed. He is said to have refused to send the Army in—'He sat down in his dug-out in Australia,' (I am quoting all Navy and Marine personnel) and let the Marines take it." Kennedy then goes on to offer his parents a realistic assessment of the bloody situation on Guadalcanal. Next, Kennedy goes on to address the impact of this a possible political future for the general, "In regard to MacArthur, there is no doubt that as men start to come back that 'Dug-Out-Doug' will spread—and I think would probably kill him off. No one out here has the slightest interest in politics—they just want to get home—morning noon and night. They wouldn't give a damn whether they could vote or not and would probably vote for Roosevelt just because they knew his name."[17]

Kennedy is confident that America will win the war but would like to see a change in the island hopping strategy (advocated by MacArthur), "this island to island stuff isn't the answer. If they do that the motto out here 'The Golden Gate by 48' won't come true." Aware that his brother is working to get himself transferred to fly fighters in the Pacific instead of the anti-U-boat patrols from England, Jack counsels resigned patience, "As far as Joe wanting to get out here, I know it is futile to say so, but if I were he I would take as much time about it as I could. He is coming eventually and will be here for a sufficiency and he will want to be back the day after he arrives, if he runs true to the form of every one else."[18]

In a letter to his parents a little over five weeks after he and his surviving crew had been rescued, Jack writes,

> It was a terrible thing though, losing those two men. One had ridden with me for as long as I had been out here . . . He had been shocked by a bomb that landed near the boat about two weeks before [the P.T. 109 sank]. He never really got over it; he always seemed to have the feeling that something was going to happen to him. He never said anything about being put ashore—he didn't want to go—but the next time we came down the line I was going to let him work on the base force. When a fellow gets the feeling that he's in for it, the only thing to do is to let him get off the boat because strangely enough, they always seem to be the ones that do get it . . . It certainly brought home how real the war is—and when I read the papers from home and how superficial most of the talking and thinking about it. When I read that we will fight the Japs for years if necessary and will sacrifice hundreds of thousands [of Americans] if we must—I always like to check where he is talking—it's seldom out here. People get so used to talking about billions of dollars and millions of soldiers that thousands of dead sounds like drops in a bucket. But if those thousands want to live as much as the ten I saw—they should measure their words with great, great care.[19]

In a letter to his father, Jack writes, "after this present fighting is over [I] will be glad to get home. When I do get out of here you'll find that you have a new permanent fixture around that Florida pool. I'll just move from it to get into my sack. Don't worry at all about me—I've learned to duck—and have learned the wisdom of the old naval doctrine of keeping your bowels—your mouth shut—and never volunteering."[20] Many of John's letters seem to be missing from the collection, but are referenced in other letters, his father reporting that Jack's letters were "cheerful, which is doing the family a lot of good," even if Jack sometimes forgot to put a date on them, making it difficult for the family to "find out what developed since they last heard" from him.[21]

These eldest three Kennedy siblings, born only a few years apart, were very close to each other. Kathleen and Joe Jr., both in England, got to see each other from time to time. If Kick was living in luxury, Joe Jr. occupied a "hut with a cement floor." He tells his parents that he is due for a week's leave in London where his sister is giving a party. After discussing his flying, his thoughts turn to his brother Jack, "I should think Jack would be due to get home anytime now. I hope he gets out before things get going there again. There seems to be a lot of activity there at present." He ends his letter with a note to his mother, Rose, who almost lost Jack when his PT boat sank and must have constantly worried about her eldest son's dangerous flying missions, "Mother, there is no sense in worrying about me over here. If I can keep my feet dry, the greatest hazard will be overcome."[22] This would prove not to be true. But there was fun to be had while he was alive. Kick reports that Joe Jr. was able to attend one of her parties with the usual constellation of interesting, well-known or titled guests, including Irving Berlin. Joe Jr., "arrived with his entire squadron who were feeling no pain."[23] Kathleen looked out for her far away brother. Writing to her parents from London, "You might tell Jack that that General Eaker's aide claims bosom friendship with him. I sat next to him last night and he is one of the Associate Editors of Life and Time. That never hurt anybody."[24]

From the family compound in Hyannisport, Massachusetts, Joseph Sr. writes a chatty letter to Jack full of news about his friends, "I'm trying to get [Jack's close friend from prep school, LeMoyne Billings] into the navy through McCormack, but his eyes are so bad it looks difficult." The elder Kennedy missed the pun but his witty son probably didn't. The father goes on to talk about family happenings, regional and national election news and informs Jack, "Your business affairs are flourishing and they have improved a great deal since you went away." Jack had been expected home by this time and his father's disappointment is palpable, "We are going to have a reunion of all the children who are here for Thanksgiving." Jack, Joe Jr, and Kick would be missing from the table that year. Joseph Sr. ends his letter, "Because we figured you'd be here for Christmas, Jack, we made no plans for sending things out to you for the Holidays, so if there is no chance of your coming, please let me know what you could use out there and I'll find some way of getting it out."[25]

In January 1944, Jack finally returned home. Joseph Sr. telegraphed the good news to Kick in England. Rose Kennedy wrote her children about their recently retuned brother Jack, "He is just the same—wears his oldest clothes, still late for meals, still [carries] no money."[26] But Joseph Sr. confided to Joe Jr. that Jack "got back having lost twenty odd pounds with his stomach in pretty poor shape . . . His back . . . in very bad shape." At that time Jack was at a hospital in Boston having x-rays of his back. "His future depends on how his back turns out," Joseph Sr. writes, "If it isn't going to be all right, I imagine he'll be through with the Navy." Mindful that enlistments were for the duration of the war and that Japan and Germany were still far from defeated, the father continued, "if he gets fixed up, I imagine he'll be on his way again, without too much enthusiasm."[27] Joseph Sr. could tell that Jack had had enough of the war. Doctors were not able to get him fixed up. Kennedy left the navy the next year. His health problems likely would have precluded service at all had he not used his father's political influence to get into the navy and into combat. Now Kennedy was a young man with a very bad back, suffering from other ailments that remain unknown, at least outside the Kennedy family, free from active duty in the navy and a little aimless. Kick wondered "for how long Palm Beach and all its comforts [could continue to] attract Brother Jack."[28] In the summer of 1944, while Jack was recuperating at Palm Beach, Joe Jr. and a colleague were killed while flying a special mission over England.

Mourning the death of his brother, nagged by his back problems, and discharged from the navy, Jack was feeling aimless. Joseph Sr. arranged for him to be hired as a special correspondent to the Hearst newspaper syndicate to report on the United Nations conference in San Francisco. He was hired to report on the UN proceedings from the point of view of the returning veteran. Around sixteen million Americans served in the armed forces during the war and they had an interest in this new international organization that was intended to help keep the peace. Hearst was one of the largest newspaper publishers in the country so Jack's by-line would be seen by millions of readers. Before work at the UN conference, Kennedy took a week or so for fun in Los Angeles. His father had been in the movie business and the son enjoyed the pleasures of what used to be called the movie colony. Operating out of the plush Beverly Hills Hotel, Kennedy and a couple of friends made the rounds of movie star parties. According to a navy buddy who was there, Kennedy made a play for actress Olivia DeHavilland, but got nowhere. Uncharacteristically his suavity left him momentarily when upon departing DeHavilland's house Kennedy, thinking he was opening the front door, "walked straight into the hall closet . . . tennis racquets and tennis balls and everything came down upon his head."[29] As Kennedy biographers Joan and Clay Blair reveal, after leaving Los Angeles for a quick visit to the famous Mayo Clinic for a checkup for an undisclosed ailment, Kennedy arrived in San Francisco to cover the conference.

Kennedy convinced a couple of friends to join him in San Francisco. Fellow PT boat captain, the ginger haired Paul B. "Red" Fay, a native of the tony San Francisco suburb of Woodside, and naval aviator Charles Spalding joined Kennedy. Spalding was a newlywed and Kennedy, managing the impossible, got the couple a room at the sold out Palace. It was at the conference that Kennedy met the woman who would marry Paul Fay. Decades later, Anita Marcus, who became Anita Fay, and ever after known as "Bride" to Fay and Kennedy, described her first meeting with Kennedy: "I was working in a hospital in San Francisco at the time of the U.N. They had a big party at what was called the Legion of Honor museum at the Presidio . . . I went to the powder room. All the girls there were talking about Jack Kennedy. When I came out . . . I sat at a table. The first person who came up was Jack Kennedy. He sat down to talk." Anita Fay described what that Stanford coed and many other women must have experienced, "I thought he was extremely attractive . . . I think the main thing was that when he talked to you, he looked you straight in the eye and his attention never wandered. He was interested in finding out what I was doing there—why I was there. It was a drawing-me-out thing. It was undivided attention. I was the most envied girl in the room. He had a way with women. There's no question about it."[30]

Kennedy did manage to do some work while he was at the UN conference. Within two days of his arrival in the city he filed his first story. Over a four-week period, Kennedy filed sixteen short pieces, each about three hundred words.[31] For this work Kennedy earned $750 from Hearst.[32] Of course, Kennedy did not need to work for a salary. His father paid many of the expenses of his nine children even as they became adults and each had trust funds from which they could spend the annual income generated.[33] But Kennedy enjoyed politics and history. He fought in and lost his brother and two crewmen in the war that was still going on. It is natural that he would want to be in San Francisco when a new model for maintaining international peace and security was being hammered out.[34] Also, he knew the publicity was good for whatever career he decided to pursue. Each story that ran featured a small photograph of Kennedy in uniform and a byline reading, "Lt. John F. Kennedy recently retired PT boat hero of the South Pacific and son of former Ambassador Joseph P. Kennedy is covering the San Francisco conference from the serviceman's point of view . . . Before the war, he wrote the best seller,

Why England Slept." That long introduction was about a quarter of the length of each short opinion piece Kennedy filed.

The columns Kennedy published, as historian Fredrik Logevall writes, "reflected his realist outlook . . . that the conference had been given too much buildup with exaggerated hopes for what it could accomplish in a world still driven by core national interests."[35] It also revealed Kennedy's recognition of continuing Russian intransigence and "stiff necked attitude." In his first article, Kennedy wrote, "There is an impression that this is the conference to end wars and introduce peace on earth and goodwill toward nations—excluding of course Germany and Japan. Well it's not going to do that." Kennedy went on to describe how there was not much news to report as yet, other than the Russians were trying to overly influence the conference. Mindful of his most recent career as a sailor he ended the article with the promised serviceman's point of view. He quoted a "bemedaled marine sergeant" he met on the street in San Francisco, whose mind likely was on the bloody invasion of Japan that looked inevitable, "I don't know much about what's going on—but if they can just fix it so that we don't have to fight anymore—they can count me in." Kennedy closed, "Me, too, Sarge."[36]

The prominent *New York Times* journalist Arthur Krock, who was a close friend of Joseph Kennedy and had been something of a midwife in helping John F. Kennedy publish *Why England Slept*, even suggesting the title which had been a play on the American title of Winston Churchill's book, *While England Slept*, was in San Francisco during the conference.[37] Krock saw journalist Kennedy up close. Krock said Kennedy enjoyed journalism, "but I think by that time he had made up his mind that the routine was uninteresting. I did see him frequently in San Francisco. He was having much more of a good time as a young man, however, than he was as a young reporter. He was not terribly diligent there. He was enjoying himself, but I think by that time he had made up his mind he did not want to be a newspaperman by profession."[38]

In his memoirs, Krock relates an anecdote that seems to capture much of John F. Kennedy's time in San Francisco. Kennedy was supposed to file a story that night. When Kennedy's friends entered his suite at the Palace,

> Jack dressed for a black-tie evening, with the exception of his pumps and dinner coat, was lying on the bed, propped up by three pillows, a highball in one hand and the telephone receiver in the other. To the operator he said, "I want to speak to the Managing Editor of the *Chicago Herald-Examiner*." (After a long pause) "Not in? Well, put somebody on to take a message." (Another pause) "Good. Will you see that the boss gets this message as soon as you can reach him? Thank you. Here's the message: "Kennedy will not be filing tonight." I think it was the same evening I saw him cutting in on Anthony Eden, the British Foreign Secretary, who was dancing with the beautiful

lady who became the Viscountess Harcourt—and promptly getting cut in on again by Eden himself.[39]

Eden could not have minded very much because Kick writes in a letter to her family, "had a first-hand report on Jack's doings at San Francisco from Guy Millard, Anthony Eden's secretary. He had glowing reports and told about how much they all liked Jack."[40]

Kennedy found time during the conference to return to Los Angeles to take out an old girlfriend, the beautiful Irish-born actress Angela Greene, then under contract at Warner Brothers. Kennedy had carried her picture in the South Pacific.[41] It was lost "deep in the heart of Ferguson Passage" when his PT boat sank, a fact that earned a mention in a letter to his parents, suggesting that Greene was not just another girl to Kennedy.[42] On their date in Los Angeles, the two made the rounds to the houses of movie star friends including Gary Cooper, who impressed her, "Being a very young starlet I thought that was smashing." Kennedy gave her suggestions for books to read and inscribed a copy of his book to her. "It was during this visit," Greene said, "that I realized he was seriously interested in politics."[43]

Kennedy's friend Chuck Spalding recalls a conversation he had with Kennedy at around this time, "I remember in the center of San Francisco one day—we were going someplace . . . and he said, 'You know, I just can't do what other people can do.' He said, 'The back bothers me and I'm sure now that Joe is dead that I'm going to go into politics.' I remember that I said to him, 'Well, that would be wonderful because who could do better? You know, you'd just be perfect for it. You'll have tremendous success.' And he asked did I think that. I reassured him that nobody could approach it with a greater chance of success. That's the only time he ever talked about it and then of course he went ahead and did it."[44]

Kennedy was not optimistic about the future of the UN or its ability to ensure global peace. With the conference underway only two weeks, Kennedy wrote in the story he filed May 7: "The world organization what will come out of San Francisco will be the product of the same passion and selfishness that produced the Treaty of Versailles. There is here, however, one ray of shining bright light. That is the realization, felt by all the delegates, that humanity cannot afford another war."[45]

In the middle of the conference, May 8, Germany officially surrendered. The next day, Kennedy reported that San Francisco took the celebration in stride and reminded his readers that in San Francisco "war" had always meant the war with Japan. He wrote, "When you have just come home from long months of fighting and are returning to the war zones in a few days, it is difficult to become excited about 'the end of the war.' V[ictory]-Day for them is a long way off." He noted the elections looming in England in which many in the British delegation were candidates and ended with the acknowledgment that Russia would not permit a hostile government along its borders. Kennedy writes, "They feel they have earned this right to security. They aim to have it come what may."[46]

In San Francisco Kennedy got to know the British delegation and interviewed them for a story about the upcoming British election that would either retain Conservative Prime Minister Winston Churchill or usher in Labour leader Clement Attlee. Churchill was a hero to much of the world and especially to John F. Kennedy for his tenacious wartime leadership. Clement Attlee had served as an able deputy prime minister during the wartime coalition cabinet, but lacked personal magnetism. Churchill memorably, if somewhat unfairly, described Attlee as a modest man with much to be modest about. The intelligence Kennedy got from these interviews, combined with the deep and nuanced knowledge he developed living in England when his father was ambassador to that country, and through his research for his book made him an insightful analyst of the state of British politics.

In an article filed on May 28, Kennedy was less certain than others about the likelihood that Winston Churchill would retain the prime ministership. Churchill had been the first and foremost to stand up to Hitler, but Kennedy noted that it was Britain's first general election since the Conservatives won in 1935 and there were millions of young people voting for the first time since that election. Most people thought Churchill would be swept back into office, but Kennedy was already skeptical of common knowledge and wrote that nobody could know whether these younger voters would support Churchill's Tories or Attlee's Labour Party.[47] Churchill lost that election in an upset. Although Arthur Krock was a cheerleader for Joseph Sr. and John F. Kennedy, he was probably truthful when he wrote in his memoir, "[John F. Kennedy] was the only source of my expectation that Churchill would be turned out of office. This he strongly indicated in his dispatches, and more definitely in a private letter to me."[48] This was an early demonstration of the skepticism that was to become a hallmark of Kennedy's approach to received wisdom later in his life.

In addition to the articles he wrote, Kennedy kept a diary discussing his stay in San Francisco. Usually typed, sometimes poorly, by Kennedy himself, the pages offer a unique and interesting look at a future president at an important moment, when he was refining the intellectual capital he would rely upon when he entered the White House only sixteen years later. In his diary entry dated July 10, 1945 (but possibly written three weeks earlier), John F. Kennedy writes:

> The Conference in San Francisco suffered from inadequate preparation and lack of fundamental agreement among the Big Three; from an unfortunate Press which praised it beyond all limit at its commencement which paved the way for subsequent disillusionment both in England and in this Country.

The finished Charter is a product of these weaknesses—but it is also the product of the hope, and even more, the realization that humanity can ill afford another war.

In practice, I doubt that it will prove effective in the sense of its elaborate mechanics being frequently employed or vitally decisive in determining war or peace.

It is, however, a bridge between Russia and the Western world and make possible discussion and a personal relationship which can do much to ease mutual suspicion.

Instead, the Big Three meeting will continue to be called to settle ticklish problems—which is good for temporary emergencies but a poor solution over long periods of time for it arouses distrust through the world and does not contribute to building a firm foundation for peace based on principle—but rather makes a virtue of expedience.

As to the future, I do not agree with those people who advocate war now with the Russians on the argument "Eventually, why not now?" Fortunately, or unfortunately, depending on how you view it, democracies have to go through a gradual disillusionment in their hopes of peace; war must be shown to be the only alternative to preserve their independence—or at least they must believe this to be true.

I think the clash with Russia will be greatly postponed. It will come perhaps, as its avoidance depends chiefly on the extent of Russia's self-restraint, and that is a quality of which powerful nations have a limited quantity.

The clash may be finally and indefinitely postponed by the eventual discovery of a weapon so horrible that it will truthfully mean the abolishment of all the nations employing it. Thus Science, which has contributed so much to the horrors of war, will still be the means of bringing it to an end.

If this is not done, the clash will take place—probably involving first the British, perhaps in Persia, for the British are in great danger of sinking to a second-class power under the onslaught of Communism both in Asia and Europe. And they may prefer to fight rather than face it.[49]

There has been some speculation that Kennedy had an inkling that the United States was close to developing a super weapon like the atomic bomb ("weapon so horrible"). Harry Truman, when he was vice president did not learn about the bomb until he became president upon Roosevelt's death. Stalin knew about the progress the United States and Britain made toward the bomb well before Truman because secrets of the "top secret" Manhattan Project had been known to the Russian through a handful of scientists and technicians sympathetic to Russia. *Time* reporter Hugh Sidey, who had many interactions with Kennedy in the Senate and the White House writes that as the atomic bomb was close to completion, more military and political leaders (if not Vice President Truman) heard about its existence and that Kennedy was well-connected enough that he might have heard rumors of an impending atomic bomb, "At the least he discerned the Soviet brutishness, the dark clouds that would turn into the cold war and the need for allied arsenals to face the challenge."[50]

Deirdre Henderson, who was hired by Kennedy as a research assistant in 1959, and in whose possession the Kennedy's diary was left, writes that it was "very unlikely" that he could have known about the atomic bomb when he wrote that column, but Kennedy's "constant thirst for information and his own powerful intuition had given him a glimpse of the horrible potentialities [of atomic weaponry] that were to dominate his own presidency."[51] Come the Cuban Missile Crisis and those perilous days thirteen days in October 1962, it is fortunate for humanity that Kennedy had been thinking about the horribleness of nuclear weapons, the arc of history and skepticism of ideology.

At the archive of the John F. Kennedy Presidential Library and Museum is a box of materials donated by Jacqueline Kennedy Onassis. There are odds and ends like a plane ticket from Qantas Empire Airways Limited for a trip to Australia, official correspondence from his congressional and Senate offices, family letters and, a letter Kennedy typed on the usual three-ring notepaper from his diary. A friend had written to Kennedy asking his opinion of the conference. His response to "Jim" (his identity is lost to time) poignantly summed up what Kennedy had learned in San Francisco:

> It would be easy to write a letter to you that was angry. When I think of how much this war has cost us, of the deaths of Cy and Peter and Orv and Gil and Demi and Joe and Billy and all those thousands and millions who have died with them—when I think of all those gallant acts that I have seen or anyone who has been to war—it would be a very easy thing for me to feel disappointed and somewhat betrayed . . . compare that sacrifice to the timidity and selfishness of the nations gathered at San Francisco must inevitably be disillusioning . . . Things cannot be forced from the top. The international relinquishing of sovereignty would have to spring from the people—it would have to be so strong that the elected delegates would be turned out of office if they failed to do it . . . We must face the truth that the people have not been horrified by war to a sufficient extent to force them to go to any extent rather than have another war . . . War will exist until that distant day when the conscientious objector enjoys the same reputation and prestige that the warrior does today.[52]

This from a man whose brother ("Joe" mentioned above) was blown up in a B-24 bomber over England and whose brother-in-law ("Billy") was killed in Belgium by a German sniper, both deaths less than a month apart.

Two men that had insight into how Kennedy's work in San Francisco helped shape him were Kenneth P. O'Donnell and David F. Powers. Both were special assistants to Kennedy when he was president and both knew him for years; O'Donnell since Kennedy's Senate campaign in 1952 and Powers even longer, joining Jack's first congressional campaign in 1946 and perhaps the person closest to Kennedy other than his brother Bobby. In their memoir of their years with Kennedy, *Johnny, We Hardly Knew Ye*, the men credit these few months Kennedy spent in San Francisco as a journalist for much that would happen later: "The thing that finally moved Jack Kennedy toward active politics, as [Kennedy] said later, was not trying to carry on for Joe or 'my father's eyes on the back of my neck,' but his own experience as a correspondent at the United Nations Conference in San Francisco . . . which sharpened his interest in the national and international issues of the coming postwar period. After getting a close look as a reporter at the postwar political leaders in action, he decided that he might be able to find more satisfaction and to perform more useful service as a politician than as a political writer or a teacher of government and history, the two careers that he had been considering up to that time."[53]

The UN Charter was signed in San Francisco on June 26, 1945. The charter was "the founding document of the United Nations," and codified the Security Council, led by the "Big Five" nations of China, France, Great Britain, the Soviet Union, and the United States. Other aims were included but the charter codified the "Great Power wartime alliance" that prevailed in World War II. In San Francisco, the young Kennedy was skeptical of the notion of collective security that the UN's most ardent supports hoped for, but later, when President Kennedy and Soviet Premier Nikita Khrushchev stood toe to toe and the world came very close to a nuclear exchange, it was fortunate that Kennedy had been thinking about these issues since San Francisco.

NOTES

1. Nick Clarke, *Alistair Cooke: A Biography* (New York: Arcade, 1999), 202. The figure 1,200 journalists is from "Press at San Francisco," *Life*, May 14, 1945, 43.
2. "Press at San Francisco," *Life*, May 14, 1945, 44.
3. "Press at San Francisco," *Life*, May 14, 1945, 46.
4. John Hersey, "Survival," *The New Yorker*, June 17, 1944.
5. "John F. Kennedy and PT 109," John F. Kennedy Presidential Library and Museum. Jfklibrary.org.
6. Letter from Joseph P. Kennedy to Joseph P. Kennedy, Jr. May 24, 1944. JPKPP Box 3. John F. Kennedy Presidential Library and Museum. Jfklibrary.org.
7. Letter from Joseph P. Kennedy, Jr. to his parents, February 19, 1944. JPKPP Box 3. John F. Kennedy Presidential Library and Museum. Jfklibrary.org.
8. Fredrik Logevall, *JFK: Coming of Age in the American Century, 1917–1956* (New York: Random House, 2020), 245.
9. Anne Garside, *Camelot at Dawn, Jacqueline and John Kennedy at Georgetown, May 1954* (Baltimore: John Hopkins University Press, 2005), 46.

10. Joan Blair and Clay Blair, Jr., *The Search for JFK* (New York: Berkley, 1976), 93–94.

11. Letter from John F. Kennedy to Camman Newberry, October 28, 1940, quoted in Nigel Hamilton, *JFK: Reckless Youth* (New York: Random House, 1992), 360.

12. Herb Caen, "It's News to Me," *San Francisco Chronicle*, December 14, 1940, 11. It is interesting to note that the column immediately adjacent to Caen's reports on developments of physicist Luis Alvarez and the transmutation of atoms going on at Berkeley, marking a synchronicity for two subjects of this book. For the definition of the slang term "pipe" and other Stanford campus lingo see John Ashton Shidler, "More Stanford Expressions," *American Speech* 7, no. 6 (August 1932): 437.

13. "National Lottery Draws Names of 24 Stanford Men, 2 Professors," *The Daily Stanford*, October 30, 1940, 1.

14. Telegraph from Lem Billings to John F. Kennedy, October 30, 1940. JFKPP-004-139-p0004. John F. Kennedy Presidential Library and Museum. Jfklibrary.org.

15. Letter from Kathleen Kennedy to her parents, January 6, 1944. JPKPP Box 3. John F. Kennedy Presidential Library and Museum.

16. Letter from John F. Kennedy to his parents, May 14, 1945. JFKPP-005-001-p0004. John F. Kennedy Presidential Library and Museum. Jfklibrary.org.

17. Letter from John F. Kennedy to his parents, May 14, 1945. JFKPP-005-001-p0005. John F. Kennedy Presidential Library and Museum. Jfklibrary.org.

18. Letter from John F. Kennedy to his parents, May 14, 1945. JFKPP-005-001-p0005. John F. Kennedy Presidential Library and Museum. Jfklibrary.org.

19. Letter from John F. Kennedy to his parents, September 12, 1943. JFKPP-005-001-p0002 and p0003. John F. Kennedy Presidential Library and Museum. Jfklibrary.org.

20. Letter from John F. Kennedy to his father, October 30, 1943. JFKPP-005-001-p007. John F. Kennedy Presidential Library and Museum. Jfklibrary.org.

21. Letter from Joseph P. Kennedy, Sr. to John F. Kennedy, November 16, 1943. JPKPP Box 3. John F. Kennedy Presidential Library and Museum.

22. Letter from Joseph P. Kennedy, Jr. to his parents, November 9, 1943. JPKPP Box 3. John F. Kennedy Presidential Library and Museum.

23. Letter from Kathleen Kennedy to her parents, November 23, 1943. JPKPP Box 3. John F. Kennedy Presidential Library and Museum.

24. Letter from Kathleen Kennedy to her parents, November 3, 1943. JPKPP Box 3. John F. Kennedy Presidential Library and Museum.

25. Letter from Joseph P. Kennedy, Sr. to John F. Kennedy, November 4, 1943. JPKPP Box 3. John F. Kennedy Presidential Library and Museum.

26. Letter from Rose Kennedy to her children, January 31, 1944. JPKPP Box 3. John F. Kennedy Presidential Library and Museum.

27. Letter from Joseph P. Kennedy, Sr. to Joseph P. Kennedy, Jr., February 21, 1944. JPKPP Box 3. John F. Kennedy Presidential Library and Museum.

28. Letter from Kathleen Kennedy to her parents, January 12, 1944. JPKPP Box 3. John F. Kennedy Presidential Library and Museum.

29. Blair and Blair, Jr., *The Search for JFK*, 369.

30. Blair and Blair, Jr., *The Search for JFK*, 373.

31. See JFK's scrapbook of articles from the SF conference: JPKPP-023-011. John F. Kennedy Presidential Library and Museum.

32. Blair and Blair, Jr., *The Search for JFK*, 377.

33. Joseph P. Kennedy's biographer David Nasaw estimates that in 1946 these trusts were worth about $8 million, or over $128 million in 2022. David Nasaw, *The Patriarch* (New York: Penguin, 2012), 586. In 1957, *Fortune* estimated Joseph Kennedy's wealth at between $200 and $400 million, which in 2022 would be between $2 billion and $4 billion (Nasaw, 693). In his oral history John F. Kennedy's close friend Paul B. Fay relates a scene he witnessed in 1959. Fay explained that Joseph P. Kennedy was complaining about how much money his children spent. [Joseph P. Kennedy] said,

> "I don't know what's going to come of all of you after I die. You're spending money as though it's going out of phase or out of fashion." He said, "You're all operating—except for Teddy; he's the only one that's operating in the black. You're all spending more than you have coming in. You're going to eat through your capital. You're not going to have anything left. There's just so much money a person can have in life, and you've got more than anybody else. And Ethel, you're the worst." He said, "Bills come in from all over the nation, every major store in every major city, practically, in the United States. Bills come in to the office to be paid." He just really harped on her, and she got up and ran out of the room in tears. Bob said, "All right, Dad, I think you've made your point." And then Bob went out and got Ethel. When they came back in, you know, it was very tense. The whole atmosphere around the table was just one where you could feel the tension and the lightening going back between these strong personalities . . . The minute Ethel came back in, [John F. Kennedy] said, "Ethel, you don't have to worry about a thing. We've decided how we're going to solve the whole thing. Dad's going to have to work harder." You know, Mr. Kennedy threw his head back and just roared. The whole thing was behind them, and we went on to something else.

James A. Oesterle, "Paul B. Fay, Jr. Oral History Interview—JFK #1 Conducted on November 9, 1970," 95–97. JFKOH-PBF-01-TR. John F. Kennedy Presidential Library and Museum.

34. At the conference Kennedy met current and future leaders, including Anthony Eden, future British prime minister; Chip Bohlen of the US State Department; Averell Harriman, US ambassador to Moscow; and Adlai Stevenson, special assistant to the US Secretary of State. The three Americans would work with Kennedy when he became president less than sixteen years later. Deirdre Henderson with an introduction by Hugh Sidey, *Prelude to Leadership: The European Diary of John F. Kennedy, Summer 1945* (Washington DC: Regnery Publishing, Inc., 1995), 86.

35. Logevall, *JFK: Coming of Age in the American Century, 1917–1956*, 392.

36. John F. Kennedy, "Kennedy Tells Parley Trends," *Chicago Herald-American*, April 28, 1945. JPKPP-023-011-p0004, box 23 JPKP. John F. Kennedy Presidential Library and Museum. Jfklibrary.org.

37. Logevall, *JFK: Coming of Age in the American Century, 1917–1956*, 255.

38. Charles Bartlett, "Arthur Krock Oral History Interview Conducted on May 10, 1964." JFKOH-AK-01, page 11. John F. Kennedy Presidential Library and Museum. Jfklibrary.org.

39. Arthur Krock, *Memoirs: Sixty Years on the Firing Line* (New York: Funk & Wagnalls, 1968), 351.

40. Letter from Kathleen Kennedy to her parents, May 27, 1945. JPKPP Box 3. John F. Kennedy Presidential Library and Museum. Jfklibrary.org.

41. Blair and Blair, Jr., *The Search for JFK*, 183.

42. Blair and Blair, Jr., *The Search for JFK*, 282.

43. Blair and Blair, Jr., *The Search for JFK*, 374.

44. John F. Stewart, "Charles Spalding Oral History Interview Conducted on March 14, 1968," John F. Kennedy Presidential Library. JFKOH-CHS-0, pages 19–24. John F. Kennedy Presidential Library and Museum.

45. John F. Kennedy, "Allied Parley Dismays Vets," *New York Journal American*, May 7, 1945. JPKPP-023-011-p0016. John F. Kennedy Presidential Library and Museum.

46. John F. Kennedy, "Peace in Europe Spurs Parley," *New York Journal American*, May 9, 1945. JPKPP-023-011-p0018. John F. Kennedy Presidential Library and Museum.

47. Henderson with Sidey, *Prelude to Leadership: The European Diary of John F. Kennedy, Summer 1945*, 99.

48. Arthur Krock, *Memoirs: Sixty Years on the Firing Line* (New York: Funk & Wagnalls, 1968), 350.

49. Henderson with Sidey, *Prelude to Leadership: The European Diary of John F. Kennedy, Summer 1945*, 6–8. The authors note that the diary entry is dated July 10, 1945. They note that this is the first entry in Kennedy's diary and that from the next entry, dated June 21, 1945, the diary proceeds chronologically.

50. Henderson with Sidey, *Prelude to Leadership: The European Diary of John F. Kennedy, Summer 1945*, xxxi.

51. Henderson with Sidey, *Prelude to Leadership: The European Diary of John F. Kennedy, Summer 1945*, 88.

52. "Dear Jim" Jacqueline Kennedy Onassis Personal Papers Box SF 64. John F. Kennedy Presidential Library and Museum. Jfklibrary.org.

53. Kenneth P. O'Donnell and David F. Powers with Joe McCarthy, *Johnny, We Hardly Knew Ye* (Boston: Little, Brown, 1972), 46.

17

Trinity and After

Three days after Roosevelt died, Oppenheimer spoke to the personnel at Los Alamos in a memorial service for the late president. Roosevelt had led the nation for twelve years, through the Great Depression and world war and to the brink of the Atomic Age. To the assembled scientists, technicians, soldiers, and others, Oppenheimer acknowledged the depth of the loss to the nation noting, "many wept who are unaccustomed to tears" and "many . . . little . . . accustomed to prayer, prayed to God." Perhaps seeking to comfort himself, he turned to the *Bhagavad-Gita*, the Hindu scripture for which he learned Sanskrit so he could read it in the original. Oppenheimer quoted from it: "Man is a creature whose substance is faith. What his faith is, he is."[1] It was faith in the strange quantum mechanics that governed subatomic particles, and faith in the industrial power of a mighty nation to create quantities of isotopes and elements that never before existed on earth that brought about the progress at Los Alamos and Oak Ridge and Hanford to that time. Not expressed, but perhaps keenly felt by Oppenheimer and others who had already contemplated the ramifications what they were creating, was the faith that they had been right to do so.

The theories developed at LeConte Hall; the products of the cyclotron and calutron at the Rad Lab and the plutonium first created at Gilman Hall; combined with industrial and intellectual power at Oak Ridge and Hanford met at a desolate desert site in New Mexico. To test the world's first fission bomb Oppenheimer selected a site two hundred miles south of Los Alamos, a corner of the Alamogordo Bombing Range in a barren area known to locals by its name in Spanish *Jornada del Muerto*, in English,

Journey of Death. Oppenheimer code-named the test "Trinity" in reference to a favorite sonnet by John Donne, *Batter my heart, three-person'd God*, that Jean Tatlock had introduced him to. Clearly she had been on his mind seven months after her death and at what he had to know would be the apex of his career, whatever further he might accomplish later in his life.[2] The sonnet begins, "Batter my heart, three-person'd God, for you/ As yet but knock, breathe, shine, and seek to mend;/ That I may rise and stand, o'erthrow me, and bend/ Your force to break, blow, burn, and make me new." If the Trinity test was successful, a new force on earth would break, blow, and burn.

There had never before been a nuclear explosion on earth and nobody at Los Alamos was sure exactly how much energy would be released by an atomic bomb. Most new weapons are thoroughly tested before they are deployed. This would be different. Oak Ridge and Hanford had not yet produced stockpiles of fissile enriched uranium or plutonium. There was not enough enriched uranium for a test and a bomb. As Groves remembered later, "Well I'll put it this way. When we exploded the Alamogordo [bomb, that was] the only one we had."[3] The gun-type trigger mechanism of the uranium bomb, the weapon destined for Hiroshima, was thought to be reliable and did not need testing. The implosion trigger mechanism of the plutonium bomb, the kind destined for Nagasaki, was novel and Oppenheimer wanted it tried out. On July 14, 1945, most of the uranium bomb, code named "Little Boy," was shipped to San Francisco and then on to the Pacific. The first use of that type of bomb would be over Hiroshima.

Two days earlier, the 13-pound plutonium-239 core had arrived at Los Alamos.[4] Groves's deputy signed for it and held the sphere in his hand. It was warm to the touch.[5] The core was returned to its container and driven to the Trinity test site in an army sedan. On Friday, 13 July, any superstitions were cast aside, and a plutonium bomb that the team at Los Alamos had long referred to as the "gadget" was assembled at an old farmhouse near ground zero of the test site. It was pouring with rain when the components of the gadget were taken to the top of a 100-foot tower, where it would be fired.

Three observation bunkers had been constructed more than five and a half miles north, west, and south of the firing tower at ground zero. Groves wanted the scientists observing the test dispersed in different locations in case an accident or miscalculation destroyed one or more of the bunkers. Equipment in these bunkers would measure the symmetry and power of the explosion and the behavior of the fireball it was expected to create—that is if it did not ignite the atmosphere, which some of the scientists still did not rule out completely. They knew that looking at the brilliance of the explosion might cause temporary blindness and even a sunburn.[6] Observers were armed with dark sunglasses. Physicist Edward Teller made "everyone nervous" by putting on suntan lotion in the pre-dawn darkness and offering it to others.[7] It was in those bunkers that some of the key scientists would witness the spectacle they worked so hard to create.

Adding to the tension of the test, the thunderstorm overhead threatened lightening. Oppenheimer knew he needed clear weather to accurately measure the strength of the detonation. He also knew that the armed gadget sitting in a shack at the top of a 100-foot steel tower had been crudely cobbled together. An earlier model of the gadget's electrical system had once been triggered prematurely by an electrical storm, like the one that just then was over at the Trinity test site.[8] Through the early morning hours Oppenheimer sweat out the weather. The test had been scheduled for 4:00 a.m. The scientists passed time the best they could. Some made wagers on aspects of the pending explosion. Oppenheimer hedged fate by betting ten dollars against George Kistiakowsky's entire month's pay that the gadget would fail to explode. The rain continued when at 3:30 a.m. Groves and Oppenheimer pushed the test back to 5:30 a.m. At 4:00 a.m., the rain stopped. Soon after 5:00 a.m., Kistiakowsky and his team armed the gadget and retreated to the south bunker. Groves left Oppenheimer and joined Ernest Lawrence, Vannevar Bush, and James Conant at base camp, about twenty-seven miles across the desert plain from tower at ground zero. The lights at ground zero were visible in the distance. The countdown began. Observers in the three bunkers heard it over a public address system, those at base camp picked it up on an FM radio signal.

At 5:30 a.m. on Monday, July 16, 1945, the gadget exploded, "vaporizing the tower and turning the asphalt around the base of the tower to green sand. Seconds after the explosion came a huge blast wave and heat searing out across the desert."[9] Observers saw an orange and yellow fireball rise and spread, followed by a second column, narrower than the first, that also rose and flattened into a mushroom shape, breaking, blowing, and burning across the Journey of Death.

Lawrence had decided to witness the explosion from an automobile because he thought the car window would filter ultraviolet light. But seconds before the explosion he grew so nervous that he changed his mind and stepped out of the car. He recalled, "just as I put my foot to the ground I was enveloped with a warm brilliant yellow white light—from darkness to brilliant sunshine in an instant." For a moment he had been "stunned by the surprise."[10] It took two minutes after the flash for the shock wave to reach him. "It was a sharp loud crack that echoed against the mountains in the far distance." Lawrence said, "the grand, indeed almost cataclysmic proportion of the explosion produced a kind of solemnity in everyone's behavior immediately afterwards. There was restrained applause, but more a hushed murmuring bordering on reverence in manner."[11]

In the south bunker over five miles away from ground zero, the blast wave knocked Kistiakowsky to the ground. Regaining his footing, he slapped Oppenheimer on the back, saying, "Oppie, you owe me ten dollars." At base camp, Bush, Conant, and Groves shook hands. When Oppenheimer returned to base camp his friend, the physicist I. I. Rabi, remembered Oppie walked with a "kind of strut." Groves said to Oppenheimer, "I am proud of you." The euphoria of the moment quickly wore off with some of the scientists. The test director, Kenneth Bainbridge, called the explosion a "foul and awesome display" and said to Oppenheimer, "Now we are all sons of bitches."[12] Later, Oppenheimer remembered, "A few people laughed, a few people cried, most people were silent." Although he code-named the test site after a holy sonnet describing a Christian tenet of the trinity of God—the Father, Son, and Holy Spirit—Oppenheimer continued, "I remembered the line from Hindu scripture, the *Bhagavad-Gita*. Vishnu is trying to persuade the prince that he should do his duty. And to impress him takes on his multi-arm form and says, 'Now I am become Death, the destroyer of worlds' I suppose we all felt that, one way or another."[13]

The Trinity test proved the novel implosion-type design for the plutonium bomb could work. The parts for the uranium-powered bomb, which would be exploded using a more conventional gun-type device, were already being shipped toward Japan. The most important piece of that bomb, its uranium core, was in the custody of Major Robert Furman, a 28-year-old Princeton-trained civil engineer who worked with General Groves on building the Pentagon. When Groves took over the Manhattan Project, be brought along Furman who he assigned to work in foreign intelligence for the project. In that role, Furman planned and often participated in missions to track and kidnap German scientists, seize uranium ore from territory abandoned by retreating German forces in Europe, and get a fix on how far along Germany was in its atomic bomb project. In short, Furman was not an ordinary courier.[14]

In July 1945, Furman was ordered to Albuquerque, New Mexico, where he was to await further instructions. At Albuquerque, Furman drove to the La Fonda Hotel in Santa Fe, New Mexico, where he met Oppenheimer. In the parking lot of the pueblo style hotel, the two men chatted in Furman's car. Oppenheimer told Furman to go to Los Alamos, where he would receive a "package." That package was one-half of the core of fissile uranium-235, produced at unfathomable cost.[15] This was the guts of the atomic bomb, which was still untested at that time. At Los Alamos, Furman was asked to sign a receipt for the package. He said, "So I signed a receipt for an atomic bomb which is kind of nice to frame. Then they decided it was too secret for me to keep the receipt, and they actually developed a receipt for a receipt that I had just given them."[16] Furman and a radiologist attached to the Manhattan Project in Los Alamos would take the package, which traveled in a shiny aluminum container resembling a milk pail with its lid bolted down, from that secret research site via armed convoy to an air force base in Albuquerque.[17] "I was in the center jeep with the [uranium core] and then there were a couple of jeeps ahead of me and a couple of jeeps behind. We were on our way to Albuquerque, the air force base there . . . The trip was pretty much without incident except we had a flat tire; this very secret very important project stood by the side of the road while some GI fixed a tire."[18] From there, the two men and their package, along with a similar dummy container flew to Hamilton Field in Marin, ten miles north of the Golden Gate Bridge. From Hamilton Field, the pair of aluminum containers proceeded to meet the *USS Indianapolis*, a heavy cruiser moored at Hunter's Point Navy Shipyard. Waiting there was the internal mechanism of the world's first uranium bomb code-named "Little Boy."

The ship had been stationed at Pearl Harbor at the beginning of the war, but it had been at sea on a training mission and escaped the Japanese attack. If that made it a lucky ship, its luck would turn disastrously bad two weeks after it completed this current mission. In the morning of July 16, 1945, just hours after the test of the atomic bomb at Trinity successfully exploded, the *USS Indianapolis* sailed under the Golden Gate Bridge to deliver the components of the "Little Boy" bomb to Tinian, one of the islands in the Northern Marianas. Located approximately 1,500 miles south of Tokyo, a B-29 bomber could make the round trip between Tinian and Tokyo in about twelve hours. In the summer of 1944, Tinian had been the site of bloody fighting between Japanese forces and American forces making their way toward Japan. Of the eight thousand Japanese soldiers defending Tinian, only 252 survived.[19] After that battle, Tinian had been turned into a giant bomber base with some of the longest runways used in the war. One Manhattan Project scientist who was sent to Tinian to assemble the second atomic bomb, the plutonium-based "Fat Man," writes: "Tinian is a miracle . . . 6,000 miles from San Francisco, the United States armed forces have built the largest airport in the world. A great coral ridge was half-leveled to fill a rough plain, and to build six runways, each an excellent 10-lane highway, each almost two miles long. Beside these runways stood in long rows [of B-29 bombers]. They were not by the dozen, but by the hundred. From the air this island, smaller than Manhattan, looked like a giant aircraft carrier, its deck loaded with bombers."[20] At Tinian, a group of specially trained crews were waiting with their massive B-29 bombers for President Truman's order to drop the bomb on Japan.

It was a typical cool San Francisco summer morning the day the *Indianapolis* departed. But before slipping under the Golden Gate Bridge any of the ship's crew on deck at the stern might have caught a glimpse of tall campanile that rises only steps away from LeConte Hall at Berkeley, where three years earlier in July 1942, Oppenheimer and his colleagues first sketched the rough technical outlines of the bomb that was sailing toward Japan.

NOTES

1. J. Robert Oppenheimer's remarks at the Los Alamos memorial Services for President Roosevelt. BANC MSS 72/117 c. Ernest O. Lawrence Papers, Berkeley Libraries.
2. Edith A. Jenkins, "Against a Field Sinister," *The Massachusetts Review* 23, no. 3 (Autumn 1982): 435.
3. Groueff, "Interview with General Leslie Groves Conducted on January 5, 1965, Part 12."
4. For the weight of the plutonium core used at Trinity see Harold Beck et al., "Accounting for Unfissioned Plutonium from the Trinity Atomic Bomb Test," Health Physics, October 2020, 504.
5. "Bomb Assembly," Trinity Test, Atomic Archive. Atomicarchive.com.
6. "Thoughts by E. O. Lawrence—Lawrence's reaction to the Trinity test, July 16, 1945," The Manhattan Project Interactive History, US Department of Energy. Otsi.gov.
7. "The Trinity Test," The Manhattan Project Interactive History, US Department of Energy. Otsi.gov.
8. Alex Wellerstein, "The First Light of Trinity," *The New Yorker*, July 16, 2015.
9. "The Trinity Test," The Manhattan Project Interactive History, US Department of Energy. Otsi.gov.
10. "Thoughts by E. O. Lawrence—Lawrence's reaction to the Trinity test, July 16, 1945," The Manhattan Project Interactive History, US Department of Energy. Otsi.gov.
11. "Thoughts by E. O. Lawrence—Lawrence's reaction to the Trinity test, July 16, 1945," The Manhattan Project Interactive History, US Department of Energy. Otsi.gov.
12. "The Trinity Test," The Manhattan Project Interactive History, US Department of Energy. Otsi.gov.
13. This was from an interview Oppenheimer gave in the television documentary, "The Decision to Drop the Bomb," directed by Fred Freed and Len Giovannitti, broadcast by NBC in 1965. Clips of this interview are available on the internet.
14. Robert Furman also has the distinction of having had access to the only private apartment in the Pentagon. During construction, he arranged to have the building's contractors build a secret space between the walls of what became the Ordnance Department. The space had a bed and a shower and was used by Furman and some of Groves's other overworked staff as a crash pad. The officers lost access when Furman was discovered exiting the apartment one day in 1943. Source: Claudette Roulo, "10 Things You Probably Didn't Know about the Pentagon," January 3, 2019. US Department of Defense. Defense.gov.
15. The other half of the core was flown to Tinian Island by the US Air Force. Source: Cindy Kelly, "Robert Furman Interview Conducted on February 20, 2008." Voices of the Manhattan Project, Atomic Heritage Foundation.
16. Source: Cindy Kelly, "Robert Furman Interview Conducted on February 20, 2008." Voices of the Manhattan Project, Atomic Heritage Foundation.

17. Lynn Vincent and Sara Vladic, *Indianapolis* (New York: Simon & Schuster, 2018) 68.
18. Kelly, "Robert Furman Interview Conducted on February 20, 2008."
19. "Reexamining Tinian's Role in Ending WWII," National Park Service. Nps.gov.
20. Rhodes, *The Making of the Atomic Bomb*, 681.

18

Gold in Peace, Iron in War

If you visit the Berkeley campus today, you won't find LeConte Hall. The building is still there and the coveted reserved curbside parking places that Nobel laureates at Berkeley receive close to their offices or labs are especially abundant there. But in 2020, LeConte Hall underwent a name change. It was a reckoning with history. The building was named for John LeConte, the university's first professor, first acting president, and third president after which he resumed teaching physics at Berkeley. It is possible that the building's name was intended to honor John's brother Joseph LeConte as well, who was also a noted professor at Berkeley. A naturalist and geographer, Joseph served as president of the prestigious American Association for the Advancement of Science and the Sierra Club. He was perhaps "the most distinguished scientist and scholar on the Berkeley campus during its early years."

Together, "the LeConte brothers were among the most accomplished scholars of the early years of the university."[1] Sadly, both men were ardent racists, Joseph appears to have been particularly so. Although the idea that Whites were superior to other races was widespread in America and elsewhere at that time, Joseph LeConte contorted science to support his opinions and biases. The LeConte name once had been prominent in California. This was changing. The Sierra Club petitioned to have the lodge in Yosemite National Park honoring Joseph LeConte renamed in 2015, and a Berkeley elementary school bearing the surname honoring the brothers was changed two years later.[2] In 2020, Cal followed suit. The LeConte name was poisoned, especially as an honorific for a science building.

It is a struggle to find anything redeeming about the experience of Japanese Americans interned during the war. The victims and the nation all were poorer for the experience. The United States spent over $4 billion adjusted for inflation on the exercise. It is harder to estimate the financial costs borne by the Issei and Nisei. The Federal Reserve Bank made an estimate of $400 million.[3] Adjusted for inflation that amounts to over $6.5 billion today. After the war many of the Issei and Nisei returned to the places they left. For those who came back to San Francisco, it was hard to find homes. Black San Franciscans had moved into the houses and apartments in Japantown, which already had become better known as the Fillmore or Western Addition. Restrictive covenants still in effect narrowed the choice of neighborhoods where non-White San Franciscans could rent or buy. Some returning Issei and Nisei ended up sleeping at Buddhist temples, single men in rows of cots on the floors of the auditoriums, married couples side by side in the balcony. One returnee to San Francisco who had to use such an accommodation remembered the snoring sounded "like an orchestra turning up."[4]

Although some quit California or the West Coast for the Midwest or East, most returned to where they had come from. By 1950, the population of Japanese Americans on the West Coast was up to 80 percent of what it had been before the war. After the war fewer Japanese Americans lived in Little Tokyos in cities. Instead, they dispersed to clusters in the suburbs. The Issei were aging and becoming dependent on their Nisei children. Multigeneration households were joined by the new generation of Sansei, children born to Nisei. Many Japanese Americans recalled going out of their way to keep a low profile in the years after the war. Japanese American communities and Japanese American identity survived internment, "but it had changed it in ways that wouldn't be understood for many years."[5]

Eighty-five percent of Black wartime migrants to the Bay Area stayed after the war. They faced a difficult time. Unlike Joseph James who had been to college and graduate school, only about 20 percent of the Black workers who came to the Bay Area had high school diplomas; half had not finished the eighth grade.[6] In her memoir, *Gather Together in My Name*, Maya Angelou writes from the perspective of a seventeen-year-old unmarried mother, "very old, embarrassingly young" but clear eyed enough to see what was going on in the Fillmore at the war's end: "Two months after V-Day, war plants began to shut down, to cut back, to lay off employees. Some workers were offered tickets back to their Southern homes. Back to the mules they had left tied to the tree on ole Mistah Doo Hickup farm. No good. Their expanded understanding could never again be accordioned into these narrow confines. They were free or at least nearer to freedom than ever before and they would not go back."[7]

After the war Joseph James returned to New York to pursue his singing career. But it did not end his activism. Before departing the West Coast in 1946 to resume his musical career, he helped cofound Marin County's first NAACP chapter. Joseph James performed in fifteen more Broadway shows before touring internationally with Leontyne Price, William Warfield, Cab Calloway, and Maya Angelou in Porgy and Bess. Later in life he became a union organizer in the Bronx. Joseph James died in 2002 at the age of ninety-one.

The era when Ernest Lawrence and Robert Oppenheimer were associated has been called the "age of personality in physics." It was a time when individuals like Einstein, Bohr, Lawrence, and Oppenheimer were widely known to people outside the sciences. It was replaced by "an age of organization" that was needed to support the high cost of "Big Science" wrought foremostly by Lawrence at Berkeley.[8] For a time Lawrence and Oppenheimer were the two biggest personalities in physics, and very close friends. Lawrence appeared on the cover of *Time* in 1937, well before Oppenheimer got that particular recognition. The Manhattan Project, however, made him a bigger celebrity with the public. *Life* put him on its cover with the caption: "Oppenheimer: No. 1 Thinker on Atomic Energy." Later, in 1954, when Oppenheimer was fighting to retain his security clearance—really, fighting the stain of treason—he was asked in a hearing under oath, "Is it true that from 1943 until recently . . . you were the most influential scientist in the atomic energy field in [America]?" Oppenheimer considered the question and replied, "I think Lawrence had in many ways more influence."[9] By that time, the friendship between the two men was over.

The celebrity both men obtained drove them to indulge different aspects of their personalities. Lawrence became the exemplar of the establishment man, joining lucrative corporate boards and socializing at the exclusive Bohemian Club and Pacific Union Club, while still overseeing research at the Rad Lab and consulting on government research and weapons projects. He also became a hawkish supporter of the hydrogen bomb and a theory of radiation warfare that repelled many, including James Conant who had helped lead the Manhattan Project.[10] Oppenheimer, once an otherworldly aesthete who lived a life of the mind and arts, reveled in his status as a hyper-connected Washington insider. His introspective and after the war sometimes brooding personality, however, did not appeal to President Truman. Oppenheimer once confided to Truman that he felt as if he—Oppenheimer—had "blood on his hands" for his role in leading the bomb project. When that meeting was over, Truman told Dean Acheson, who was soon to be promoted to secretary of state, "I don't want to see that son of a bitch in this office ever again."[11] Truman's successor, Dwight Eisenhower, also disliked Oppenheimer. But many other powerful government officials did seek out his counsel in the first years of the Cold War. Oppenheimer's left wing background and evasions about his relationships with people the government considered suspect were overlooked because he had been so valuable to the country. This came to an end in 1954 when after a sham hearing Oppenheimer's security clearance was revoked. General Groves testified on behalf of Oppenheimer. So did Vannevar Bush, who had been in charge of all government research during the war.

Speaking about Oppenheimer's work at Los Alamos, Bush said, "He did a magnificent piece of work. More than any other scientist that I know of he was responsible for our having an atomic bomb on time."[12] Several physicists who had been essential to the Manhattan Project defended Oppenheimer. I. I. Rabi testified that because of Oppenheimer's work, America had an arsenal of atomic bombs and hydrogen bombs, asking Oppenheimer's antagonists, "What more do you want, mermaids?"[13] Other physicists, like Oppenheimer's friend and colleague Edward Teller, who had been with Oppenheimer and the handful of physicists he gathered in that small office in LeConte Hall to sketch the theoretical outline of an atomic bomb in the summer of 1942, testified against him. Ernest Lawrence had been scheduled to appear at the hearing, but a bout of colitis, which began troubling him after the war and would contribute to his death four years later at the age of fifty-seven, prevented him from traveling from Berkeley to Washington, DC, for the hearing. Had Lawrence participated in the hearing, he would have testified against his old friend. In interviews with prosecutors, Lawrence concluded that Oppenheimer "should never again have anything to do with the forming of policy."[14] Oppenheimer lost his security clearance.[15] President Eisenhower ordered a "blank wall" to be erected between Oppenheimer and nuclear secrets.[16] Told about the outcome of the hearing, Albert Einstein said, "The trouble with Oppenheimer is that he loves a woman who doesn't love him—the United States government."[17]

John F. Kennedy knew when to leave a party. Skipping the final days of the UN conference in San Francisco, he headed to England. Britain was holding its first election since the beginning of the war. Winston Churchill's Conservative Party was vying against the socialist Labour Party. Filing his last story as a journalist, Kennedy explained to his readers why the Conservatives were badly beaten, despite how beloved Churchill was as a wartime leader. Exquisitely well connected because of his father's wealth and influence, Kennedy joined the secretary of the navy to see the Potsdam Conference underway in Germany. This was the meeting of the leaders of the United Kingdom, Untied States, and Soviet Union to negotiate terms for ending World War II. It was at this conference that President Harry Truman received news of Oppenheimer's successful test at the Trinity site. When the "Little Boy" atomic bomb exploded over Hiroshima, Kennedy was in the secretary of the navy's airplane flying back to Washington. His own brush dealing with nuclear annihilation during the Cuban Missile Crisis was only seventeen years in the future.

Most of the crew aboard the *USS Indianapolis*, the ship that departed San Francisco with half of the core of uranium-235 that powered the "Little Boy" atomic bomb, did not live to celebrate the end of the war the atomic bombs hastened. The ship sped from San Francisco to Tinian Island to deliver pieces of the world's first atomic bomb. That journey had been uneventful. Its cargo delivered, she sailed on to Guam and was headed to Leyte when, minutes after midnight on July 30, 1945, she crossed the view of the periscope of a Japanese submarine. The sub fired six torpedoes at the *Indianapolis*. Two of those torpedoes hit their mark, nearly rending the ship in half. As she listed to her side, the order was given to abandon ship. Nearly nine hundred crewmembers who survived the torpedo attack watched in the water as their ship sank beneath them in a little over ten minutes, taking with it three hundred dead crewmates.[18] A worse fate awaited most of the survivors in the water. Hundreds of sharks found them, drawn by the bloody pieces of human bodies thrown into the sea by the exploding ship. The men suffered in the ocean for four days and five nights with no food or drinking water, all the while being attacked by sharks. Hundreds of the sailors were killed in the feeding frenzies before rescuers arrived. Only 317 crewmembers survived.[19]

Almost everybody in the United States was touched by World War II. Unlike today, most people had a son or daughter, cousin, neighbor, uncle or friend in the military. Over sixteen million men and women served in the armed forces during the war. More than four hundred thousand American service members were killed and more than one and a half times that number were wounded. If that pain and loss was close to home, the war itself had been far away from the homeland. Vast swaths of Europe and Asia had been devastated during the war. An estimated forty-five million civilians had been killed, three time the number of deaths suffered by the various militaries in the war. By contrast, only six American civilians had been killed in the continental United States as the result of enemy action.

In Europe and Asia most of the industries had been destroyed and national economies wrecked. In stark contrast, America had been built up by investments in infrastructure and manufacturing in service to the war. There was full employment after the lean years of the Great Depression. The American economy boomed during the war, growing by around 4 percent a year. The economic gains were widely shared and lasting, the size of the middle class increased by 50 percent in the decade and a half after the war.[20] America stood at the summit of the world.

Wallace Stegner, the novelist laureate of the West, said "California is like the rest of America, only more so."[21] In the years around World War II, San Francisco and the Bay Area amplified California's exceptionalism. This was because the region, to steal a phrase from Hollywood, was ready for its close-up. The investments made by Californians to build free universities at Berkeley and elsewhere, and commitments to continue supporting them through thick and thin times, created an environment that could attract outstanding young talented scientists like Lawrence and Oppenheimer, who in turn attracted future generations of gifted scientists that made California's universities great. The creative public-private financing and entrepreneurial spirit exhibited by Lawrence and Sproul that funded the big science that Lawrence created characterized the scrappy university on its way up. Much of that private money came from East Coast philanthropies that for the first time was spent heavily to support research in the West, buying into Lawrence's vision and quiet charisma.

The cultural ferment of San Francisco supported an opera, symphony, museums, and restaurants, clubs of all description, and varied nightlife. It attracted talented people of different ethnicities, races, incomes, talents, and perspectives. It speaks well of the city that Maya Angelou, Joseph James, Ernest Lawrence, and Robert Oppenheimer could all thrive. The city of San Francisco has an official motto: *Oro en Paz. Fierro en Guerra.* This is Spanish for "Gold in Peace. Iron in War." It was coined in 1898 when the city was an embarkation point for American soldiers heading to fight in the Spanish-American War. The motto was particularly apt in describing San Francisco during World War II. Iron and steel were produced here and made into war-fighting ships. And a new kind of fire was created too. The sparks of the inferno released for the first time on earth at the Trinity test site and unleashed over Hiroshima and Nagasaki ending the war, were first fanned across the bay. The war and the tenuous peace that followed brought long lasting wealth to the city, the Bay Area, and California. The gold and fire produced in and around San Francisco changed the world.

NOTES

1. "UC Berkeley Building Name Review Committee," June 26, 2020. Chancelor.berkeley.edu.

2. Gretchen Kell, "UC Berkeley's LeConte and Barrows Halls Lose Their Names," Berkeley News. News.berkeley.edu.

3. "By the time WRA finally closed its books, it had spent $160,037,030. It had cost the army $56,482,638 just to build the ten relocation centers. Since the army

had spent a grand total of $88,679,716 in the evacuation, the overall cost to the American taxpayer was $248,716,746—nearly a quarter billion dollars in cash outlay . . . There is no way to estimate the long-term economic loss to the evacuees themselves, although the Federal Reserve Bank made an arbitrary estimate of $400,000,000. Briones, *Jim and Jap Crow: A Cultural History of 1940s Interracial America*, 440.

4. Brian Niiya, "Return to West Coast," Densho Encyclopedia. Encyclopedia.densho.org.

5. Niiya, "Return to West Coast."

6. Wollenberg, "James vs. Marinship: Trouble on the New Black Frontier," 277.

7. Maya Angelou, *Gather in My Name* (New York: Random House, 2009), 228–229.

8. Davis, *Lawrence and Oppenheimer*, 11. Davis uses the phrase "Big Science" in quotes, perhaps coining the phrase that has gained circulation since.

9. Davis, *Lawrence and Oppenheimer*, 11.

10. Herken, *Brotherhood of the Bomb*, 185.

11. Bird and Sherwin, *American Prometheus: The Triumph and Tragedy of J. Robert Oppenheimer*, 332.

12. Vannevar Bush "Testimony, United States Atomic Energy Commission," in The Matter of J. Robert Oppenheimer, vol. 10, April 23, 1954, 1962.

13. I.Rabi, "Testimony, United States Atomic Energy Commission," in The Matter of J. Robert Oppenheimer, volume 8, 1554.

14. "Lawrence in the Cold War," American Institute of Physics. Aip.org.

15. In December 2022, the US Secretary of Energy nullified the 1954 decision calling the hearing a "flawed process." William J. Broad, "J. Robert Oppenheimer Cleared of Black Mark after 68 Years," *New York Times*, December 18, 2022, 16.

16. William J. Broad, "Transcripts Kept Secret for 60 Years Bolster Defense of Oppenheimer's Loyalty," *New York Times*, October 11, 2014.

17. Bird and Sherwin, *American Prometheus: The Triumph and Tragedy of J. Robert Oppenheimer*, 503–504.

18. Scott Neuman, "Wreckage of USS Indianapolis, Sunk by Japanese in WWII, Found in Pacific," The Two-Way, National Public Radio. Npr.org.

19. Jessie Kratz, "The Sinking of the USS Indianapolis," Pieces of History, National Archives. Prologue.blogs.archives.gov.

20. David M. Kennedy speech given at Humanities Texas, June 7, 2011. Kennedy uses home ownership as a proxy for middle class.

21. Wallace Stegner, "California: The Experimental Society, an Editorial," *The Saturday Review*, September 23, 1967, 28.

Bibliography

"200 Million Volts of Energy Created by Atom Explosions." *San Francisco Chronicle*, January 31, 1939.

"320 Americans Killed in WWII Naval Magazine Accident." Port Chicago Naval Magazine National Memorial. National Park Service.

Adams, Stephen B. "Regionalism in Stanford's Contribution to the Rise of Silicon Valley." *Enterprise and Society* 4, no. 3 (September 2003): 521–543.

Adler, Jerry. "1934: The Art of the New Deal." *Smithsonian Magazine*, June 2009.

Alvarez, Luis W. *Adventures of a Physicist*. New York: Basic Books, 1987.

Angelou, Maya. *Gather in My Name*. New York: Random House, 2009.

Angelou Maya. *I Know Why the Caged Bird Sings*. New York: Ballentine Books, 2015.

"Architecture and Environs. The Historic Research Campus in Dahlem, Berlin." Harnack House, Conference Venue of the Max Planck Society.

Atkinson, Rick. "Ten Things Every American History Student Should Know about Our Army in World War II." Foreign Policy Research Institute.

Badash, Lawrence, Hodes, Elizabeth, and Tiddens, Adolph. "Nuclear Fission: Reaction to the Discovery in 1939." *Proceedings of the American Philosophical Society* 130, no. 2 (June 1986): 196–231.

Bamford, James. *Body of Secrets*. New York: Anchor, 2002.

Bartlett, Charles. "Arthur Krock Oral History Interview Conducted on May 10, 1964." JFKOH-AK-01. John F. Kennedy Presidential Library and Museum.

Beck, Harold et al., "Accounting for Unfissioned Plutonium from the Trinity Atomic Bomb Test." *Health Physics* 119, (October 2020): 504–516.

Beebe, Lucius. "San Francisco: Boom Town De Luxe." *American Mercury*, January 1942.

Benedict, Ruth. "Letter to Milton S. Eisenhower, June 11, 1942." bk0013c8x6r -FID1. University of California, Berkeley Bancroft Library.

Bernstein, Barton J. "The Oppenheimer Loyalty-Security Case Reconsidered." *Stanford Law Review* 42, no. 6 (July 1990): 1383–1484.
Bernstein, Jeremy. "Oppenheimer's Beginnings." *New England Review* 25, no. 1/2: 38–51.
Bethe, H. A. "J. Robert Oppenheimer, 1904–1967." *Biographical Memoirs of Fellows of the Royal Society* 14 (November 1968): 390–416.
Biddle, Francis. *In Brief Authority*. Garden City, NY: Doubleday & Company, Inc., 1962.
"Big Science, Neptunium." American Institute of Physics.
Billings, Lem. "Telegraph to John F. Kennedy, October 30, 1940." JFKPP-004-139-p0004. John F. Kennedy Presidential Library and Museum.
Bird, Kai and Sherwin, Martin J. *American Prometheus, The Triumph and Tragedy of J. Robert Oppenheimer*. New York: Vintage Paperback, 2006.
Birge, R. T. "Address." Nobel Prize in Physics Ceremony in Berkeley, February 29, 1940. Nobelprize.org.
Blair, Joan and Blair, Clay, Jr. *The Search for JFK*. New York: Berkley, 1976.
Blum, John Morton, ed. *From the Morgenthau Diaries, Years of War, 1941–1945*. Boston: Houghton Mifflin, 1967.
Blum, John Morton. *V Was for Victory: Politics and American Culture during World War II*. San Diego: Harcourt, Brace & Company, 1976.
"Bomb Assembly." Trinity Test, Atomic Archive. Atomicarchive.com.
Brechin, Gray. "Guttering the Promise of Public Education." UC Berkeley Department of Geography Commencement, May 16, 2009.
Brechin, Gray. *Imperial San Francisco*. Berkeley: University of California Press, 2006.
Briones, Mathew M. *Jim and Jap Crow: A Cultural History of 1940s Interracial America*. Princeton: Princeton University Press, 2012.
Broad, William J. "Transcripts Kept Secret for 60 Years Bolster Defense of Oppenheimer's Loyalty." *New York Times*, October 11, 2014.
Broek, Gertjan. "The (Im)possibilities of Escaping. Jewish emigration 1933–1942." Anne Frank House.
Broussard, Albert S. *Black San Francisco: The Struggle for Racial Equality in the West, 1900–1954*. Lawrence: University Press of Kansas, 1993.
Broussard, Albert S. "Interview with Aurelious P. Alberga conducted on December 7, 1976." *Afro-Americans in San Francisco Prior to World War II*. San Francisco Public Library Oral History Project.
Bush, Vannevar. "Testimony to the United States Atomic Energy Commission. In the Matter of J. Robert Oppenheimer." United States Department of Atomic Energy, 1954.
Caen, Herb. "Days of Our Years." *San Francisco Chronicle*, May 16, 1995.
Caen, Herb. "It's News to Me." *San Francisco Chronicle*, December 14, 1940.
Carter, Stephen L. "What Thurgood Marshall Taught Me." *The New York Times Sunday Magazine*, July 18, 2021.
Cassidy, David C. *J. Robert Oppenheimer and the American Century*. New York: Pearson, 2005.
Childs, Herbert. *An American Genius: The Life of Ernest Orlando Lawrence*. New York: E. P. Dutton & Co., 1968.

Clarke, Nick. *Alistair Cooke: A Biography*. New York: Arcade, 1999.
Compton, Arthur Holly. *Atomic Quest*. New York: Oxford University Press, 1956.
Conn, Stetson, Engelman, Rose C., and Fairchild, Byron. *Guarding the United States and Its Outposts*. Office of Military History, Department of the Army, Washington, DC, 1964.
Corbyn, Zoë. "Why Nobel Laureates are Getting Older." Scientific American website. Scientificamerican.com.
Cremer, Peter with Brustat-Naval, Fritz. *U-Boat Commander*. Translated by Lawrence Wilson. Annapolis: Naval Institute Press, 1984.
Daniels, Douglas Henry. *Pioneer Urbanites: A Social and Cultural History of Black San Francisco*. Berkeley: University of California Press, 1990.
Davis, Nuel Pharr. *Lawrence and Oppenheimer*. New York: Simon and Schuster, 1968.
DeWitt, J. L. "Letter to Henry Stimson, September 12, 1942." University of California, Berkeley Bancroft Library, Japanese American Evacuation and Resettlement Records 1930–1974. BANC MSS 67/14 c, folder D2.046.
Edises, Pele. "Joe James Is a Busy Man." *People's World Daily*, January 6, 1945.
"Einstein Letter." The Manhattan Project, an interactive history, US Department of Energy, Office of History and Heritage Resources.
"Einstein's 'Spooky Action at a Distance' Paradox Older Than Thought." *MIT Technology Review*.
Eisenhower, Milton S. "Letter to Cole E. Morgan, April 30, 1942." bk0013c8x6r-FID1. University of California, Berkeley Bancroft Library.
Eisenhower, Milton S. "Letter to E.H. Wiecking, March 26, 1942." bk0013c8x6r-FID1. University of California, Berkeley Bancroft Library.
Eisenhower, Milton S. "Letter to Harold D. Smith, April 5, 1942." bk0013c8x6r-FID1. University of California, Berkeley Bancroft Library.
Eisenhower, Milton S. *The President is Calling*. New York: Doubleday and Co., 1974.
"Electromagnetic Separation." The Manhattan Project Interactive History, US Department of Energy.
"E.O. Lawrence Wins Nobel Prize in Physics." Lawrence Berkeley National Laboratory.
Eschner, Kat. "Old Particle Accelerator Tech Might Be Just What the Doctor Ordered." *Smithsonian Magazine*, February 20, 2017.
"Executive Order 8802: Prohibition of Discrimination in the Defense Industry (1941)." Milestone Documents, National Archives.
"Federal Theatre Project, U. S. (1939) Federal Theatre on Treasure Island 'Swing Mikado' A cast of 100: Sensational success: Hot from New York: The big hit of the Golden Gate International Exposition." Library of Congress.
"Fortnight," *The Newsmagazine of California* 6, no. 4, February 18, 1949.
Garside, Anne. *Camelot at Dawn, Jacqueline and John Kennedy at Georgetown, May 1954*. Baltimore: John Hopkins University Press, 2005.
Glines, Carroll V. *The Doolittle Raid*. New York: Orion, 1988.
Goluboff, Risa Lauren. "Let Economic Equality Take Care of Itself: The NAACP, Labor Litigation, and the Making of Civil Rights in the 1940s." *UCLA Law Review* 52, (2005): 1393–1486.

Goodchild, Peter. *J. Robert Oppenheimer: Shatterer of Worlds*. Boston: Houghton Mifflin, 1981.
Goodman, Jack, ed. *While You Were Gone*. New York: Simon and Schuster, 1946.
Gratzer, Walter. *Eurekas and Euphorias: The Oxford Book of Scientific Anecdotes*. Oxford: Oxford University Press, 2002.
Grodzins, Morton. *Americans Betrayed, Politics and the Japanese Evacuation*. Chicago: University of Chicago Press, 1949.
Groueff, Stephane. "Interview of Eleanor Irvine Davisson Conducted on February 8, 1965, at Berkeley, CA." Voices of the Manhattan Project, Atomic Heritage Foundation.
Groueff, Stephane. "Interview with General Leslie Groves Conducted on January 5, 1965, Part 6." Voices of the Manhattan Project, Atomic Heritage Foundation.
Groueff, Stephane. "Interview with J. Robert Oppenheimer Conducted on September 12, 1965." Voices of the Manhattan Project, Atomic Heritage Foundation.
Hamilton, Nigel. *JFK. Reckless Youth*. New York: Random House, 1992.
Hayashi, Doris. "Diary." Vol. 1, Japanese Americans—Evacuation and Relocation, 1942–1945, Japanese American Evacuation and Resettlement Study, University of California, Berkeley Bancroft Library.
Heilbron, J. L. and Seidel, Robert W. *Lawrence and His Laboratory: A History of the Lawrence Berkeley Laboratory*. Volume 1. Berkeley: University of California Press, 1989.
Henderson, Deirdre with an Introduction by Sidey, Hugh. *Prelude to Leadership: The European Diary of John F. Kennedy, Summer 1945*. Washington DC: Regnery Publishing, Inc., 1995.
Herken, Gregg. *Brotherhood of the Bomb: The Tangled Lives and Loyalties of Robert Oppenheimer, Ernest Lawrence, and Edward Teller*. New York: Henry Holt and Company, 2002.
Hersey, John. "Behind Barbed Wire." *The New York Times Magazine*, September 11, 1988.
Hersey, John. "Survival." *The New Yorker*, June 17, 1944.
Hiltzik, Michael. *Big Science: Ernest Lawrence and the Invention That Launched the Military-Industrial Complex*. New York: Simon and Schuster, 2015.
Hobart, John. "'The Swing Mikado' Makes Hit, 'De Punishment Fits De Crime.'" *San Francisco Chronicle*, June 16, 1939.
Hoopes, Townsend and Brinkley, Douglas. *FDR and the Creation of the U.N.* New Haven: Yale University Press, 1997.
Horiuchi, Lynne and Sankalia, Tanu, eds. *Reinventions: San Francisco's Treasure Island*. Honolulu: University of Hawaii Press, 2017.
Iijima, Ben. "Diary." Japanese Americans—Evacuation and Relocation, 1942–1945 Japanese American Evacuation and Resettlement Study, University of California, Berkeley Bancroft Library.
Inada, Lawson Fusao. *Only What We Could Carry*. Berkeley, CA: Heyday Books, 2000.
James, Joseph. "Marinship Negroes Speak to Fellow Workmen." *The Marin-er*, August 21, 1943.
James, Joseph. "Profiles: San Francisco." *The Journal of Educational Sociology* 19, no. 3 (November 1945): 166–178.

Jenkins, Edith A. *Against a Field Sinister*. San Francisco: City Lights Books, 1991.
"Jewish Emigration from Germany." The United States Holocaust Memorial Museum.
"John F. Kennedy and PT 109." John F. Kennedy Presidential Library and Museum.
Johnson, Charles S., Jones, Grace, Long, Herman. "The Negro War Worker in San Francisco: A Local Self-Survey." May 1944.
Johnson, Marilynn S. *The Second Gold Rush: Oakland and the East Bay in World War II*. Berkeley: University of California Press, 1993.
Johnson, Richard W. "Mention San Francisco's Top of the Mark to Service Men—That Brings on Nostalgia." United Press International, February 22, 1944.
"J. Robert Oppenheimer." Part 01. The Federal Bureau of Investigation. Vault.fbe.gov.
Keegan, John. "Peace in Their Time." *Washington Post*, December 15, 2002.
Kell, Gretchen. "UC Berkeley's LeConte and Barrows Halls Lose Their Names." *Berkeley News*. News.berkeley.edu.
Kelly, Cindy. "Interview with Edward Gerjuoy Conducted on April 13, 2008." Voices of the Manhattan Project, The Atomic Heritage Foundation.
Kelly, Cindy. "Robert Furman Interview Conducted on February 20, 2008." Voices of the Manhattan Project, Atomic Heritage Foundation.
Kennedy, David M. "Speech given to Humanities Texas, June 7, 2011."
Kennedy, John F. "Allied Parley Dismays Vets." *New York Journal American*, May 7, 1945.
Kennedy, John F. "Dear Jim." Jacqueline Kennedy Onassis Personal Papers Box SF 64. John F. Kennedy Presidential Library and Museum.
Kennedy, John F. "Kennedy Tells Parley Trends." *Chicago Herald-American*, April 28, 1945.
Kennedy, John F. "Letter to his parents, September 12, 1943." JFKPP-005-001-p0002 and p0003. John F. Kennedy Presidential Library and Museum.
Kennedy, John F. "Letter to his parents, May 14, 1945." JFKPP-005-001-p0004. John F. Kennedy Presidential Library and Museum.
Kennedy, John F. "Letter to Joseph P. Kennedy, Sr., October 30, 1943." JFKPP-005-001-p007. John F. Kennedy Presidential Library and Museum.
Kennedy, John F. "Peace in Europe Spurs Parley." *New York Journal American*, May 9, 1945.
Kennedy, Jr., Joseph P. "Letter to his parents, November 9, 1943." JPKPP Box 3. John F. Kennedy Presidential Library and Museum.
Kennedy, Jr., Joseph P. "Letter to his parents, February 19, 1944." JPKPP Box 3. John F. Kennedy Presidential Library and Museum.
Kennedy, Kathleen. "Letter to her parents, November 3, 1943." JPKPP Box 3. John F. Kennedy Presidential Library and Museum.
Kennedy, Kathleen. "Letter to her parents, November 23, 1943." JPKPP Box 3. John F. Kennedy Presidential Library and Museum.
Kennedy, Kathleen. "Letter to her parents, January 6, 1944." JPKPP Box 3. John F. Kennedy Presidential Library and Museum.
Kennedy, Kathleen. "Letter to her parents, January 12, 1944." JPKPP Box 3. John F. Kennedy Presidential Library and Museum.

Kennedy, Kathleen. "Letter to her parents, May 27, 1945." JPKPP Box 3. John F. Kennedy Presidential Library and Museum.
Kennedy, Rose. "Letter to her children, January 31, 1944." JPKPP Box 3. John F. Kennedy Presidential Library and Museum.
Kennedy, Sr., Joseph P. "Letter to John F. Kennedy, November 4, 1943." JPKPP Box 3. John F. Kennedy Presidential Library and Museum.
Kennedy, Sr., Joseph P. "Letter to John F. Kennedy, November 16, 1943." JPKPP Box 3. John F. Kennedy Presidential Library and Museum.
Kennedy, Sr., Joseph P. "Letter to Joseph P. Kennedy, Jr., February 21, 1944." JPKPP Box 3. John F. Kennedy Presidential Library and Museum.
Kennedy, Joseph P. "Letter to Joseph P. Kennedy, Jr., May 24, 1944." JPKPP Box 3. John F. Kennedy Presidential Library and Museum.
Kim, Tammy E. "An Asian-American Reimagining of Gilbert and Sullivan's 'The Mikado.'" *The New Yorker*, December 27, 2016.
Kosowsky, Arthur B. "Edward Gerjuoy." *Physics Today*, March 31, 2018.
Kratz, Jessie. "The Sinking of the USS Indianapolis." Pieces of History, National Archives. Prologue.blogs.archives.gov.
Krock, Arthur. *Memoirs: Sixty Years on the Firing Line*. New York: Funk & Wagnalls, 1968.
Lathrop, Judith M., ed., "Los Alamos Science." (Winter/Spring 1983): 6–25.
Lawrence, E.O. "Letter to Compton, A.H dated October 14, 1941." Ernest O. Lawrence Papers, University of California, Berkeley Bancroft Library.
Lawrence, Ernest. "Award Ceremony Speech for the Nobel Prize in Physics, 1939." February 29, 1940.
Lawrence, Ernest O. "The Evolution of the Cyclotron." Nobel Lecture, December 11, 1951.
"Lawrence in the Cold War." American Institute of Physics. Aip.org.
Lewis, Hilary. "Oscars: Who Came up with the Name Oscar?" *The Hollywood Reporter*, February 18, 2015.
"Life Visits the Top of the Mark." *Life*, July 31, 1944.
Lippmann, Walter. "The Fifth Column." *Los Angeles Times*, February 13, 1942.
Logevall, Fredrik. *JFK: Coming of Age in the American Century, 1917–1956*. New York: Random House, 2020.
"Los Angeles with 575,480 of Population Passes San Francisco and Leads the West." *New York Times*, June 9, 1920.
Lotchin, Roger W. *The Bad City in the Good War*. Bloomington: Indiana University Press, 2003.
Mawdsley, Evan. "Sinking the SS Athenia." August 4, 2020. Yalebooks.yale.edu.
McCaffrey, Deb. "Lawrence and the Cyclotron: the Birth of Big Science." February 26, 2016, Public Library of Science Blogs, ECR Community.
McCormick, Anne O'Hare. "His 'Unfinished Business'—And Ours." *The New York Times Magazine*, April 22, 1945.
McCormick, Anne O'Hare. "San Francisco: Battlefield for Peace." *The New York Times Magazine*, May 6, 1945.
McWilliams, Carey. *Brothers under the Skin*. Boston: Little, Brown & Co., 1964.
Messer, Krystal. "Dainty Distractions: the Japan Pavilion at the Golden Gate International Exhibition." *UCLA Thinking Gender Papers* (January 4, 2014).

Miller, Leta E. "Elmer Keeton and His Bay Area Negro Chorus: Creating an Artistic Identity in Depression-Era San Francisco." *Black Music Research Journal* 30, no 2 (Fall 2010): 107–140.
Miller, Leta E. *Music and Politics in San Francisco*. Berkeley: University of California Press, 2012.
Miller, Paul T. *The Postwar Struggle for Civil Rights: African Americans in San Francisco 1945–1957*. New York: Routledge, 2010.
Miller, Sherman. "Barbary Coast Is Recalled by Frisco Boom." *Variety*, November 4, 1942.
Morrow, Irving F. "Golden Gate Bridge Report on Color and Lighting." April 6, 1935.
Nachmansohn, David. *German-Jewish Pioneers in Science, 1900–1933*. New York: Springer-Verlag, 1979.
Nasaw, David. *The Patriarch*. New York: Penguin, 2012.
Nash, Gerald D. *The American West in the Twentieth Century*. Englewood Cliffs: Prentice-Hall, 1973.
Nash, Gerald D. "Stages of California's Economic Growth, 1870–1970: An Interpretation." *California Historical Quarterly* 51, no. 4 (Winter, 1972): 315–330.
Nash, Gerald D. *The American West Transformed: The Impact of the Second World War*. Bloomington: Indiana University Press, 1985.
"National Lottery Draws Names of 24 Stanford Men, 2 Professors." *The Daily Stanford*, October 30, 1940.
Neuman, Scott. "Wreckage of USS Indianapolis, Sunk by Japanese in WWII, Found in Pacific." The Two-Way, National Public Radio.
Newton, Jim. *Justice for All, Earl Warren and the Nation He Made*. New York: Riverhead Books, 2006.
Niiya, Brian. "Return to West Coast." Densho Encyclopedia. Encyclopedia.desho.org.
Noble, John Wesley. *Never Plead Guilty: The Story of Jake Erlich*. New York: Farrar, Straus and Cudahy, 1955.
"Not So Golden Gate." *Time*, June 19, 1939.
O'Donnell, Kenneth P. and Powers, David F. with McCarthy, Joe. *Johnny, We Hardly Knew Ye*. Boston: Little, Brown, 1972.
"One Foe Is Vanquished." *San Francisco Chronicle*, May 9, 1945.
Oppenheimer, J. Robert. Interviewee in "The Decision to Drop the Bomb." Directed by Fred Freed and Len Giovannitti, broadcast by NBC in 1965.
Oppenheimer, J. Robert. "Remarks at the Los Alamos Memorial Services for President Roosevelt." BANC MSS 72/117 c. Ernest O. Lawrence Papers, Berkeley Libraries.
Oppenheimer, J. Robert. "Testimony to the Atomic Energy Commission." In the Matter of J. Robert Oppenheimer, 1954.
"Party Ship Is Sent to Parley by Soviet." *New York Times*, March 21, 1945.
Petrin, Katherine and Davis, Matthew. "South San Francisco Opera House." National Register of Historic Places Registration Form, Bayview Opera House. Bvoh.org.
Powers, Thomas. *Heisenberg's War*. Boston: DeCapo Press, 2000.

Presidential Speeches. "Franklin D. Roosevelt, February 23, 1942: Fireside Chat 20: On the Progress of the War." Miller Center, University of Virginia.
"Press at San Francisco." *Life*, May 14, 1945.
Rabi, I. I. "Testimony, United States Atomic Energy Commission." In The Matter of J. Robert Oppenheimer. Volume 8.
"Race Not Mutiny Is Issue in Trial of 50 Negro Seamen." October 13, 1944. NAACP Press Release.
"Reexamining Tinian's Role in Ending WWII." National Park Service. Nps.gov.
Rhodes, Richard. *The Making of the Atomic Bomb*. New York: Simon and Schuster, 1986.
Riess, Suzanne. "Interview with Mary Blumer Lawrence Conducted in 1984." Robert Gordon Sproul Oral History Project. Volume 2.
Roberts, Edith. "Letter to Milton S. Eisenhower, May 9, 1942." bk0013c8x6r-FID1. University of California, Berkeley Bancroft Library.
Roberts, Lesley. "JFK in Scotland: Former US President Began Journey to White House with Public Speech in Scottish Hotel in 1939." *Daily Record*, September 8, 2013.
Rossi, Angelo. "Testimony to the Select Committee Investigating National Defense Migration." House of Representatives, Seventy-Seventh Congress, February 21, 1942.
"Sally Rand (1904–1979)." The Museum of the City of San Francisco. Sfmuseum.org.
Sanders, Robert. "UC's First Nobel Prize Presented in Berkeley 75 Years Ago." February 17, 2015, Berkeley News, Press Release, UC Berkeley.
Schiller, Reuel. *Forging Rivals: Race, Class, Law, and the Collapse of Postwar Liberalism*. New York: Cambridge University Press, 2015.
Schlesinger, Stephen C. *Act of Creation: The Founding of the United Nations*. Cambridge: Westview, 2004.
"Science in the Service of Man." University of California Committee in Cooperation with the Golden Gate International Exhibition, San Francisco, 1939–1940.
Seaborg, Glenn T. with Seaborg, Eric. *Adventures in the Atomic Age: From Watts to Washington*. New York: Farrar, Straus and Giroux, 2001.
Serber, Robert with Crease, Robert P. *Peace and War Reminiscences of a Life on the Frontiers of Science*. New York: Columbia University Press, 1998.
"S. F. Clear of All But 6 Sick Japs." *San Francisco Chronicle*, Thursday, May 21, 1942.
Sherwin, Martin J. "Interview with Haakon Chevalier's Interview, Part 2, Conducted on June 29, 1982." Voices of the Manhattan Project, Atomic Heritage Foundation.
Sherwin, Martin J. "Interview with Harold Cherniss, Part 1, Conducted on May 23, 1979." Voices of the Manhattan Project, The Atomic Heritage Foundation.
Sherwin, Martin J. "Interview with Robert Serber Conducted on January 9, 1982." Voices of the Manhattan Project, Atomic Heritage Foundation.
Shibutani, Tamotsu. "The Initial Impact of the War on the Japanese Communities in the San Francisco Bay Region—A Preliminary Report." Japanese American Evacuation and Resettlement Records, UC Berkeley Bancroft Library.

Shibutani, Tamotsu. "Letter to Virginia Galbraith, dated May 4, 1942." bk0013c8x2j-FID1.pdf. Japanese American Evacuation and Resettlement Study, University of California, Berkeley Bancroft Library.
Sime, Ruth Lewin. "Science and Politics: The Discovery of Nuclear Fission 75 Years Ago." *Annalen der Physik* (Berlin) 526, no. 3–4, A27–A31.
"Sinking." California Department of Fish and Wildlife. Wildlife.ca.gov.
Smith, Alice Kimball and Weiner, Charles, eds. *Robert Oppenheimer: Letters and Recollections*. Cambridge, Harvard University Press, 1980.
Smith, Jack. "Raising Caen to the Level of an L.A. Idol." *Los Angeles Times*, August 17, 1988.
Smith, Jr., J. Clay, ed. *Supreme Justice: Speeches and Writings; Thurgood Marshall*. Philadelphia: University of Pennsylvania Press, 2003.
Smith Jr., J. Clay. "Thurgood Marshall: An Heir of Charles Hamilton Houston." *Hastings Constitutional Law Quarterly*, 20, no 3 (Spring 1993): 503–519.
Sproul, Robert G. "Opening Remarks." Nobel Prize in Physics Ceremony in Berkeley, February 29, 1940.
Starr, Kevin. *The Dream Endures*. Oxford: Oxford University Press, 1997.
Starr, Kevin. *Endangered Dreams: The Great Depression in California*. New York: Oxford University Press, 1996.
Starr, Kevin. "The Gold Rush and the California Dream." *California History* 77, no. 1 (Spring, 1998): 56–67.
Starr, Kevin. On the Same Page Lecture given at the San Francisco Public Library, June 19, 2012.
Stegner, Wallace. "California: The Experimental Society, an Editorial." *The Saturday Review*, September 23, 1967.
Stewart, John F. "Charles Spalding Oral History Conducted on March 14, 1968." JFKOH-CHS-01, John F. Kennedy Presidential Library and Museum.
Stilwell, Joseph W. arranged and edited by White, Theodore H. *The Stilwell Papers*. New York: Shocken Books, 1972.
Streshinsky, Shirley and Klaus, Patricia. *An Atomic Love Story*. Nashville: Turner Publishing, 2013.
"Sub Shells Santa Barbara Coast." *The San Diego Union*, February 24, 1942.
Summerscale, Owen. "A History of Plutonium." Actinide Research Quarterly, September 21, 2022. Los Alamos National Laboratory.
Tanaka, Togo W. "Journal, Japanese Americans—Evacuation and Relocation, 1942–1945." Japanese American Evacuation and Resettlement Study, University of California, Berkeley Bancroft Library.
"Tanforan (detention facility)." Densho Encyclopedia.
Taylor, Quintard. "African American Men in the American West." *The Annals of the American Academy of Political and Social Science*. Vol. 569, May 2000: 102–119.
"The Conference: The Second Beginning." *Time*, May 07, 1945.
"The Courier's Double 'V' For a Double Victory Campaign Gets Country-Wide Support." *Pittsburgh Courier*, February 14, 1942.
"The Great Jazz Revival." The San Francisco Traditional Jazz Foundation Collection, Stanford Libraries. Exhibits.stanfprd.edu.
"The Plutonium Path to the Bomb." The Manhattan Project Interactive History, US Department of Energy.

"The San Francisco Conference Will Go On as Planned." *Life*, April 23, 1945.

The Totalizer, June 20, 1942.

"The Trinity Test." The Manhattan Project Interactive History, US Department of Energy.

"Thoughts by E. O. Lawrence—Lawrence's Reaction to the Trinity Test, July 16, 1945." The Manhattan Project Interactive History, US Department of Energy.

"To Meet the Delegate from . . . Visitors Continue to Hold Spotlight." *San Francisco Chronicle*, May 9, 1945, 8.

Thomas, Dorothy Swaine and Nishimoto, Richard S. with Hankey, Rosalie A., Sakoda, James M. Grodzins, Morton, Miyamoto, Frank. *The Spoilage*. Berkeley: University of California Press, 1946.

Top of the Mark Squadron Bottle log book.

Thomas, Dorothy Swaine and Nishimoto, Richard S. with Hankey, Rosalie A., Sakoda, James M. Grodzins, Morton, Miyamoto, Frank. *The Spoilage*. Berkeley: University of California Press, 1946.

Tretkoff, Ernie. "December 1938: Discovery of Nuclear Fission." This Month in Physics History, American Physical Society News, December 2007.

Tuchman, Barbara W. *Stilwell and the American Experience in China, 1911–1945*. New York: Grove Press, 1985.

Tushnet, Mark V., ed. *Thurgood Marshall: His Speeches, Writings, Arguments, Opinions, and Reminiscences*. Chicago: Lawrence Hill Books, 2001.

"UC Berkeley Building Name Review Committee." June 26, 2020. Chancellor.berkeley.edu.

Van Der Zee, John, *The Greatest Men's Party on Earth: Inside the Bohemian Grove*. New York: Harcourt Brace Jovanovich, 1974.

Vincent, Lynn and Vladic, Sara. *Indianapolis*. New York: Simon & Schuster, 2018.

Warren, Earl. "Testimony to the Select Committee Investigating National Defense Migration." House of Representatives, Seventy-Seventh Congress, February 21 and 23, 1942.

Weeks, Linton. "The 1940 Census: 72-Year-Old Secrets Revealed." National Public Radio.

Weiner, Charles and Richman, Barry. "Luis W. Alvarez Oral History Conducted on February 14, 1967." Niels Bohr Library and Archives, American Institute of Physics, College Park, MD USA.

Wellerstein, Alex. "The First Light of Trinity." *The New Yorker*, July 16, 2015.

Whitman, Alden. "Robert G. Sproul, 84, Dies." New York Times, September 12, 1975.

Whitman, Alden. "Walter Lippmann, Political Analyst, Is Dead at 85." *New York Times*, December 15, 1974.

Whitson, Dana and Clinton, Larry. "Joseph James, Entertainer." Sausalito Historical Society, February 13, 2019.

Williams, Juan. "The Courts: Poetic Justice." *New York Times*, January 18, 2004.

Witwer, David. "Who Was Westbrook Pegler?" *Humanities* 33, no. 2 (March/April 2012).

Wollenberg, Charles. "James vs. Marinship: Trouble on the New Black Frontier." *California History* 60, no. 3 (Fall 1981): 262–279.

Wollenberg, Charles. *Marinship at War: Shipbuilding and Social Change in Wartime Sausalito*. Berkeley Western Heritage Press, 1990.
Yarris, Lynn. "Ernest Lawrence's Cyclotron: Invention for the Ages." Lawrence Berkeley National Laboratory.
Yarris, Lynn. "Ernest Orlando Lawrence—The Man, His Lab, His Legacy." Science Beat, Lawrence Berkeley National Laboratory.

Index

Abelson, Philip H., 45
Acheson, Dean, 195
air raid blackout in San Francisco, 55
Alamogordo bombing range, 185
Alberga, Aurelious P., 120–21, 127–28,
Alley, Vernon, Fig.10, x
Alvarez, Luis W., 31, 42, 43, 45–47, 73,
American Federation of Labor's
 Boilermakers Union Local, 123
American Legion, 70, 108–10
American Prometheus, biography of J.
 Robert Oppenheimer, 149, 155, 199
Andersen, George R., 134, 138
Angelou, Maya, 6, 57, 59, 115–16, 119,
 122, 126–28, 194–95, 198–99; *Gather Together in My Name* memoir of,
 194; *I Know Why the Caged Bird Sings* memoir of, 5–6, 59, 115, 126–28. See also Marguerite Johnson
anti-Japanese-American sentiment in California, 52, 68
assembly centers, 95, 97–98, 101–105, 109–110, 112, 116
atomic bombs, 47, 76, 189, 197. *See also* "Little Boy;" "Fat Man"
Atomic Energy Commission, 155–56
atomic explosion, possible ignition of earth's atmosphere, 88

Attlee, Clement R., 163, 178

B-24 bomber, 180
B-25 bomber, 77
B-29 bomber, 189
Bainbridge, Kenneth, 188
Bank of America, 2
Barbary Coast in San Francisco, 157, 164; international settlement, 161
"Battle of Los Angeles," 57, 64
Bayview, San Francisco working-class neighborhood, 118
Bayview Opera House, 127
Beasley, Delilah L., 119–20
Beaver, Floyd, 159
Bechtel Corporation, 125
Beebe, Lucius, 157, 159, 164, 201
Bendetsen, Karl R., 95
Benedict, Ruth, 100, 112, 201
Benner, Roger, 159
Berkelium, 5n1
Bethe, Hans A., 31, 42, 81–82, 87–88, 91
Biddle, Francis B., 50, 51–52, 63-65, 66, 70–72, 94–95, 97, 111, 138
big science, 4, 18, 28, 31, 47, 195, 198–99
Bird, Kai, 149
Birge, Raymond T., 16–18, 23–24

Black Americans: San Franciscans, 4–5, 8, 50, 115, 118, 121, 194; ship workers, 133–34, 139, 141; war work in the Bay Area, 116, 118, 121, 123, 142; working class, 8
Blair, Clay Jr. and Joan, 174–75
Bloch, Felix, 30
Bohemian Club, Fig.10, 89, 162, 195
Bohemian Grove campsite, 21, 89–90, 92, 147
Bohr, Niels, 24, 45, 89
Boilermakers Union Local 6 (A.F.L.), 124, 132, 133-34, 138, 139–40, 141; as a Jim Crow union, 131–43
bombs, V-1 rockets and V-2 missiles, 168
boom town San Francisco, 157, 164
Boston University, 36
Brode, Robert B., 155
Broussard, Albert S., 119
Bush, Vannevar, 78, 80, 81, 84, 187, 188, 196
Butler, Edward, 139

Caen, Estelle, 151
Caen, Herb, 151, 155, 182
Cal. *See* University of California, Berkeley
California Supreme Court, 139–40
Californium, 5n1
California Institute of Technology, 3, 11, 24, 28, 46, 87, 151
Caltech. *See* California Institute of Technology
Cambridge University, 15, 23, 31, 42, 100, 165, 208–209; Cavendish lab, 42
Challenger, Union Pacific steam locomotive, 121
Cherniss, Harold F., 27–28
Chevalier, Haakon M., 87, 153
Chou, Lupei, ix, 159
Churchill, Winston S., 161, 178, 196
City College of New York (CCNY), 80
Claflin College, 36
Clark, General Mark W., 65
closed shop, 132, 139, 141; shipyards, 123
Coconut Grove ballroom, 13
Collins, Daniel, 121–22

Columbia University, 15, 83
columnists, 69
Commission on Wartime Relocation and Internment of Civilians, 112
Communist Party, American, 86, 138, 150, 153
Compton, Arthur H., 78–79, 82, 88, 91–92, 203, 206
Conant, James B., 78, 187, 195
Cooper, Sheldon, 76
Cremer, Peter, 125, 129
Crocker, William, 28
Curie, Joliot Irène, 43
Curie, Marie, 43
Curie, Pierre, 43
cyclotron, 11, 14, 16, 18, 21, 25, 43, 45, 73, 76, 206, 211; *Crocker Cracker*, 28; expense of, 14, 15, 17; power of, 14, 25, 43, 46, 79

Daily Stanford, 182, 207
Daniels, Douglas Henry, 120, 127–28, 203
Depression-Era San Francisco, 8–10, 39
DeWitt, John L., 62–64, 67–69, 70, 99, 112
Dixon, Maynard, 7, 11
Donne, John, 186
Doolittle, James H., 77; "Doolittle Raid" bombing of Tokyo, 82
Doudna, Jennifer, 13
DuBois, W.E.B., 120

Eden, Anthony, 176–77, 183
Einstein, Albert, 12, 24–25, 31, 73–74, 195–96
Eisenhower, Dwight, 195
Eisenhower, Milton S., 94, 95–100, 105, 110–12, 114
executive orders, presidential, 4, 95, 97, 128; Executive Order 8802, 124, 136; Executive Order 9066, Figs.4–5, 69, 93, 96
evacuation and relocation of Japanese-Americans, 111–14
Evans, Arthur R, 169

Index

Fair Employment Practices Commission. *See* FEPC
Fairmont Hotel in San Francisco, 157, 160, 162
"Fat Man," atomic bomb, 76, 189
Fay, Anita Marcus, 175
Fay, Paul B., "Red," 175, 183
Federal Bureau of Investigation, 51, 61–62, 64–65, 67, 81, 85–86, 94, 145, 152–53, 163
Federal Theater Project, 10, 37, 38; Joseph James performances, 36
FEPC (Fair Employment Practices Commission), 124, 128, 136
Fermi, Enrico, 43, 45, 78, 89, 146
Fillmore district of San Francisco, 5, 8, 50–51, 69, 115, 117, 118–19, 122, 134, 160, 194; nightlife of, 160
fission, nuclear, 41, 43–47, 73, 75; weapon, 46, 78–79, 83, 88, 145–47
Fleming, Thomas C., 142
Ford, Leland, 98
Frank, Edith, 41–42
Frisch, Otto, 44–46, 73
Furman, Robert, 188, 190

Gadles, Merle, 122
Galbraith, Virginia, 102, 112–13
Gasa, Biuku, 168, 169
General Strike in San Francisco, Fig.3, 9, 134, 150
George VI, King, 164
Gerjuoy, Edward, 31–32, 79–80, 82, 205–206
German army (*Wehrmacht*), nuclear research, 46
German and Italian immigrants, 51, 67–68, 95
German scientists, 18, 46, 188; dominance in chemistry and physics, 14, 42
German U-boats, 74, 168
Germany's anti-Semitic laws, 41
Giannini, A.P., 3; Giannini Hall at Berkeley, 97
Gibson, Phil S., 141
Gilbert and Sullivan productions, 10, 37, 39

Gilman Hall at Berkeley campus, 22, 76, 89, 147, 185
Golden Gate Bridge, Fig.1, 7, 50, 77, 119, 124, 142, 157–58, 165, 189
Golden Gate International Exhibition, 7, 9, 12, 37, 39
Golden Gate International Exposition, 12, 38
Goleta, California, 57
Göttingen University, 23, 42, 147
Great Depression, 3-4, 8, 10, 11, 15, 28, 30, 35, 38, 54, 85, 98, 149, 151, 157–58, 185, 197
Great Migration of Black Americans, 116, 120
Greene, Angela, 177
Grodzins, Morton, 97
Grove, Andrew S., "Andy," 79
Groves, Leslie R., 83–85, 89–91, 145–46, 153–54, 156, 186–88, 190, 196; and Oppenheimer, 146, 187; tolerance for left-wing views, 85

Hahn, Otto, 43–44, 46, 73, 75
Hall Johnson Choir, 36–37, 131, 142
Hall, Mike, 159
Hamilton Field Air Force Base, 117, 189
Harvard University, 16, 23–24, 28, 75, 78, 169–70
Hayashi, Doris Shigeko, 104–107, 113,
Heisenberg, Werner, 27, 88, 154
Henderson, Diedre. 179
Hiroshima, 47, 186, 197–98
Hobart, John, 38–39
Hoover, Herbert C., 64
Hoover, J. Edgar, 87
Hopkins, Harry L., 35
Houston, Charles H., 136, 143, 209
Howard, John Galen, 22, 136–37
Howard University, 136
Hunter's Point neighborhood of San Francisco, 117–18
hydrogen bomb, 88, 195–96

Iijima, Ben, 107–9, 113–14, 204
Immigration Act of 1924, 49
internment of Japanese Americans, 110, 115; drive for internment in

California, 69, 101; fear of sabotage by Issei or Nisei-Americans, 52, 65–67, 100; Japanese-American internees, 95, 97–99, 101–102, 104–105, 110, 112
invasion panic in California, 49–59
Issei, 49–53, 61, 66–67, 70, 93–95, 97–98, 101–103, 110, 116, 194. *See also* Japanese Americans; Nisei

Jack's, San Francisco restaurant, 30, 167–74, 176
James, Alberta, 119
James, Joseph, Fig.9, 35–37, 116–17, 126–27, 131–35, 138–43, 144, 194–95, 198–99; Broadway performances, 36, 195; career as a performer, 10, 36–38; committee led by, 134; growing up under segregation, 35–36; Hollywood performances, 36, 131; *James v Marinship*, 136–37, 138–40; trains as a welder, 131
Japanese American Evacuation and Resettlement Study (JERS), 58, 96, 111–14
Japanese Americans, 4–5, 8, 63–64, 66–69, 93–96, 98, 101, 108–16, 194; apartheid against, 50; communities in California, 8, 50, 51, 102, 194; Fillmore district homes of, 5; immigrants, 2, 49–50; population of, 8, 194; resettlement of, 94–95. *See also* internment of Japanese Americans; Issei; Nisei
Japanese Imperial Navy destroyers, 54, 168
Japanese Imperial Navy submarines, 56–57, 64, 197
Japan pavilion, Golden Gate International Exhibition, 10–11
JERS. *See* Japanese American Evacuation and Resettlement Study
Jewish physicists escape Nazi Germany, 73
Jim Crow, 5, 36, 120, 132–33, 141
Johnson, Charles S., 118–19, 123–24, 126–28, 158
Johnson, David, Fig.10
Johnson, Hiram, 50
Johnson, Marguerite, 5, 115
Johnson, Richard W., 158, 164
Johnson, Robert Sr., 158
Joliot, Frédéric, 43

Kaiser, Henry J., 123, 125,
Kaiser Wilhelm Institute, 42–43
Kawahara, Sachi, 109
Keeton, Elmer, 37, 39, 207
Kennedy, Joseph P. Jr., "Joe Jr.," 167, 169, 171, 173–74
Kennedy, John F., Fig.8, 75, 167–70, 175, 176 178, 181–84, 196; attractive qualities of, 175; combat experience, 168, 172; consoles survivors of *Athenia*, 75; diary 179, 184; influence of UNIOC upon, 181; newspaper column, 176–79; Stanford University experience of, 170
Kennedy, Joseph P. Sr., 75, 169–70, 173–74, 176, 178, 181–83, 183
Kennedy, Kathleen, "Kick," 173, 182–83
Kennedy, Rose F., 174
Kibei, 94, 101, 103–104
Kistiakowsky, George, 148, 187
Krock, Arthur, 176, 178, 183–84
Khrushchev, Nikita, 181
Kumana, Eroni, 168, 169

Lange, Dorothea, Figs.4–5, 8, 35,
Lawrence, Ernest O., Fig.6, 11, 13, 14, 15, 16–19, 21–31, 42–43, 73–75, 78–81, 84, 86–87, 89–91, 145, 147–48, 150, 154–55, 187, 190, 195–96, 198–99; and Atomic bomb, 12; arrival at Berkeley, 22; career summarized, 16; confidence in Oppenheimer, 145; Groves assessment of, 84; in the Cold War, 199, 206; offers from other universities, 16; personal appearance of, 21; personal taste, 80; vision and quiet charisma, 198; wife's recollections of, 22, 79, 206; witnesses atomic bomb test, 187; wins Nobel prize, 18, 203
Lawrence, John H., 74

Index

Lawrence, Mary Blumer, "Molly," 16, 18, 30, 208
Lawrence Berkeley National Laboratory, 18, 30–31, 203–204, 211
LeConte, John, 193
LeConte, Joseph, 193
LeConte Hall at Berkeley, 22, 45, 77, 80, 87–89, 146, 185, 189, 193, 196
Lewis, Gilbert N., 29, 30
Lippmann, Walter, 65–66, 71
"Little Boy," atomic bomb, 189, 197
Logevall, Fredrik, 169
Los Alamos, 80, 90, 146–47, 152–53, 154, 185–86, 188, 196
Lyon, Frederick G., x

MacArthur, Douglas, 171
Manhattan Project, 30–32, 81–82, 83–84, 87, 90–91, 145, 148, 152, 154–55, 188–90, 195–96
Mare Island Navy Shipyard, 140
Marin City, 134
Marin County, 117, 195
Marin County Superior Court, 139
Marinship shipyard, 125–26, 128–29, 131–35, 138–42, 144, 199; Liberty ship construction, 125–6; employees, 126; *Marin-er* magazine, 133; management, 139; Negro Advisory Board, 133; officials, 134
Mark Hopkins Hotel: Top of the Mark bar, Fig.11, ix, 77, 157–58, 164; Oppenheimer and Tatlock tryst at, 152
Marshall, Thurgood, 4, 135, 137–38, 140, 142–44, 209–210, 134–41, 143; education of, 136–37
Maxwell, James Clark, 42
McCloy, John J., 95
McCormick, Anne O'Hare, 161
McLemore, Henry, 53, 58
McMillan, Edwin M., 76–77
Meitner, Lise, 43–44, 46
Meneweather, Martel, 120
Mielziner, Jo, 162
The Mikado, 37, 39
Miller, Irving, 7
Miller, Leta, 36, 37

Mooney, Joseph, 158

NAACP (National Association for the Advancement of Colored People), 4, 117, 120–21, 133–38, 140–44; national, 135; and Thurgood Marshall, 135
Najima, Haruo, 107
Nash, Gerald D., 117
National Association for the Advancement of Colored People. *See* NAACP
National Defense Research Committee (NDRC), 78
Newton, Jim, 66
Nisei, 49–53, 58, 61–62, 64, 66–67, 69, 93–94, 96–98, 100–106, 111, 118–19, 122, 194. *See also* Japanese Americans; Issei
Nishimura, Rhoda, 109
Nobel Prize, 13, 15–18, 25, 29, 45, 84–85, 148; in physics, 19, 42, 73, 78; ceremonies in Berkeley, 13, 18
nuclear fission, 46–47, 78; discovery of, 47
nuclear research, 46, 73, 76

Oakland California, 7, 37, 50–51, 57, 68, 115–16, 119, 123, 126, 132, 158
O'Donnell, Kenneth P., 180
Ogawa, Tatsu J., 109–110
oil industry, Californian, 54
Office of Scientific Research and Development (OSRD), 78, 82
Oliphant, Marcus E., 78–79
Olson, Culbert L., 51, 67, 69, 93, 100
Oppenheimer, J. Robert, Fig.7, 11, 17–18, 21–33, 45–46, 73–75, 77–82, 83–92, 145–56, 185–90, 195–96, 198–99; arrival at Berkeley, 22; attractiveness of, 148; Chevalier and, 153; communism and, 81; dual appointment to Berkeley and Caltech, 24; Groves and, 84, 145; intelligence and personality of, 26; loyalty to the United States, 85, 199; Oppie nickname, 23, 26, 29, 187; personal wealth, 30, 149; security

clearance, 196; sense of urgency after Pearl Harbor, 80; study of the Bhagavad-Gita, 185, 188; students of, 26, 79; summer conference at Berkeley, 88–89; surveilled by FBI, 152; Tatlock and, 150–52
Oppenheimer, Frank F., 25, 81, 85, 150
Oppenheimer, Katherine Harrison, "Kitty," 147, 151–53
OSRD (Office of Scientific Research and Development), 78, 82

Pacific Heights neighborhood of San Francisco, 118, 157
Pacific Union Club, 195
Palace Hotel San Francisco, 159–60, 175–76; Maxfield Parrish Pied Piper bar, 159
peacetime draft lottery, 170
Pegler, Westbrook, 65
physics: classical laws of, 24; theoretical, 23–24, 26–27, 29, 86
plutonium bomb, 88, 186, 188
Powers, David F., 180
Porgy and Bess, 37, 195
Port Chicago, explosion disaster, 140–41
Potsdam Conference, 196
Powell, Colin, 79
Pyle, Ernest T., "Ernie," 66

quantum theory, 23–24

Rabi, I.I., 188, 196
Randolph, A. Philip, 124
Redwood City California, 107–108
relocation centers, 69, 198
relocation of Japanese-Americans, 70, 93, 95–96, 107, 109, 111–14
Resner, Herbert, 134, 138, 144
restrictive covenants, race-based, 50
Richardson, Friend, 121
Roberts, Edith, 100
Roberts, Owen, 66
Roosevelt, Eleanor, 10, 35
Roosevelt, Franklin D., 3, 4, 9, 49, 52, 53, 57, 59, 63–65, 69, 70, 73, 74, 77–78, 82, 93, 94–95, 100, 124, 161–62, 170, 171–72, 185; selection of San Francisco as site of UNIOC, 161
Rossi, Angelo J., 52, 68
Run, Little Chillun' production, 36–37
Ryder, Arthur, 27

S-1 Committee, 80, 89–90; attended by Lawrence, 147
Sachs, Alexander, 74
San Bernardino California, 55
San Bruno California, 97, 102, 107
San Francisco: Bohemian Club, 89; Black population, 117; Committee Against Segregation, 133, 135; Embarcadero, Fig.3, 7; Polo Club, 53; nightlife, 198
San Francisco Bay, 7, 9, 28, 77, 124–25
San Francisco Bay Region, 58–59
San Francisco-Oakland Bay Bridge, Fig.2, 7, 11,
Sausalito California, 128–29, 142, 211
Schiller, Reuel, 141
Seaborg, Glenn T., 29, 31–32, 43, 47, 55, 59, 75–77, 79, 82, 146–47; caught air raid blackout, 55
"seeing the elephant," 160
Seidler, Aaron, 158
segregated union lodges, 132
Serber, Robert, 25–26, 30, 31–33, 87–88, 150–51
Sherwin, Martin J., 149
Shibutani, Tamotsu, "Tom," 52, 53, 58–59, 102–104, 110, 112–13
Sidey, Hugh S., 179
Sierra Club, 193
Silicon Valley, 8, 42
Sime, Ruth Lewin, 44
Smith, Alice Kimball, 24
Smith, Harold, 95
Smolny (Russian ship), 163
Southern California, 2–3, 10, 67
Spalding, Charles F., 175, 177
Sproul, Robert G., 15, 17, 18, 83, 97
S.S. Athenia, 74
S.S. Montebello, 56–7
S.S. William A. Richardson, 131
Stanford University, 1, 3–4, 11, 30, 107, 146, 149, 170, 175

Stark, Harold R., 65
Starr, Kevin, 5–6, 11
Stegner, Wallace E., 198
Stilwell, Joseph W., "Vinegar Joe," 54–56, 59
Stimson, Henry L., 63–64, 70, 171
Strassmann, Fritz, 43–44, 46, 73
straw bosses, 8–9
"Swing Mikado," 10, 12, 37–39, 203–204
Szilard, Leo, 42, 74

Tanforan assembly center, Fig.5, 102–7, 109–10; "Tanforan Tooters," jazz band, 109; *Tanforan Totalizer* newspaper, 107–109, 114
Tatlock, Jean F., 149–54, 186; Oppenheimer and, 149, 150; suicide, 153; Telegraph Hill home, 152–53
Teller, Edward, 18, 42, 87–88, 186, 196
Thomas, Dorothy Swaine, 97, 104, 107, 111–12
Tinian Island, 189
Tolan, John H., 68; Tolan Committee, 68–69
Top of the Mark. *See* Mark Hopkins Hotel
Treasure Island, 9–10, 12, 35, 37–39, 41, 117
Trinity atomic bomb test, 186, 188, 190, 197, 198; test site, 185–91, 198
Truman, Harry S., 128, 179, 189, 195–96
Tushnet, Mark, 135–36

U-235 Uranium isotope, 46, 75, 79–80, 146–48, 197
U-238 Uranium isotope, 76
UC. *See* University of California
UCLA. *See* University of California, Los Angeles.
Ulam, Stanislaw M., 42
United Nations International Organizing Conference in San Francisco (UNIOC), 1945, 161–62, 165, 174, 181, 208; delegates, 161–63, 165, 167, 177, 210
United States Atomic Energy Commission, 91–92, 199, 202, 208
United States Supreme Court, 4, 66

University of California (UC), 3, 13, 15, 18, 58, 111–14, 201, 203–204, 206, 208–209, 215
University of California, Berkeley, 3, 11, 15, 16–17, 18, 25–26, 28–29, 80, 83, 97, 107, 138, 144, 147–48, 193; building name review committee, 198, 210; chemistry department, 29; physics department, 14, 16, 23–24, 32
University of California, Los Angeles, 3, 11, 15, 29
University of Cambridge, 15, 23, 42
University of Chicago, 42, 78, 146
University of Göttingen, 23, 42
University of Southern California, 3
uranium bomb, 46–47, 186
Uranium Committee, 74, 78, 80
USC. *See* University of Southern California.
USS Bullhead, 159
USS Hornet, 77
USS Indianapolis, 189, 197, 199

Vertigo, 159
von Neumann, John, 42, 167

War Relocation Authority, 94–95, 97–100, 110; operating out of the Whitcomb Hotel in San Francisco, 96, 98
Warden, Gentry, 37
Warren, Earl, 8, 63, 67, 69–72, 93, 137
Weaver, Robert C., 123
Weiner, Charles, 24
Western Addition. *See* Fillmore district of San Francisco
Whitmore, Dave, 159
Wollenberg, Charles, 125, 138
Works Progress Administration, 10, 38; artists, photographers and writers employed by during the Depression, 35
WRA. *See* War Relocation Authority

Yale University, 23
Yalta Conference, 161

About the Author

Philip E. Meza is a strategy consultant, researcher, and writer. As a consultant and researcher, he has worked with first, second, and third generation leaders in Silicon Valley to study and help shape their businesses.

He is the author or coauthor of three books dealing with strategy, technology, and media: *Strategic Dynamics, Concepts and Cases* (McGraw-Hill/Irwin, 2006); *Hollywood, High Tech and the Future of Entertainment* (Stanford University Press, 2007); and *Becoming Hewlett-Packard* (Oxford University Press, 2017). These books are used at universities and business schools around the world. Philip's most recent book, *Inventing the California Look* (Rizzoli, 2022) is about twentieth-century photography and design.

Philip has an MBA from The Wharton School of the University of Pennsylvania. When he was an undergraduate at the University of California at Berkeley he met some of the key chemists and physicists discussed in this book. They were long into retirement but still part of the vital scientific community they helped shape at Berkeley.

Philipmeza.com

www.ingramcontent.com/pod-product-compliance
Lightning Source LLC
Chambersburg PA
CBHW021352300426
44114CB00012B/1199